HOUSTON COUGARS IN THE 1960s

SWAIM-PAUP-FORAN SPIRIT
OF SPORT SERIES

Sponsored by James C. '74 and Debra Parchman Swaim,
Nancy and T. Edgar Paup '74, and Joseph Wm. and Nancy Foran

HOUSTON COUGARS IN THE 1960s

Death Threats, the Veer Offense, and the Game of the Century

Robert D. Jacobus

Texas A&M University Press
College Station

This paper meets the requirements of ANSI/NISO
Z39.48-1992 (Permanence of Paper).
Binding materials have been chosen for durability.
△ ∞

Library of Congress Cataloging-in-Publication Data

Jacobus, D. Robert, author.
    Houston Cougars in the 1960s: death threats, the veer offense, and the game of
the century / Robert D. Jacobus.—First edition.
        pages cm.—(Swaim-Paup-Foran spirit of sport series)
    Includes bibliographical references and index.
    ISBN 978-1-62349-347-9 (cloth: alk. paper)—ISBN 978-1-62349-348-6
(ebook) 1. University of Houston—Sports—History—20th century. 2. College
sports—Texas—Houston—History—20th century. 3. Discrimination in sports—
Texas—Houston—History—20th century. 4. African American basketball
players—Texas—Houston—Biography. 5. African American football players—
Texas—Houston—Biography. 6. Houston (Tex.)—Ethnic relations—History—
20th century. I. Title.

    GV691.U535J33 2015
    796.04309764'1411—dc23
                                        2015019545

For my mother,
Lilyan Jacobus,
and Eva

CONTENTS

FOREWORD
WADE PHILLIPS

They got to the University of Houston one year ahead of me. They were great athletes, all three of them. And they certainly proved it, changing the course of college football and basketball history. Looking back on that history, Warren McVea proved to be one of the greatest running backs in America in the mid-1960s, and you can't say enough about what Elvin Hayes and Don Chaney did for college basketball in Houston, the state of Texas, and the National Collegiate Athletic Association (NCAA). "Wondrous Warren" put excitement into the game like few players before him; "the Big E" and "the Duck" taught basketball fans across America the meaning of the term *dunk* and displayed the strategy and ability to win the Game of the Century in Houston's Astrodome.

The route to success required the normal pain and sacrifice that every coach from grade school to the pros talks about daily. But these great athletes experienced extraordinary pain and suffering far beyond that of their teammates, for they were the first African American scholarship athletes at an urban university still getting its figurative feet wet in the budding institution known as integration. I hailed from an all-white high school at Port Neches-Groves, east of Houston in the shadows of Beaumont. This background didn't affect my attitude in the least. I am the son of a football coach who worked in locker rooms and on football fields all over Texas. I learned from my dad, a lifelong football coach named Bum Phillips, that colors of skin and economic backgrounds make no difference.

In 1965, my dad served as the defensive coordinator under UH head coach Bill Yeoman. Coach Yeoman had been an assistant at Michigan State and had an equal respect for the abilities of black and white players. In Southeast Texas, my dad coached all-white teams but knew African American coaches such as Willie Ray Smith, the coach at Beaumont Charlton-Pollard, whose son was All-Pro defensive end Bubba Smith. When coaches scout players, they don't see color; they evaluate size, strength, desire, and potential. With his unprecedented recruitment of Warren McVea, Coach Yeoman provided an opportunity no other college football coach in a high-profile Texas university had previously offered. This was a historic move. The Southwest Conference, arguably the best group of football teams in the United States, hadn't yet taken that step. He made it a goal to get all the good players, regardless of color. He made Houston a force to be reckoned with and saw his Cougars win many games, one season after another. He definitely opened everyone's eyes and showed them that football players come in all shapes, sizes, and colors. His outstanding record proves that he was right.

A written history of Bill Yeoman's pioneering spirit on the UH football field and Guy V. Lewis's courageous recruitment of Hayes and Chaney for work on the basketball court is long overdue, in my opinion. No doubt, many sports fans in Texas and all over the South know many parts of the story, but now a high school and college history teacher and UH graduate, Bob Jacobus, has taken us back in time to detail the thoughts of these brave coaches as well as expand on what went through the minds of the major characters in these great football and basketball dramas.

Like I have pointed out, I got to the UH football scene a year later than Warren, Elvin, and Don. They had already endured a year of racial abuse. I was not there for the more serious episodes, but I do recall in detail what it was like being a teammate of Warren McVea and, later, Elmo Wright. I learned like the coaches and the rest of my teammates that once the fans recognized the players's abilities and got past the racial issue, they changed their attitude altogether. A great example of this happening was the University of Kentucky game played in the then-segregated state of Kentucky. The fans were throwing things at Warren when we went out on the field to play the first half. After witnessing his superior athletic abilities, some of those same people were cheering him in the second half.

It didn't take the UH players long to accept Warren and other African Americans. I experienced this and know it to be true. After all, we were putting the Cougars on the national football map and winning about eight games a year. By my sophomore year, we took it personally when obnoxious fans said bad things about our teammates. I've been coaching for more than 40 years now, many of them as a head coach, and that's the main reason I have a more vivid recollection of the positives instead of the negatives. Accentuating the negative seldom, if ever—I might even say *never*—gets your team in the win column.

We became family at UH, both on and off the field and in that locker room that became our home away from home. We cared about each other. We were deeply concerned when feelings were hurt. We took up for each other! Family means trust, loyalty, and common purpose. I have to say that we worked hard and pulled together in those pioneering UH days and played like brothers. The skin color—then, as now—didn't matter. So what we have in these pages is a great family success story. I hope you enjoy reading it as much as I did living it with my family members.

FOREWORD

JAMES KIRBY MARTIN

We've all asked questions like this one: Where were you on this or that day when some memorable, but often tragic, event occurred—you know, the day President Kennedy was shot or the morning of 9/11 being prime examples. But such memorable days and events are not always tragic. Certainly this was the case with college basketball's "Game of the Century," which took place on January 20, 1968. Played at Houston's famous Astrodome with nearly 53,000 people in attendance and a national viewing audience numbering in the millions, the game featured No. 1–ranked UCLA and No. 2–ranked University of Houston. The Bruin team featured Lew Alcindor (Kareem Abdul-Jabbar), and the Cougars had Elvin Hayes and Don Chaney, all three future basketball legends. UCLA had won 47 games in a row before UH stopped them that night by a final score of 71–69. The huge television audience loved the game, so much so that it launched the modern era of big-time college basketball on regional and national networks, the progenitor of what we have come to know each year as "March Madness."

That January, I was a third-year graduate student studying American history at the University of Wisconsin. My wife, Karen, and I lived in a modest apartment in Madison, and my days consisted of taking classes and doing research for my doctoral dissertation. On the evening of the 20th, I remember telling Karen that a basketball game was going to be on TV, nationally televised no less! We turned on our aging black-and-white set to view this event and sat there in rapt attention as this gladiator-like contest unfolded before our eyes. Like so many viewers, we started rooting for UH, the underdog. When Elvin Hayes made those two free throws with under a minute to go, we held our breath to see whether mighty UCLA could work its basketball magic to overcome the two-point lead. We cheered when the Bruins failed and celebrated a victory for the underdogs from a young, emerging Texas public university.

At that time, I knew virtually nothing about the University of Houston. It didn't dawn on me that in another 12 years I'd become a member of the UH faculty. When offered the position in 1980 to become a history professor and department chair, what most appealed to me was an opportunity to join an institution that was striving to gain serious academic recognition among the great universities in America. Then comfortably situated as a full professor at dear old Rutgers University in New Jersey, I could have vegetated there the rest of my life, teaching classes and writing a few more books. But future dynamism and greatness in higher education, I believed, lay in the American South and West. The University of Houston, etched most positively in my memory because of the "Game of the Century," was like a diamond in the rough waiting to be polished brightly. To become a part of that polishing process was the kind of challenge that appealed to me. Karen and I moved with our three young daughters to the Bayou City.

Since 1980, I've taught an impressive array of UH students. One in that number is Robert Jacobus, who enrolled in our master's degree program back in the early 1990s. Bob was teaching school locally and wanted to expand his knowledge of US history. Even though I served as his program adviser, I didn't get to know Bob very well and had no idea that several years later he would contact me about a book he was writing. Bob wondered if he could send me a copy of the manuscript and get my reactions. Sure, why not? I'd be happy to take a look, I told him—and look I did, reading the pages in utter amazement as the story unfolded.

Based on almost 250 interviews with the likes of Hayes and Chaney, Bill Yeoman, Guy V. Lewis, Bum Phillips, Wade Phillips, Warren McVea, and so many other key sports-related figures, the story line features an athletic department that, in an age of rampant discrimination against African Americans in the American South, dared to challenge that pattern. What Bob has compiled in these pages is the background story about coaches and players who broke through the rigid, apartheid-like color lines in Southern college sports just a few years before the "Game of the Century." Enduring venomous commentary, personal abuse, and even death threats, these heroes had the courage to take on society's racist taboos in seeking to make a better, more tolerant world through the medium of college athletics.

This compelling story played itself out in a racially divided city at a fledgling, upstart university wanting to win football and basketball games, but something of far greater significance took place than a few noteworthy victories here and there. The participants demonstrated that equality of opportunity should be a function of ability and talent, regardless of color. As such, these heroes struck a blow against a still-dominant apartheid social structure in the American South, thereby opening the door for African American athletes to become a vital part of college sports wherever discrimination against their participation remained a reality.

As Bob Jacobus shows, it was not just African American athletes, despite all the short-term abuse, who benefited in the long run in terms of opportunity; so did those bigoted fans who had hurled their racial slurs and made their threats. Amid their shouts, they began to realize that integrated teams, like the two that participated in the "Game of the Century," were invariably of a higher performance quality than those that remained segregated. The effect was to promote greater tolerance in the face of mindless bigotry. Over time, the jeering turned to cheering, thus significantly improving the athletic landscape while also helping to heal America's racial divide.

Yes, the "Game of the Century" was a capstone event of sorts. Of greater importance, which never crossed my mind back in January

1968, was the struggle that was going on before and long after that game to open up college athletics in the South to all players, black and white. In many ways, the bigger game of the century was that struggle, and the big winner was a more tolerant and fair-minded nation.

Bob Jacobus has given us a compelling story, sometimes disturbing but also uplifting in its presentation. I can't thank Bob enough for sharing his manuscript with me—and now with you. It's been a great honor for me to work with Bob in learning that it wasn't just the famous clash of basketball titans that mattered when Karen and I turned on the TV that freezing winter evening in Madison, Wisconsin. It was also the background story so cogently captured in the pages of this book.

PREFACE

Dr. King did a great thing, but he owes an
awful lot to the University of Houston.
   —UNIVERSITY OF HOUSTON FOOTBALL COACH BILL YEOMAN

I have devoted most of my adult life to teaching history in high school and community college, primarily in and around Houston. Having been around this great city and state since 1972, whenever I heard stories about the integration of college athletics in Texas in the 1960s, I kept hearing the same two stories of integration—both of which occurred in 1966. That spring, Texas Western University in El Paso, with an all–African American starting five, defeated all-white University of Kentucky for the NCAA title, 72–65.

The other story from the fall of 1966 was about when Jerry LeVias, from Beaumont, became the first African American scholarship football player for Southern Methodist University in the now defunct Southwest Conference, and the many challenges he faced on and off the field.

When the 40th anniversary of Texas Western's win was highlighted by the film *Glory Road* in 2006, I started getting curious about when UH integrated its athletic teams in the mid-1960s. I heard many stories about University of Houston sports in the 1960s and their rise to prominence. This rise was in no small part thanks to the recruitment of black athletes to Cullen Boulevard. Undoubtedly, the most fascinating stories centered around football's Warren McVea and basketball's Elvin Hayes and Don Chaney.

While both the Texas Western and Jerry LeVias stories were inspiring and needed to be told, I proceeded in 2007 to delve into the story of the University of Houston's integration of its athletic department. What I found, besides the fact that the story had never been fully told before, was that the city of Houston also underwent a transformation.

An avid sports fan around Houston during the pioneering Civil Rights years couldn't help but know the names Bill Yeoman and Guy V. Lewis. They were the truly insightful coaches that showed courage in recruiting star players McVea, Hayes, and Chaney. These were not just any star players; they were the first African American players recruited to play on the red-and-white-clad University of Houston Cougars football and basketball teams. They were picked not to fulfill a quota or merely signal an end to segregation in the South's largest segregated city; they became Cougars because these coaches cared nothing about the color of their faces and everything about the talent God gave them and the further development of that talent that could help a team win some football and basketball games.

The UH story is both a team history and a history of integration of college athletics throughout the South. To tell this story, I had to find all the primary sources—the coaches, players, administrators, and even as many fans and community leaders as possible. I started with an interview with Coach Bill Yeoman (long retired after his glorious UH coaching tenure) on August 10, 2007. I spent a few hours with the father of the Veer offense and similar amounts of time in mostly phone interviews with Coach Guy V. Lewis, Warren McVea, Elvin Hayes, and Don Chaney.

These five are the main characters but not the only standouts in this great American sports success story. I interviewed more than 240 others in the ensuing years, piecing together impressions, both good and bad. I developed an accurate and very moving understanding of the actions of such unsung heroes as Marvin Blumenthal and Lloyd Wells. These are two almost forgotten men who played pivotal roles in the integration of not just UH but the city of Houston itself. Blumenthal directed the recreation program at the Jewish Community Center, which was integrated years before UH and other colleges in the vaunted Southwest Conference. Blumenthal hailed from the East and walked the talk in Houston when he made it clear that it wasn't a big deal for blacks to be playing against whites in pick-up basketball games just minutes from the UH and Texas Southern University campuses. Wells was a sports writer and columnist for the *Forward Times* and the *Informer*, two of Houston's African American newspapers. Wells, recognized as pro football's first African American full-time scout, served as a facilitator and conduit for talented black high school players who were unsophisticated about the ins and outs of securing college scholarships. The list of black players Wells recruited for colleges and the National Football League draft would fill many pages herewith.

I also learned through interviews and research that Blumenthal and Wells were just two of a growing number of individuals—both blacks and whites—who formed a subculture dedicated to tiptoeing around the integration land mines around Houston and other nearby environs, such as East Texas and Louisiana. Examples are numerous and will warm the hearts of Houstonians interested in their city's history.

In the pages to follow, this book recounts many courageous decisions that put the UH Cougars near the top of America's college football and basketball world. You will learn from these pages that no one—not McVea, Yeoman, Hayes, Chaney, Lewis, nor anyone else—backed away from the dangers, most of which were kept out of the news media's coverage. The UH freshman basketball team, the Kittens, with Hayes and Chaney as members, integrated numerous East Texas junior college gyms their freshman year. The Cougar football team quietly blazed a trail of integration in college football venues throughout the South, integrating stadiums in Tennessee, Kentucky, Florida, Mississippi, and Georgia from 1965 to 1968.

Due to Yeoman and Lewis recruiting these black players, the Cougars rose from athletic obscurity to the highest level of college athletics by McVea, Hayes, and Chaney's senior year in 1967–68. The football team captured their greatest win in school history with a 37–7 win over mighty Michigan State in September 1967, with McVea having his greatest game as a Cougar. The basketball team, led by Hayes and Chaney, became the nation's top-rated team after winning the "Game of the Century" over UCLA, owner of a 47-game winning streak, in the Astrodome on January 20, 1968.

The history of the UH coaches is another great sports story told here. When Yeoman arrived from Michigan State University in December 1961, he teamed up with Lewis, who took over the basketball coaching reins in 1956, for the next 24 seasons. This formed the longest and most successful tenured duo in the two major college sports in NCAA history. (The closest to these two is Ohio State University, where football coach Woody Hayes and basketball coach Fred Taylor together roamed the sidelines and courtsides for 18 seasons from 1958 to 1976).

This book is primarily intended for sports enthusiasts and people interested in the history of University of Houston athletics. Since this is the case, I opted to present the facts in a narrative form without breaking them up with footnotes, as would be the case in a more academic work. The documentation of all game statistics and other facts is located in the sources cited in the bibliography.

In addition, anyone wanting to view the actual handwritten notes of all 240-plus interviews used for this book can see them in the Department of Special Collections at the M. D. Anderson Library on the main campus of the University of Houston.

However, this book doesn't just tell a story about athletics, pioneering coaches, and courageous players; it also documents the significance of the city of Houston's role in the Civil Rights era—a still largely untold story that deserves more credit and attention as we look back on sporting events of the 1950s and 1960s. The book should appeal to a wide audience. It is not just pigeonholed into one idea or topic.

Sports enthusiasts may enjoy reading about many of the famous names from the 1950s and 1960s in football and basketball, like Oscar Robertson or Bubba Smith. The saga of the 1971 Major League Baseball Most Valuable Player (MVP) and Cy Young Award winner, Vida Blue, who was most likely headed to the University of Houston on a football scholarship in 1967 until circumstances made him pursue a baseball career, may also be of interest to readers.

But besides sports, Civil Rights enthusiasts can learn how Houston, the largest segregated city in the South, was desegregated beginning in the late 1950s. They may like reading about some of the actual people in Houston who broke down racial barriers, people like the aforementioned Marvin Blumenthal and Lloyd Wells. Arthur Gaines, the man who integrated Houston hotels in 1962 and restaurants in 1963, recounts his story as well in these pages.

And for fans of oral history, there is much of a human element in the book, with the more than 200 interviews from people, both black and white, about relations between the races and obstacles that needed to be overcome on both sides.

In the end though, besides talking about Civil Rights, the desegregation of Houston, human relations between the races, and so on, this book is a story about two Hall of Fame coaches, Guy V. Lewis and Bill Yeoman, and the role they had in integrating the University of Houston athletic department, as well as desegregating college sports venues throughout East Texas and the South from 1964 to 1968.

As Bill Yeoman said to me during one of our interviews, "You know, Dr. King did a great thing, but he owes a lot to the University of Houston." As you will hopefully find in these pages, Yeoman was not exaggerating when he said this.

ACKNOWLEDGMENTS

I could not have written this book without the help and encouragement of many people. This book would not have been started without former Houston Cougar football coach Bill Yeoman returning my phone call and subsequently meeting with me in August 2007 to get this project off the ground.

Thank you to the other four major people in this book—Guy V. Lewis, Warren McVea, Elvin Hayes, and Don Chaney—for their candid interviews early in the project to help carry this book forward.

Also, many thanks to the following:

- The more than 240 former players, coaches, administrators, and fans who granted me interviews. I'm forever grateful, because this book would not have been possible without their cooperation.
- Former Cougar basketball player John Moore, who early on let me spend the afternoon at his house so I could interview UH legends Bo Burris and Don Schverak.
- Ted Nance, UH sports information director during the years the book focuses on, for constantly and patiently pointing me in the right direction when I had questions about that time period.

- Tom Kennedy, as I quickly found out that an author is only as good as his editor when he made the early manuscript come alive.
- Former UH quarterback Dick Woodall, who helped answer questions several times along the way.
- The fine people at the M. D. Anderson library at the University of Houston's Department of Special Collections: Pat Bozeman, Mary Manning, Matt Richardson, and Greg Yerke.
- Butch McReynolds, who provided some of his photos for the book.
- Jeff Conrad of the UH Athletic Department, for providing photos for the book.
- Don Schverak, who was a wealth of information, answered my questions with candor, and provided me with photos for the book.
- Dr. Martin Melosi and Dr. Debbie Harwell at the University of Houston Center for Public History.
- My history professor and advisor at UH, Dr. James Kirby Martin, for teaching me more than 20 years ago how to be a historian—and also, in the past few months, for his unwavering support in the quest to get this book published.

HOUSTON
COUGARS
IN THE 1960s

1 AMERICA'S SEGREGATED CITY

*We heard the N-word coming from the crowd, and we
even heard some of it from the Houston players. This was
the only game of my college career that I heard this.*
— AFRICAN AMERICAN LINEBACKER
FREDDIE JAMES OF OREGON STATE

Houston was a typical Southern city after World War II—
typical in every part of life as far as black and white social
interaction. There just was not a lot of contact between the
races. There were white neighborhoods and there were those
dedicated to African Americans. Unless you were a maid or
worked for a white man or his family in some other capacity, black people really had no contact with the white world.
Arthur Gaines, a native Houstonian and longtime black edu-
cator, grew up in this environment. "We had our part of town
and they had theirs," he said. "About the only time we might
mix was on public transportation." Houston had streetcars in
its earlier days, and Gaines recounted the years when there

was a "colored" section in the back. The same segregated sections were present later in city buses.

When stories have been told about the postwar Civil Rights movement in the South, the role of Houston and its move toward integration has been rarely mentioned alongside the more notable stories from Birmingham, Memphis, Jackson, Atlanta, Greensboro, and New Orleans. One apparent reason was Houston's geographic location on the western edge of what will always be considered the "Deep South." Although slow to integrate, Houston did not see the violence prevalent in many Southern cities in the 1950s when the roots of the Civil Rights movement were being planted. The Bayou City simply was not in the national limelight and quietly remained the largest segregated city in America—remote and out of the sight and mind of the movement's leaders.

Gaines graduated from the all-black Phillis Wheatley High School and went on to work for the Houston Independent School District for 61 years as a teacher, principal, deputy superintendent, and school-board member. In the latter capacities, Gaines made decisions that affected the nation's third-largest fully integrated school district. Yet in his public school days, he never had a white classmate. A white counterpart and fellow Houston native, Joel Williams, the son of a University of Houston golf coach, attended Lora B. Peck Elementary School on South Park (which came to be known as Martin Luther King Boulevard), Cullen Middle School on Scott Street, and Austin High School, where he was a member of the 1964 state championship basketball team. "In all my years of school," Williams recalled years later, "I never went to school with a black person. The races never socialized. It was like we were over here and they were over there. It was two separate worlds. It was just the times. I didn't know any better and it was just the way it was back then."

Integration at any level of Houston society was nonexistent; white athletes participating in any sporting endeavor involving African American players was totally unheard of. It would only be made possible by the slow-moving Civil Rights efforts in the Lone Star State, where the National Association for the Advancement of Colored

People (NAACP) and staff lawyers like Thurgood Marshall challenged segregation in higher education through lawsuits in federal court. Several cases reached the United States Supreme Court. One example had Houston ties. *Painter v. Sweatt* involved Heman Sweatt, an African American mail carrier from Houston who applied to the University of Texas School of Law in 1946. In order to prevent Sweatt from attending this traditionally all-white institution, the Texas legislature created what became Texas Southern University in 1947, complete with a new law school for blacks. Not satisfied with this, Thurgood Marshall eventually won Sweatt's case before the Supreme Court in 1950, thus integrating the UT law school.

After the success of this case and others, the NAACP began attacking segregation at the public school level. The event that began to expedite change in the South was the landmark Supreme Court decision known as *Brown v. Board of Education of Topeka, Kansas*. Chief Justice Earl Warren and the eight other justices unanimously struck down segregation in public schools across the United States with that decision on May 17, 1954.

Although Houston was in transition like the rest of the South after *Brown v. Board of Education*, it was still very much a Southern city. Segregation and racism were still the way of life there. Mickey Herskowitz, a native Houstonian and longtime sports columnist for the now defunct *Houston Post* and later the *Houston Chronicle*, well recalled the racial attitudes at the *Post* in the 1950s: "The paper 'covered' black sports teams only by occasionally printing a high school or college score and not much else. In 1954, the Houston Buffs's Texas League franchise, a Class AA farm team of the St. Louis Cardinals, signed their first black ballplayer, a first baseman and future Major League player named Bob Boyd."

Herskowitz remembered, "We actually had a copy editor resign because he did not want to report on or edit articles that mentioned black ballplayers." Even after the Buffs integrated, it was an unwritten policy at the *Post* not to run pictures of black players. For example, the editors thought that a picture of a black player sliding into third base on the front page of the sports section would be offensive to white readers.

This racist attitude persisted throughout the 1950s and beyond, as illustrated by another event Herskowitz recalled from the inaugural season of the Houston Oilers football team in an October 9, 1960, game against the New York Titans at Jeppesen Stadium on the campus of the University of Houston. Titan offensive lineman Howard Glenn, 24, suffered a broken neck in the first half of play. The press box learned that Glenn died from the injury and announced the news to the sportswriters covering the game. In the early days of the American Football League, the writers always chose a "Player of the Game." Herskowitz heard one of his colleagues remark, "I can't cast my vote until I find out who killed that nigger!" It was taken as a joke but reflected the attitude toward black athletes on any field of play during this time period.

This attitude surfaced in almost every way. Galena Park, a blue-collar suburb east of downtown Houston, often showed flashes of bigotry. Billboards around the city in the late 1950s and early 1960s proclaimed, "Impeach Earl Warren," alluding to the chief justice's leadership in the Brown decision. Galena Park was producing outstanding all-white football teams during this period. School administrations had no problem getting their bond elections approved. One resident, who grew up to earn a law degree from UH and reach the top of his profession in Houston, verified that these elections always had a catch. "Whenever bond elections came up to improve the schools in Galena Park," Jim Perdue recalled, "all of the white citizens would vote YES to improve the white schools but would vote NO to any improvements to the black schools. Also, since there were poll taxes, very few blacks were able to vote in elections." Galena Park also had local chapters of the White Citizens Council, an organization that appeared throughout the South shortly after the *Brown v. Board* decision in 1954. The goal of the organization was to maintain segregation and promote the extreme right-wing group known as the John Birch Society.

The attitudes described by Herskowitz and Perdue extended into most areas of Houston life in the 1950s and early 1960s. Racist attitudes particularly became apparent at UH football and basketball games against opponents that had African American players on their rosters. These opponents first appeared in 1953 and faced blatantly racist home team fans until 1963, the year before the Cougars had football player Warren McVea and basketball players Elvin Hayes and Don Chaney—the individuals who integrated UH athletics. Until their first year on campus, 1964, Houston was one of the most challenging places in the South for opposing black players to come and play. Most of the issues facing football players were the individual and team accommodations they experienced when they came into town with their teams. For basketball players, the games were extremely intimidating and threatening because of the close proximity of the fans to the small arena on campus.

In spite of these harsh attitudes, by the early 1960s the city of Houston and the University of Houston stood at the forefront of change in college athletics. College football and basketball were the de facto agents for these changes in 1964 when UH became the first major college in the South to integrate its athletic program with the recruitment of McVea, Hayes, and Chaney. These recruits and the daring coaches who brought them to campus broke down the walls of segregation in the largest city in the South. Events that happened at UH sporting events before Bill Yeoman took over Cougar football and Guy V. Lewis became the crown prince of UH basketball still linger in the minds and hearts of those African American players who experienced them and went on to see changes that led to national prominence of the highest order.

Before this great sports era began, African American players from opposing colleges had to face many of the same hardships in the 1950s and 1960s that Jackie Robinson experienced in the 1940s when he became the first black to play Major League baseball with the Brooklyn Dodgers. All they had to do was travel with their teams to Houston.

The first college football team with African Americans on its roster to enter this mighty segregated city to play football against UH was the Arizona State Sun Devils, who made their appearance against the Cougars at Rice Stadium on October 24, 1953. The Cougars won, 24–20. Two Arizona State players have never forgotten what happened, both on and off the field. They not only faced a potent UH team; they also lost a battle against segregation.

One of them was junior running back James Bilton, a Phoenix native and the Sun Devils's leading rusher his senior season, a talent that earned the attention of the Pittsburgh Steelers, who later drafted him. He lasted until the final cut before the 1955 NFL season. Bilton was somewhat of an integration pioneer. The football field in Houston was not the first he integrated in the South. In 1951, he was the first black to play in Fayetteville at the University of Arkansas. He integrated El Paso that same year when the Sun Devils played Texas Western College. In 1952, Bilton, along with tackle John Jankans and future NFL Hall of Fame running back John Henry Johnson, was one of the first African Americans to play at Hardin-Simmons University in Abilene. In 1953, Bilton and Jankans became the first African Americans to play at North Texas State University in Denton, Texas. Finally, in 1954, Bilton and Jankans integrated Midwestern State College in Wichita Falls. The pioneers also officially integrated hotels in Abilene and Wichita Falls while they were at it.

Jankans was the other player who took the field against the Cougars that Saturday at Rice Stadium. He was a sophomore, future team captain, and future All–Border Conference tackle. He hailed from Reading, Pennsylvania, and had played high school football with Baltimore Colts Hall of Famer Lenny Moore. Houston's mainstream newspapers made no mention of these two young black men coming to play the Cougars. But the October 31, 1953, edition of the *Informer*, a historically black newspaper, caught on to the significance of the event. The paper spotlighted an engaging columnist, Lloyd Wells, who not only wrote about star black athletes but also helped them reach higher levels of play when he could. Wells described the significance of the appearance of Bilton and Jankans: "Before approximately 20 Negro fans last Saturday night, gridiron history was made on Rice Field here in Houston, where Negroes performed for the first time against white players on a college or school level."

Wells went on to tell his readers that Bilton and Jankans were on the Sun Devils's roster. He said Bilton was the leading ground gainer for Arizona, scoring one touchdown, and "played brilliantly on defense," since two-way starters, or one-platoon football, was the rule in 1950s college football. "On one occasion," Wells wrote, "Bilton made a brutal tackle on a UH halfback, almost tearing his jersey off in the process . . . I think that this was the instant where the whites underwent the period of transition and accepted seeing white and colored athletes come in physical contact with each other." Regarding Jankans, the columnist noted that he "played the entire game in the line and was conspicuous only by his sterling play."

Wells reflected genuine optimism about the promise of things to come: "In the future, we are going to check the rosters of all white college teams coming here and inform our readers of the fact. One thing that is remarkable and noteworthy . . . Houston has accepted Negro college football players."

Jim Bilton, a great integration figure in the annals of Texas football, died of heart failure on July 24, 1984, after serving as a school administrator for many years. However, Jankans responded to a request for an interview detailing his feelings about the historic game at Rice Stadium. "There wasn't anything that was done any different," Jankans recalled. "We stayed together at the same hotel. Coach Clyde Smith, a Michigan State man, spoke to the team ahead of time so we were prepared. The agreement was made ahead of time that the team was to stay together. I remember the hotel we stayed at had black elevator operators. When we walked into the hotel, they were happy we were there. They asked us, though, what we were doing staying in the hotel."

Hotels were segregated by law in 1953, but Jankans insisted that both white and black players stayed at the same hotel, which was most likely the famed Shamrock Hilton, just down the street from Rice Stadium. Jankans remembered seeing many black fans coming out to see Arizona State practice at the stadium, and he thought he saw a man matching Lloyd Wells's description. "As far as the game was concerned," he recalled, "there was nothing discriminatory at the game."

After Bilton and Jankans broke the color barrier in Houston's college football world in 1953, other teams with African American players followed suit. They all shared the same problem: Where would they stay?

The answer to this key question varied. If the whites on the team stayed in a hotel, the black players were quartered elsewhere. Sometimes

the teams stayed together in the campus dorms at the University of
Houston and even the very segregated Rice University. The Cougars
played their home games in Rice Stadium until the 1965 opening of
the Harris County Domed Stadium, or—as it became more commonly
known—the Astrodome. Occasionally, the integrated visiting teams
actually stayed on the campus of Texas Southern University. Segregated
or not in this time period, Houston had the rare distinction of having
four institutions of higher learning spaced like close-in suburbs, south
of downtown and only a few miles apart. The University of St. Thomas
was the only one of these four at that time that did not field any athletic teams. UST was the closest to downtown, Rice was further south,
and Texas Southern was situated to the east between Rice and UH.
So accommodations at any of the three major schools at least had the
potential for glossing over the issue of segregated hotels.

*   *   *   *   *   *   *

The next integrated football team to visit Houston was the Cougars's Missouri Valley Conference (MVC) rival from the University
of Detroit in both 1954 and 1956. Those two Detroit teams had some
unique accommodations, both times staying at a yacht club about 40
miles south of the city and situated on Galveston Bay. Frank O'Connor
was the quarterback in 1954 when the Cougars won 19–7 on December 4, wrapping up a 5–5 season. "We stayed at the Houston Yacht
Club," O'Connor said. "I don't think it was open, since we were the
only ones there. We didn't realize until years later why it was done.
The coaches didn't tell us anything. We thought it was a special thing
for us to stay there. Since we weren't from this part of the country, we
were unaware of the prejudice. There was no conversation among us
about there being segregation. We just thought we were a team staying
together."

Two years later, team member Al Korpac thought the team had
rented a country club near the water. He never suspected that the accommodations were just another gambit in the segregation game. On both
visits to Houston, Detroit had two African American players, backfield
mates Billy Russell and Richard White. Great accommodations that

were far away from the field were one thing, but the name-calling by fans during the game was another. Russell and White were heaped with abuse. Russell started out having a pretty good game, often gaining 10 or 15 yards on his carries. "On one play, I was going out of bounds and a Houston player clothes-lined me," Russell remembered. "I jumped up and got in the player's face. After that the fans chanted, 'He's a dirty nigger' over and over. I felt an extra jolt of adrenaline. Now I was ripping off runs of 20 yards a crack. After the game we had to get a police escort off the field."

On top of police help, Detroit suffered a 39–7 loss to the Cougars, thus enabling UH to finish with a 7–2–1 season record and the Missouri Valley Conference championship.

White said that in the years he and Russell played together (1954–57), they never competed against a black player. "Even the Air Force Academy never lined up a black player," White said. "I did see some black basketball players from other teams when they used to come in to Detroit to play." By all measures, Houston stood out as the most racist city. And the measure that counted the most was the fans's use of the N-word as the Detroit players ran underneath the bleachers to the locker room. "That was the only racial bias I heard from fans my whole college career," White said.

Villanova was another college with an African American player on its roster when the team visited Houston on November 17, 1956, and lost to the Cougars, 26–13. Rollie West was the Wildcats's first-ever black player and held the distinction of integrating Kyle Field earlier that same season, the home of the Texas Aggies, who were then led by Coach Paul "Bear" Bryant, in College Station, 90 miles up the road from Houston. West got a bad taste of prejudiced fans in the nonconference pairing with the Aggies, who won 19–0 on September 22.

No black player had ever taken Kyle Field, and many powerful alumni wanted to maintain the strong segregation stance. Herskowitz remembered that one of the Aggies's star players, future Heisman Trophy–winner John David Crow, intervened during a luncheon the day before the game. Both teams were present. "John David helped diffuse the situation by saying to the crowd at the luncheon, 'If us white boys can stand it here in College Station, then they can come down here and play, too!'" Crow was alluding to the fact that the white Aggie men had to endure A&M being an all-male military school at this point in time.

John Lammers, one of West's white teammates, said every team member but West stayed at the Shamrock Hilton in 1956, as "Rollie was unable to stay with us." The team was told that West stayed at the A&M president's home. "Rollie not getting to stay with us was something we weren't used to. Being from the Philly area, we had no clue as to what was going on in the South."

"I didn't stay at the president's home," West said, setting the A&M cover story straight. "I stayed with a local black family. When we came to Houston later, I also stayed with a black family." The team went to a movie in Houston, and when his fellow team members learned West was being forced to sit in "the colored balcony," they took a stand. "The whole team sat with me, which was nice," West said. "Before we came down to Texas, the coaches explained the situation to me. I just didn't know anything about this kind of prejudice, being from Philly."

The Wichita State Shockers were another MVC opponent of UH with African American players: Roland Lakes, Willie Mallory, and Bob Blackwell. Another player, star running back Ted Dean, was injured and did not make the the October 11, 1958, game, which the Cougars won, 44–0. A white player, linebacker Nelson Toburen, was a future member of the Green Bay Packers championship teams in 1961–62 under Vince Lombardi. Toburen was one of the many teammates who were upset that these three young men had to stay in private homes during road trips to the South. "We were from the North and we hadn't seen this before," Toburen said. "But it was an issue that players like Dean and Lakes never really talked about with us."

Mallory said that he, Lakes, and Blackwell stayed in a black hotel near Texas Southern and got to eat with their teammates at their more upscale hotel. "We also got some extra spending money while we stayed at TSU, so that was good," he said. They both stayed with black families on football trips to North Texas State in Denton and Hardin-Simmons in Abilene. Fans weren't kind to them at the UH game, but

Mallory added, "I do remember there were no problems at all with the Houston players."

Blackwell walked away from his experience with a whole new understanding of the South, especially of its black citizens. "Being from Philly originally," he said, "I didn't have any idea there were historically black colleges like Texas Southern University in the South. At Hardin-Simmons, I stayed with a local black family. I had no idea there was such a thing as a rich black guy."

In 1959, the Washington State Cougars became the first West Coast team with African American players to venture into the South to play a football game. They were the better Cougar team on the field, taking a 32–18 victory home with them to wrap up a 6–4 season on Thanksgiving Day in Rice Stadium. The crowd was estimated to be only six thousand fans. Washington State, under Coach Jim Sutherland, had a very talented team that included future American Football League All-Star running back Keith Lincoln (Los Angeles / San Diego Chargers), 1960 NFL Rookie of the Year wide receiver Gail Cogdill, and the Canadian Football League's second all-time leading rusher and Hall of Fame member, George Reed.

The Houston trip was Cogdill's first experience with segregation. "The schools we had played out West had never dealt with the black issue or segregation," he said. "We didn't find out our black teammates weren't going to be staying with us until we got off the plane. Keith Lincoln and I were shocked. It was like, 'What? They're going somewhere else to stay and we're staying at a hotel?' What's kind of funny, though, is that during and after the incident, we never sat down and talked about it with each other. It was never brought up. Looking back, I kind of wish we would have."

The Houston trip also was a first-in-a-lifetime experience for Reed, who had accommodations at Texas Southern. "We had never come face to face with that stuff," he recalled. "I had been taught growing up playing ball that the team stays together and plays together." He didn't learn of this common segregation practice until right before the team plane landed at the airport. However, he could cite no rude awakenings at the stadium from either the fans or the players. "In fact," he said, "a few of the Houston players shook my hand after the game. One play that stood out was when I was blocking on a kickoff return and I wiped out about five guys with one block. It felt there was something pent up inside of me—I wanted to prove I belonged on the same field as everyone else."

Reserve running back Perry Harper, the first black player at Washington State, joined as a walk-on after military service, having been convinced that it was the place for him by his company commander. Harper said, "Even though I had been around a lot because of my military experience, I did not realize Houston was not integrated. We were not told about the segregated conditions in Houston until Coach Sutherland finally told me on the plane when we were about an hour out of Houston. I was playing cards in the back of the plane, and Coach sat down next to me and said he wanted to talk to me. He said when we got to Houston, we would be picked up by a group from Texas Southern University, and that's where we'd stay."

Sutherland then prevailed upon Harper to break the news to Reed about the arrangements. At 22, Harper was almost four years older than Reed. The segregated arrangement did have its benefits. When Harper and Reed got off the plane, they were provided $200 apiece, and off they went. "I had never been to an all-black university before," Harper said. "They accepted us right away and we actually had a pretty good time. This was a learning experience, though. The racism wasn't totally new to me, being in the military before Washington State. I think it was all new to George, though. There was one thing that Coach Sutherland did at the game that stood out. He actually had me start this game. Usually I backed up Keith Lincoln, but when the lineup was announced, I came running out. I think coach did it to prove a point."

As the 1960s approached, Houston remained a segregated city, but times were changing. In March 1960, about a month after North Carolina A&T students had tried to integrate lunch counters in Greensboro, Texas Southern University students led by Eldrewey Stearns and Quentin Mease, director of the Houston's African American YMCA, attempted to integrate several Houston lunch counters. Later that summer, the TSU students attempted to integrate the downtown Houston lunch counter at Woolworth's.

With this backdrop of change, football teams from the North and West continued to come to Houston with their African American players to compete against the Cougars. In 1960, UH dropped out of the Missouri Valley Conference to become an independent. At the end of the 1961 season—in the last game before Bill Yeoman became head coach of the Cougars—Oregon State University was scheduled for a season-ending matchup. The Beavers were led by future Heisman Trophy–winner Terry Baker as quarterback. However, the Cougars ended up with a 23–12 victory that gave them a 5–4–1 record, compared to Oregon State at 5–5. The Beavers had several African Americans on their roster, including Art Gilmore, Gene Hilliard, John Thomas, and Charlie Marshall.

Another black Oregon State player, linebacker Freddie James, recounted the trip: "Houston was our last game of the year. The year before in Portland, we had beaten them badly. None of us had ever faced segregation before. Coach [Tommy] Prothro told the whole team beforehand what our travel plans were. We would not be staying in a hotel but on the University of Houston campus. Usually when we flew to an away game, we would spend two nights away from home. In Houston, we only stayed on Friday night and flew home right after the game on Saturday. I found the whole thing distasteful."

"During the game," James continued, "we heard the N-word coming from the crowd and we even heard some of it from the Houston players. This was the only game of my college career that I heard this. It was not a pleasant experience. One thing that did stand out, though, was how well the team joined together. They were disgusted that Oregon State would enter into that contract to play in Houston. There was nothing pleasurable about that weekend. It was a mediocre season capped by a loss at the end, and I remember it was a quiet plane ride home."

The last two teams that came to Houston with African American players were old Missouri Valley Conference foes: the University of Cincinnati and the University of Detroit. The Bearcats came to Houston in 1962 with lineman Rufus Simmons and Al Nelson, later a defensive back for the Philadelphia Eagles for nine seasons. Nelson and Simmons recalled that the team stayed together in Rice University dormitories. Otherwise, there weren't any unpleasant on-field incidents. "My older teammates warned me to keep my helmet on because sometimes the Houston fans would throw things like Coke bottles from the stands," Simmons said.

The coach of the Bearcats was Chuck Studley, who later became the interim head coach of the Houston Oilers for ten games in 1983. Studley recalled trying to "shield our players" by staying on the Rice campus. "The night before the game, the team went to a movie, and we had to sit in the balcony as a team because that was where the black players had to sit," Studley said. "I also remember cautioning our players that there were certain restaurants they couldn't go to. The whole ordeal was kind of interesting. Neither myself nor the team had ever experienced anything like that before."

The last team to come to Houston to play the Cougars before they integrated in 1964 was the University of Detroit Titans on November 2, 1963. The Cougars, in the midst of a 2–8 season, blasted the Titans, 55–18. Detroit had only one African American player on its roster, tackle Robert Rice. The year before Detroit came to play UH, they had been involved in an ugly racial incident and a five-minute brawl on the field against Memphis State University, where several Detroit players had defended Rice because of the racial slurs and cheap shots delivered his way by opposing players.

The Detroit players experienced no on-field incidents with Cougar players. However, when the visiting Titans showed up at their hotel, they ran into a slight problem. During the registration process, the hotel manager saw Rice, who was waiting outside. The manager was not planning to register a black player. But then Coach John Idzik went to the manager and stated, "You go out there and tell that young man to his face he can't stay here!"

Years later, when Coach Idzik's son, John Idzik, the present-day general manager of the New York Jets, heard of this incident involving his father, he explained, "Back when my dad was a coach, he was color blind. He cared about his players. What he said that day sounds exactly like what he would have done in that situation."

The manager relented, and Bob Rice got to stay with the rest of the team. It proved to be a sign that things were changing for the better in the South's largest segregated city.

2 DORM BUNKS AND CRAMPED ARENAS

They screamed, booing, questioning my ancestry, yelling every
name in the book. Programs flew down from the stands.
Hot dogs and cinnamon buns—all of it directed at me.
—OSCAR ROBERTSON, CINCINNATI BEARCATS

African American college basketball players coming to play
in Houston had to deal with the same dual hardships as their
football counterparts. They, too, were subjected to different
accommodations because of segregation and the taunting and
verbal abuse by the Houston fans. Some of the biggest-name
players and teams appeared in Houston from 1953 through
1963. Although Jim Bilton and John Jankans of Arizona
State were the first two African Americans to play college
football in the South's largest segregated city, they were not
the first black athletes to play a college sport there.

That distinction belongs to Wichita State University star
forward Cleo Littleton, who played in Houston on February 25, 1953. Littleton was followed a week later by Ben

Bumbry of Drake University, with both games against the Cougars at the old Sam Houston Coliseum in downtown. Littleton played twice in Houston: as a sophomore in 1953 and a senior in 1955. In the latter game, he became only the seventh player in college basketball history to score more than two thousand points in a career. He scored 30 points against the Cougars in an 82–79 loss. In 2014, at the time of this writing, Littleton was still the all-time leading scorer in Wichita State history with 2,164 points.

Several of Littleton's white teammates recalled the 1955 trip to Houston, in which the game was played on the UH campus at Public School Gym (later known as Jeppesen Field House), which had a capacity of only 2,500. Littleton stayed with a black family. Once on the court in the cramped arena, he was extremely close to the fans and could hear their every word. A white teammate, James Strathe, recalled, "The fans kept hollering, *'Nigger go home!'* Being from Kansas, we were sort of integrated, so we weren't used to this." Another teammate, Gary Thompson, said, "It was all very degrading. We hadn't been exposed to that stuff in Kansas. Cleo handled it very well. We talked about the situation a little bit as a squad. The white guys knew that we couldn't afford to lose our tempers. I thought overall the whole team handled the situation with class."

Another white Shocker player, Glen Boyer, called Houston "the worst place as to how Cleo was treated. They called him every name in the book." The team's train arrived at midnight, and Littleton was picked up by a black family, with whom he spent the night. Boyer did concede that when Littleton scored his 2,000th point and was removed from the game, "he did get applause from the Houston crowd."

"It was getting toward the end of the season," Littleton remembered, "and I needed 22 or 23 points to get to 2,000. When we got to Houston, I stayed with an African American family—she was a teacher and he was a postal employee. The game was played in that little gym on campus and I only made four field goals in that game, but I was 22 out of 25 at the free throw line, so I got the record.

"They tried their best to keep me from the record. They beat me up. Houston was the worst. In this gym there was a little tunnel to the court. The fans threw cups at me—some empty, some with ice or what-ever else was in them. They called me every name but Cleo Littleton. I also remember that after the game we went to the train station, and I had to wait in the 'Colored' waiting area. All of my teammates moved in there with me, though, and sat with me. That made me feel good."

Ben Bumbry had similar experiences five days later when he became the second African American to take a college basketball court in Houston. Bumbry helped to lead Drake University to a 73–64 victory over the Cougars, ending a 13–12 season on a positive note. He was the team's leading scorer, averaging 17.4 points per game, and was later selected to Drake's 1950s All Decade Team.

"It was the only time I couldn't stay with the team," Bumbry said, in recalling his trip to Houston. "I stayed with a professor from Texas Southern University at his house. Houston was a bad experience. Ear-lier in the year, we had played them at Drake. Our old field house there had two landings. On the landing one of the Houston players said, 'We're going to get you, nigger, when you come to Houston.' John England, my teammate, grabbed the Houston guy and almost got into a fight. When we did go to Houston, I got spit on, hit in the face, and I remember one time I drove the baseline and got clobbered and nothing was called. It was just a bad time there."

Bradley University of Peoria, Illinois, a Missouri Valley Confer-ence member, visited the Cougars on several occasions from the early 1950s to 1961, the year after the Cougars dropped out of the MVC to become independent. The Braves had several African American players that were recruited by coaches Bob Vanatta and Chuck Ors-born during those years, which happened to be some of the most successful seasons in Bradley history. The first were Shellie McMillon and Curley Johnson, both out of Chicago. They helped lead Bradley to the 1957 National Invitation Tournament (NIT) championship. Another prominent black player in the era was Joe Billy McDade, a sophomore on the 1957 NIT title team and senior on the 1959 NIT runner-up squad. The 1960 NIT championship team also included Bobby Joe Mason, Al Saunders, Mack Herndon, Chuck Granby, and All-America sophomore and future NBA All-Star Chet Walker.

When the Braves came to Houston during this time period, they were subjected to the same treatment other African American players commonly faced.

Bradley came to Houston in 1957 to face the Cougars in Coach Guy V. Lewis's first year as head coach. Surprisingly, UH won this home game, 88–79, although the team ended the season at just 10–16. One of the white players from this Braves team was Gene Morse. He recalled that veteran players Curley Johnson and Shellie McMillon warned their younger teammates what might happen courtside in what for many of them was their first appearance in Houston. "I was from the small town of Havana, Illinois—about 4,500 people," Morse said. "We didn't get involved in that racial stuff."

When it first came time for a meal together, the Bradley team entered the restaurant through a side door with their black teammates. At the game, things got much worse. "Besides getting on the black players," Morse said, "the Houston fans were calling to the white players, 'nigger lovers, nigger lovers, nigger lovers!' Houston was the worst place we ever played. Early in the game, McMillon went over a Houston player's back. The fans very quickly let us know what they thought of us. I was a sophomore, only 18 years old. Even though it was tough, I'm glad I went through that era. We were pioneers, but we didn't make a big deal out of it. It makes a better person out of you. We knew it was the right thing to do."

Joe Billy McDade, a Bradley forward from 1957–59, likely had the most unique perspective of any African American player when he came to Houston. Today a US District Judge in Peoria, McDade was a native Houstonian who wound up at Bradley almost by accident. McDade grew up in the predominately black Third Ward in Houston, "at 2817 E. Alabama, right by the old Jack Yates Senior High School on Elgin and Delano, not far from the UH campus." He received only one college basketball scholarship offer—from Huston-Tillotson College in Austin, 170 miles west of Houston.

Graduating from Yates in 1955, McDade won the E. E. Worthing Scholarship, worth $4,500. "I wanted to get out of Texas," he said. "You can understand why. My high school civics teacher told me there was a small liberal arts college in Illinois called Bradley. Turns out I got accepted, and the day I went over to Texas Southern University to send off the $50 matriculation fee to the college, the lady at TSU who helped me, Naomi Washington, said, 'Bradley! I just graduated from there! Do you play basketball?' I honestly hadn't thought about playing basketball at Bradley. For sure, no one on the team knew I was coming up there."

McDade caught a train to Chicago at Union Station and met Shellie McMillon and Curley Johnson when they got on the same train. The two basketball recruits immediately wanted to know who McDade was and what his plans were, assuming he was a noted recruit from Texas that Bradley coach Charles "Ozzie" Orsborn had somehow discovered. "They took me out that night and I had my first beer," McDade said. "The next night I got a call from the Peoria paper. The reporter started asking, 'Who are you? Did Ozzie recruit you? Don't lie to us.' Coach Orsborn had no idea I was even on campus. He tracked me down in the registration line and asked me if I'd like to come out for basketball. I went out for the freshman team, and I got a partial scholarship halfway through my sophomore season."

The player from Houston, McDade, wasn't eligible for varsity basketball as a freshman, so he didn't get to go with the team on its trip to his hometown. McMillon and Johnson clued him in on what happened. They hadn't been able to stay with the team at what McDade described as "the finest hotel in the South"—the Shamrock Hilton. Instead, they were sent to a rundown black hotel on Dowling Street in the Third Ward. McDade said, "I had to tell the guys that the hotel they stayed at, the Ajapo, was a well-known whorehouse."

Once on the varsity team and bound for Houston, McDade told Orsborn he wasn't staying in the whorehouse. Coach Lewis opened up the UH dorms for the black players, but Orsborn declined the offer. He made arrangements for McDade, McMillon, Johnson, and Bobby Joe Mason—in McDade's words, "a fantastic player"—to stay with black families. The Bradley–UH game was played at the very cramped Jeppesen Field House. "It was the first time my grandmother had seen me play—it was a small place," McDade said of the venue, which was virtually in his boyhood neighborhood. "The fans called us *nigger*, spit on us, and we got into a slight brawl with the Houston players. We got our payback the next year when we beat them 116–80 in Peoria. To my amazement, just a few years later these same fans were cheering on Elvin Hayes. I saw the power of sports change the outward expressions of racial prejudice."

Future seven-time NBA All-Star Chet Walker and the 1960 Bradley NIT championship team made a late-season visit to Houston and suffered a 63–58 loss on February 22, 1960, one of only two losses that season, the other a road defeat to the Oscar Robertson–led Cincinnati Bearcats. Playing in Houston was part of a three-game road trip through the South—St. Louis, Houston, and Denton, home of the North Texas State University Eagles.

Walker and his teammates encountered problems in all three cities. "I remember the deal was we couldn't stay in hotels in Houston," he said. "We stayed in the girls's dorms. After the game, we went over to TSU to eat. We were treated in a hostile way at the game. We were called names and I remember cowbells ringing. After the trip through those three cities, I wanted to transfer. We had also played at North Texas. We had gotten in a fight up there, so that was even worse than Houston."

Before Bradley's first trip to the South, the season started impressively for Walker. He scored 111 points in the first three games of the 1959–60 season, elevating Bradley to be ranked as the No. 4 team in the nation. Walker felt pretty confident by the time the three-city road trip to the South came around. Coach Orsborn well knew what was in store and reminded Walker and three other black players—Al Saunders, Bobby Joe Mason, and Mack Herndon—to expect racism and offensive treatment. "That was just the way things were and there was nothing we could do about it," Walker recalled.

In St. Louis, the home team band played "Dixie" while the fans waved Confederate flags. Once in Houston, Bradley's black players got what really amounted to a Christmas present. As expected, the team was refused admission to the Shamrock Hilton, but every player, both white and black, was allowed into dorms at the University of

Gary Phillips of UH shoots over Bradley's Chet Walker (#31), January 1961
(Courtesy of Don Schverak)

Houston. "The only reason the black players got to stay with the white players was because it was Christmas vacation time at the university," Walker said. "We still had to get our meals at Texas Southern University, a black school."

During warm-ups for the Houston game, fans threw lit cigarette butts on the floor at the Bradley players and screamed, "Nigger!" The experience confounded Walker and the other blacks. "I was in a state of great confusion and frustration," he said, "and I scored only one point in the first half, wondering why I was subjecting myself to such abuse." Although he got control of himself in the second half, scoring 20 points, Walker and the Braves lost a close game. Then the team went up to Denton and got into the fight with the North Texas fans.

Walker recounted, "I will never forget those games, those fans, those towns, and the way I felt. After we returned to school, I called my mother and told her I wasn't sure that I could keep going.

Everything had turned so ugly. I said I couldn't stay at Bradley. I was going to transfer, but that didn't work out. I then became desperate enough to consider flunking out. If I couldn't play for another school, I would just fail and go home. Eventually, I found the resolve to stay and get everything I could from the experience."

Like Bradley, the University of Cincinnati made several visits to Houston while a member of the Missouri Valley Conference, first from the late 1950s to 1960 with the Oscar Robertson–led Bearcats and then in 1961 and 1962, when Cincinnati won back-to-back NCAA national championships. Robertson's senior year was 1959–60, so he was in the NBA when the Bearcats got the glory with three black stars in 1961 and four in 1962. "The Big O" and two black sophomores, Tom Thacker and Paul Hogue, anchored the 1960 team. By the 1962 championship season, the Bearcats had four black starters: Thacker, Hogue, Tony Yates, and George Wilson.

Obviously, teams were becoming basketball powers in the NCAA with the recruitment of and steady reliance on African American players.

*   *   *   *   *   *   *

The name Oscar Robertson was golden on the NCAA basketball courts by 1960. Robertson came to Houston for the first time as a sophomore on December 21, 1957, when the UH Cougars hosted the Cincinnati Bearcats at Public School Gym. Fans in Houston weren't used to seeing a highly rated team like this one, and a growing number of them didn't care that much about rooting for the home team, which lost to the Bearcats, 70–53.

One of the Robertson fans was a high school kid named Bill Worrell, but he wasn't just any sports fan. He later attended UH, becoming a cheerleader and playing for the baseball Cougars. After graduation, he went to work as a field reporter for the NBC affiliate in Houston, KPRC/Channel 2, and soon began serving as a full-time sports reporter. In 2014, Worrell was serving as the play-by-play announcer for the Houston Rockets for Fox Sports Southwest. He said that his one and only purpose for attending the Cincinnati game at UH was to see Oscar Robertson. "In fact," Worrell said, "we were cheering for him. Cincinnati had a terrific team. I really don't remember him being treated badly."

A couple of Robertson's white teammates, however, Spuds Hornsby and Dave Tenwick, had different memories. So did Robertson himself. Hornsby and Tenwick had helped recruit Robertson in a part of the nation that had general knowledge of the Civil Rights movement but seldom felt the need to pay much attention to it—that is, until they came to Houston. The white players stayed at the Shamrock; their star, Oscar Robertson, did not. Earlier in his career, he had broken the color barrier at Cincinnati in the same year the school entered the Missouri Valley Conference. Like Bradley, Cincinnati made the same trek through the South to St. Louis, Houston, and Denton, while under the tutelage of Coach George Smith.

"In Houston, we stayed at the Shamrock Hilton, a plush, downtown hotel," Robertson recalled. "At around midnight, the hotel manager called Coach Smith's room. He said Coach Smith had to get that black kid down at the end of the hall and get him out of the hotel.

"I was in my room. I'd been lying down on the bed for a little while, when a knock on the door interrupted. Coach Smith came in and said that I couldn't stay here. Well, I thought the whole team was moving."

"What do you mean?" the star asked. "Where are we going?"

Smith told him the rest of the team was staying put, but Robertson had to go to a nearby "blacks-only" college, Texas Southern University.

"They don't want blacks staying here," Smith said.

Robertson continued, "I didn't know what to say or do. The Texas Southern basketball coach got out of his bed in the dead of night, helped me out, and found me a spare dorm room. In that dorm room, I laid down on a little bunk bed. 'What just happened?' I asked myself. 'What the hell is going on here?' I had forgotten momentarily that this was America."

At the game the next night, the packed house exploded. It wasn't cheers for Oscar Robertson; it was abuse being hurled at him, along with everything else some members of the crowd could find. He thought he had trouble enough being matched against Gary Phillips, who later became the first All-America basketball player at UH and a first-round draft pick of the Boston Celtics in 1961.

Upon reflection many years later, Robertson said that had the crowd known what he had endured the previous night, cheers would have filled the air for a hotel manager just doing his job. "They screamed, booing, questioning my ancestry, yelling every name in the book," Robertson said. "Programs flew down from the stands. Hot dog and cinnamon buns. All of it directed at me.

"I didn't take any warm-up shots or get loose, but just stood in the middle of the court, my arms crossed. I didn't know if I was going to play, did not know what to do, but the longer I stood there, the angrier I became.

"Something inside me said, '*Play the game.*' So I did. I scored only 13 points, my low for the season, and some papers would make it out as if this kid Gary Phillips had a lot to do with stopping me. The truth is, under the circumstances, it was one of my best performances in college.

"I hadn't gotten any sleep the night before, hadn't warmed up, and was mad as hell, really not in the right state of mind to play the way I usually did. We still pounded them, 70–53. Afterwards, a newspaperman asked how it felt to be the star, yet forced to live away from his teammates. I answered, 'How would you feel if you were me?'

"Then I waited until we were back in Cincinnati and went to see Coach Smith. I told him I did not think he had anything to do with what happened. If I thought he had, I would have left school and never come back. But, I also said, he'd checked me into that room. The university and the athletic department, and *yes*, the coaching staff—all of them knew the travel plans; they were responsible for making and OKing them.

"I said I did not want to go anywhere again with the team and yet be kept separate from them. I did not want to attend any civic functions or any public team functions. I didn't blame the players on my team for what happened. But if I couldn't stay with them, I wanted nothing to do with team functions that promoted this school, and I didn't want any questions about it.

"If anything like this happened again, I told him, I would leave UC. From that day forward, I grew up fast."

After Houston left the Missouri Valley Conference in 1960, Cincinnati again played the Cougars on their home court in 1961 and 1962 at the conclusion of the two seasons the Bearcats won national championships. The growing number of black players suffered the same abuse as Oscar Robertson.

On February 23, 1961, the Bearcats beat the Cougars, 85–80, at Jeppesen Field House. Black players stayed in a UH dormitory. "We barely got out with our lives, though," Mark Altenau, a 1961 letterman for Cincinnati, said. "Houston was the worst. I was scared."

Starting center Paul Hogue became the New York Knicks's second overall pick in the 1962 NBA draft. Hogue also recalled the 1961 trip to Houston. "To be honest, a lot of that stuff in Houston didn't bother me. I had been born and raised in the South in Knoxville, Tennessee. I remember we had to stay in the dorm. At the game, there was a section where about 20 black fans were sitting in the corner.

"I remember it was a close game, and Ted Luckenbill of Houston took a shot and as it was going down into the basket, I took it out and the ref didn't see it. The fans didn't like it. After the game, we had to stay in the dressing room, and they brought in all the sportscasters and announcers down to talk to us.

"When we left, we had a police escort back to the dorm. I had also heard that players from other MVC schools like Drake and Bradley had been treated badly. Houston was the worst place we went, and what's funny is a couple of years later they had Hayes and Chaney and everything changed."

Another black player for the Bearcats, Tom Thacker, later had a seven-year professional basketball career with the Cincinnati Royals, Boston Celtics, and the Indiana Pacers of the fledgling American Basketball Association. Thacker was on the Houston trips in both 1961 and 1962. "I remember elbowing a Houston player, and the fans started throwing ice at us and calling us names," Thacker said of his 1961 experience. "Eventually we had to be escorted back into the locker room." The following year, UH played its games in the only slightly more spacious Delmar Field House across town, where Cincinnati won, 60–52. "When they introduced the starting lineup, they introduced the four black starters first and then Ron Bonham last. The crowd gave him a standing ovation for being the only white starter."

Cincinnati had a growing number of black players, each of whom detailed his experiences for this study of the last big city in America to integrate its college basketball courts and other sporting arenas.

Forward/center George Wilson, another Cincinnati player who amassed a seven-year pro career, also remembered the TSU accommodations, the "cracker box gym," and the "mock cheer" for Ron Bonham. "I also remember towards the end of the game, I flipped a pass to a teammate for a layup, but I ran into a Houston player," Wilson said. "The Houston crowd started throwing stuff on the floor, including a lot of coins, some as big as half dollars. When the game was over, I said to Thacker and Yates, 'Let's get out of here!' I have nothing positive to say about our visit to Houston."

Thacker told his teammate, "I got called 'nigger' so much I thought they were calling Roy Rogers's horse—Trigger!"

Reserve Larry Elsasser, a sophomore in 1962, was a white player who hailed from an integrated neighborhood in Cincinnati. He was taken aback by black players having to stay away from the team in the TSU dorm and also somewhat leery of Shasta, the University of Houston's live cougar mascot who made regular appearances at athletic events. "The Houston fans were chanting, 'Feed 'em to Shasta,' about my black teammates. The whole experience was an eye-opener. The one place I remember in my career at Cincinnati was Houston."

The Cincinnati game brought out the worst in the UH fans. Junior center Dale Heidotting recalled an incident in 1962. "I remember fans throwing money at us," he said. "In fact, I picked some up and put it in my shoe. I remember after the game, the fans were angry. Coach [Ed] Jucker got hit by an orange on the way to the locker room."

"Coach went up to a state cop and told him if he had any balls he would go up into the stands and get the guy who did it," senior reserve forward Fred Dierking said. "Luckily our athletic director had made the trip, and he intervened to downplay the incident."

Dierking explained, "I remember when we flew into Houston, we had been told stories beforehand about the prejudice down there. When we got off the plane and went into the terminal, one of the first things we saw was the 'White' water fountain and the 'Colored' water fountain."

Junior guard Larry Shingleton said, "I was scared in Houston. We had to run off the floor after the game." He and other players found it to be a unique "first" that Jucker had to bend the state trooper's ear about getting hit with the orange. But there were many "firsts" for this group of players from the Midwest.

Bonham went on to play two NBA seasons with the Boston Celtics and one with Indiana of the American Basketball Association (ABA). He recalled that the mock cheer made him feel uneasy. "I got loud applause as I was introduced last," he said. "It was strange. All through high school I had played with black players and I didn't think about it. What happened in Houston affected me. I felt very uneasy about the whole situation and I'd never felt that way before."

* * * * * * *

Another college team that came to Houston in the 1961–62 season was just beginning to make its mark on the national scene under a coach that college basketball fans everywhere grew to love and admire for his winning ways. Coach John Wooden's 1962 UCLA Bruin team was his first to make the Final Four, where they lost in the national semifinals in Louisville to the Cincinnati Bearcats, 72–70. Two key players on that Wooden team were African American sophomores Walt Hazzard from Philadelphia and Fred Slaughter from Kansas City. When they were seniors in 1964, they helped lead UCLA to an undefeated 30–0 season and their first of ten national titles under Wooden.

UCLA came to Houston on December 22 and 23, 1961, to play in the Lions Club Tournament at Sam Houston Coliseum in downtown. Little did the players know when they hit this Southern city that it would be where they truly became a *team*. It would be the only time that Hazzard and Slaughter ever played a game in the Deep South. The players, such as reserve Jim Milborn, had been raised in places like

Long Beach, where they had never experienced the need to segregate a team based on the fact that it had black players. "It was kind of a shock, what transpired," Milborn said.

The Bruins had a dismal 2–4 record going into the first game of the tournament. The record initially became even worse. The Cougars destroyed the team from California, 91–65, with their zone press. Apparently believing that Hazzard and Slaughter were not getting fair treatment from the referees in the first half, Wooden held out both players the rest of the game. The next night, he didn't play either one against Texas A&M.

None of the Houston newspapers mentioned the offbeat—some would say *strange*—strategy. But United Press International, one of the nation's two leading newspaper wire services at the time, contacted Wooden. (Or it could be that Wooden contacted the wire services.) United Press International (UPI) prepared a story after interviewing Wooden about the incident. The next day's issue of the *Modesto (California) Bee* exclaimed, "UCLA Coach Blasts Race Issue in Texas." The wire story said Wooden "insists he's not trying to be a crusader but emphasizes that because of racial problems, 'I don't think we'll be taking another team to Houston—at least not for a while.'"

The following Tuesday, the coach told the Southern California Basketball Writers luncheon, "They treated us well. There was no trouble from the crowd. There was no picketing of any kind outside. There was no segregation inside." Then he went on to say that he had held out his two Negro players against A&M "because I felt everyone would be better off."

The article also said Wooden "did not know until the team arrived in Houston for the two-day tourney that UCLA had different arrangements" than some of the other teams in the tournament. "We stayed on campus," Wooden said. "I thought that's where everyone stayed until I found out Auburn and Texas A&M were staying at a hotel. Then I learned that other teams with Negro players like Cincinnati and Bradley also had to stay on campus."

Wooden concluded, "We held them out the next night. They [Hazzard and Slaughter] just didn't feel comfortable. It's hard to explain.

Walt Hazzard (#42) of UCLA looks to rebound against the Cougars, December 1961
(Courtesy of Don Schverak)

But we just felt everyone would be better off." The article went on to say that the University of Southern California would be making a trip to Houston in February 1962. The Trojans had one Negro player on its roster: Vern Ashby.

"John Wooden waited until he got back from California before he said anything about the race issue," longtime UH sports information director Ted Nance asserted decades later in an interview for this history. Nance tells a different story: "Truth is, his team had been destroyed by our zone press. They got frustrated and got some fouls called on them. Walt Hazzard was hot-dogging, trying to dribble behind his back, and kept getting the ball stolen.

"Wooden conveniently blamed everything on something else. At Sam Houston Coliseum, the stands were a long way from the benches, so I don't know how they could have heard anything. Ever since that day, I've had a problem with John Wooden."

"We absolutely killed them with the zone press," UH sophomore forward Donnie Schverak remembered. "Every time we would get Walt Hazzard in the air, we would take the ball away from him and then he would foul someone. The reason he didn't play the second half was because he had pretty much fouled out in the first half and we were so far ahead. There was nothing racial about it. We were just kicking their asses."

Schverak then added, "After that game, John Wooden went over to Guy Lewis's house, and Guy showed him the zone press we used to beat them. It was the same zone press Wooden used to start winning national championships in 1964."

Former Wooden player Jerry Norman, then in his first year as an UCLA assistant coach, backed up Nance's contention about the racial accusations: "There really wasn't anything out of the ordinary when we went to Houston. We stayed on campus. I don't remember anything racial coming from the stands. I think [the racial situation] was perception more than reality. These games brought a lot of anxiety to the sophomores—Hazzard, Slaughter, and Larry Gower, too. They had never been away from the West Coast. This was their first road trip. I think that had a hand in the racial thing. I think it may have been a perceived problem when there wasn't one."

After their weekend in Houston, the UCLA team pulled together and ended their regular season on a 14–4 run. Then they won their first two games in the NCAA Tournament before losing to Cincinnati. Many of the UCLA players credit their experience in Houston for bringing the team together.

An almost forgotten figure on the UCLA team that year was the third African American player on the Bruins's roster—sophomore reserve guard Larry Gower, a Los Angeles product. "I couldn't forget that trip," Gower said. "We were not allowed to stay in downtown Houston. We stayed on campus. One incident I remember before the game was that the NAACP was going to be at the game and was going to picket over segregated seating. They asked us [himself, Hazzard, and Slaughter] not to cross the picket line and play. I was only 19 or 20 years old and I wanted to play ball, so I played. Houston was the first place I had ever been where I had seen blatant discrimination.

"The main thing I remember about the game were the fouls called on Hazzard and Slaughter in the first half. I guess, as a form of protest, Coach Wooden sat us down the second half of the game and the game the next night. Nothing was directly said by Coach Wooden to the team about it.

"What's funny is that up until the Houston game, we had been a pretty mediocre basketball team. In a curious way, that experience knitted the team together—a purely unintended effect. That was the first year we went to the Final Four. Almost 50 years later, and I still remember it. It definitely left an impression on me."

Gower later had a conversation with Mike Warren, who played in the famous UCLA–UH game in the Astrodome in 1968. "He goes to my church. When I told him what had happened to us, he couldn't believe it. He said that when UCLA went there to play in the Dome in '68, there were no problems, and it was funny how fast things could change in just a little over six years."

Senior Pete Blackman was a starting forward on the 1961–62 UCLA team and eventually worked for UCLA as administrative vice chancellor before moving into an emeritus capacity. Blackman's feelings about the Houston weekend eventually got him mentioned in the March 19, 1962, edition of *Sports Illustrated*. Blackman said, "I was 20 years old, and we were playing in a segregated arena. I remember there was some issue before the game on segregation. We stayed at the UH dorms. I don't remember any cackling between us and the UH players. The refs, though, started in on Walt and Fred. It was like foul

on Walt, run down the floor, foul on Fred, run down the floor, and
so on. They just wouldn't let them play.

"I was put in the game, and they nailed me with a bunch of fouls
as well. Coach Wooden was such a careful and thoughtful man—he
wouldn't lash out—so he decided not to play Walt and Fred anymore
while we were there. We had never encountered anything like this
before. The way we came together and handled it bonded us together
as a team. In fact, Walt said to me that it meant a lot to him that the
team went out and won the game the next night against Texas A&M.

"Walt was the catalyst. That brutal weekend in Houston bonded us.
Us coming together as a team was a source of great pride, and it helped
us grow both as individuals and as a basketball program. I believe it was
the springboard that helped us win our first NCAA title two years later.
The whole thing was just so shocking to us. They [the black players]
were just so unwelcome.

"The poem that was mentioned in *Sports Illustrated*—I was an En-
glish major, and the afternoon before the Texas A&M game, I scratched
out a poem on an envelope that was a comment on society in Texas—
was a parting shot. I knew Coach Wooden would not approve, so I put
it on the locker-room chalkboard on our way out.

"The players liked it—it was not obscene. It just commented on
society in Texas. *Sports Illustrated* got a hold of it later in the year and
printed part of it." The article was titled "Wizards in the Land of
Oz." Of Blackman, it said, "After UCLA was thrashed at Houston, he
composed an ode on why it is hard to be a visiting team using Negro
players in the Southwest. He noted that he had a tough time, and it
was only his name that was 'half-Black.' This effort ended up with
Blackman exulting, in masterful meter, over the Mexican victory at
the Alamo."

"It was part of the ethic of the ball club," Blackman said. "It was
how we grew together and became friends. I think Walt, Fred, and
Larry liked it that I took up their cause."

To quote one of the more notable lines of the poem, "They laid me
out upon the rack, and only my name was half-Black."

Blackman continued, "Yes, it was a miserable affair. It was an institutional thing, that being the city of Houston. We never had a problem with the players at UH."

Sophomore center Fred Slaughter from Topeka, Kansas, hadn't experienced being a target of the Jim Crow laws that remained a Houston practice. He and Hazzard got into a segregated taxi cab and were briefed on the facts of life in the Bayou City. "The black driver told us that Houston was still very bad when it came to segregation and that we would just have to learn to live with it," Slaughter said. "When the game against Houston started, the refs started dropping fouls on me that weren't warranted. We were held out of the second half of the Houston game and the whole second game."

"It didn't bother us that much. We did come together as a team, though, sitting in those dorms—it was only us on campus. It had a bonding effect. I recall that when we got back to UCLA, it was shortly thereafter that the college came out with a policy that we would no longer travel to places that were not racially sensitive.

"What's kind of funny about the whole thing is that years later I was walking around the UH campus with Clyde Drexler, since I was representing him after he was drafted by Portland. And we walked around the campus and I thought to myself how badly I had been treated in Houston just a few years before."

Hazzard grew up in Philadelphia. He matured after the Houston experience and went on to a 1964 senior season to clearly demonstrate the leadership that would help UCLA win the national championship. Then he became a territorial first-round draft pick of the Los Angeles Lakers, going on to play ten NBA seasons. Hazzard was also a member of the United States gold-medal basketball team in the 1964 Olympics, and after his playing days, he served as the Bruins's head coach in the mid-1980s.

Hazzard remembered the segregated conditions, his first and only time to experience such treatment while a college player. He also recalled that while UH was assessed only 16 fouls in the first game, UCLA got 33. "The game was not fairly officiated. I didn't play in the second half. It was obvious to me why we didn't play. Coach Wooden didn't have to explain it to us.

"He didn't want us to play anymore down there. Before we came to Houston, Coach Wooden had given us some indications that there might be some problems down there. I do remember Larry Gower and I going to a party somewhere near campus after the game. The event upset a lot of people, though. The incident bothered me. It wasn't the first time I had been exposed to it.

"Even though I grew up in Philly, my parents—and myself a little bit—had been exposed to racism back in Delaware, where they were from. My parents grew up in segregation. The whole incident in Houston hurt and I didn't like it. It made you not want to go there again. The whole incident made a bond with the players and the team. The incident spoke well of the white players's character. Guys like Pete Blackman were more upset about it than we were."

The last two games of the 1962 regular season for both Houston and Southern California took place at Delmar Field House on February 23 and 24, with the Cougars taking 56–51 and 76–68 victories to propel them into the National Invitation Tournament, where they lost their first-round game to Dayton, 94–77.

Vern Ashby had become the first black basketball player in USC history three years before, and the game with Houston was the only time Ashby played in the South. "I remember before we went to Houston, one of the assistant coaches held a meeting with the team to explain what the situation was," Ashby said. "We couldn't stay together in a hotel. We could either stay on campus or not go at all. My teammates said they weren't going to Houston without me, so we decided to stay in the dorms.

"It's funny that one of my friends on the USC football team, Ben Wilson, the starting fullback and captain of the 1962 national championship team, was from Houston and said, 'You know, that place is segregated.'

"I really don't remember any particular problems at the games. We played on back-to-back nights. I don't remember anything going on. My teammates were very protective of me."

The 1962–63 season brought the eventual NCAA champion, Loyola of Chicago, to Houston on February 28, 1963. What transpired was one of the worst incidents involving black players on a visiting team before integration. At the time, Sonny Yates was a columnist for the UH student newspaper, the *Daily Cougar*. In an article titled "Jeppesen Crowd Unbearable," Yates described the incidents of that night, in which Loyola prevailed, 62–58, before a packed house of 2,638 fans.

"It's the worst I've ever seen and a big discredit to the school itself," Loyola coach George Ireland told Yates, referring to the unsportsmanlike conduct of the Jeppesen crowd. The unruly fans not only used harsh language but also took on the job of tossing cups, paper, and even pennies onto the playing area. In addition, fans sitting close to the railing near the Loyola bench blurted out derogatory statements concerning the eight Negro athletes on the Ramblers team. Ireland stressed emphatically that it wasn't the players's fault; it was the fans that were unsportsmanlike. "Of course, it was probably fans other than students involved. But things such as this are bad for any school," Ireland said.

Yates's article continued, "Ireland was correct. Half the wild fan antics was done by Houston area fans and not students. These fans (some adults) were not only behaving themselves in a childish manner, but they were ruining UH's reputation all over the nation."

The article went on to quote Loyola's star player, Jerry Harkness, as saying, "It was the worst I've seen in high school or college." Ireland said he thought a lot of Coach Guy Lewis and the Cougar players and wanted to return to Houston for future games. "But I just can't put up with the fans," he said. The incident was still clearly etched into the memories of both Sonny Yates and the Loyola-Chicago players decades later. Yates said, "It was February of 1963 and we hosted Loyola of Chicago. This was less than a year before Elvin Hayes and Don Chaney came to UH."

Several Loyola players recalled the abuse they endured that night. Jerry Harkness was the star of the Loyola team and later drafted by the New York Knicks, lasting three professional seasons with the Knicks and the Indiana Pacers of the ABA. He remembered, "We had a lot more talent than Houston did. I remember we were up by a lot at the half. We were playing in a small gym and the fans from the city came to watch. As we went back on the court for the second half, the fans threw things at us and on us. I didn't play well in the second half and Houston made it close at the end.

"It was very tough on me emotionally. I had grown up in New York City. Les Hunter, who was from the South and was used to this, pulled us through. To me, the whole thing was shocking. I also remember that Les, myself, and Ron Miller went out to eat after the game, but where we went they said they couldn't serve us."

Houston restaurants were not integrated until June 1963. Hotels were officially integrated on April 1, 1962.

Harkness then added, "It's funny how life is sometimes. I was originally supposed to go to Texas Southern to play ball. I wasn't a good student, and I had only been playing ball for about a year. What happened was that the dorm I was going to stay at burned down—at least that's what I was told—and so now I was stuck with no place to play. At the time, I thought it was not good. In [TSU's] yearbook I had seen some pretty girls, and I had talked to their star player, Bennie Swain.

"I was excited, but now my scholarship was gone. My mentor, Walter November, a New York insurance man who organized and coached playground teams in New York, would recommend area players to Rambler coach George Ireland. Coach Ireland contacted Loyola and I worked my butt off to improve my grades. I ended up majoring in Sociology. I started out making C's, but I got my grades up to A's before I graduated."

Guard John Egan was the only white starter on Loyola's team in 1963. A Chicago native, Egan also was a part of college basketball integration history. In an earlier 1963 game against Wyoming, Egan fouled out, and Coach Ireland replaced him with a black substitute, Pablo Robertson. This move made Loyola of Chicago the first team in NCAA history to have five black players on the floor at the same time.

Egan recalled his team's Houston trip: "We didn't know how bad it was going to be—at least, I didn't. It was worse than anywhere as far as the fans and the bullshit you had to go through. It was just at the game itself and it was just a few of the fans. It was not the city of Houston, the UH players, or the university. Interestingly enough, I had been recruited by Houston, and I took a recruiting trip there to see Guy Lewis, Gary Phillips, and Ted Luckenbill. I loved it there. I came this close to going there."

White reserve Chuck Wood said, "I do remember the team meal before the game was at a black restaurant. I also remember we had to take separate cabs to the game. At the game, things were pretty dicey. All of us white players were called 'albinos' and 'nigger lovers.' The fans threw money while we were shooting free throws. Easily the worst place I had played in. We had also played in New Orleans. I was pretty naïve at the time as to what was going on in the South—I was only 19 or 20 years old."

An African American reserve on the 1963 Loyola-Chicago team was junior center Rich Rochelle, who said, "Houston was extremely bad. We were called names. They threw pennies at us. At least in the South, though, the racism was blatant, so you knew exactly what you were going to face and where it was coming from. Growing up in the North, you didn't know who was going to stab you in the back.

"For example, in Evanston, Illinois, where I played ball in high school, we had an unspoken set of rules, like no more than three minorities on the team and no more than two on the floor at the same time. Coach Ireland let us know what we were going to face when we went to the South. After a couple of trips, we knew what to expect. In fact, Coach Ireland liked to run up the score on teams from the South to humiliate the people in the stands. When I played for Loyola from 1961–63, it was a time of upheaval, of change, about not accepting the status quo."

Junior guard Ron Miller was a New York City native unexposed to the sort of treatment he received in Houston and the South. "I didn't think much about going to Houston before we went there," Miller said. "I didn't think Texas was like that. In fact, one of my high school teammates was playing at Houston: Reno Lifschutz. I had met Houston coach Guy Lewis up in New York when he was recruiting Reno. After the game in Houston, Coach Lewis came up to me and apologized for the way the fans acted. I'll always remember that.

"I also remember at the game the fans calling John Egan 'albino' and a bunch of other names. At one point during the game, I chased a ball out of bounds and a lady fan yelled at me, 'You nigger!' Chuck Wood told me when he was standing in the huddle, he got hit in the chest by a piece of ice, and at first he thought he had been shot. Les Hunter told me that Houston had the toughest crowd of all. When I've told my own kids what happened to me and my teammates in Houston, they thought I was exaggerating."

The last time a team with African American players played in Houston before the arrival of Elvin Hayes and Don Chaney to UH in the fall of 1964 was on December 2, 1963, at Delmar Field House, when the Minnesota Golden Gophers arrived to defeat the Cougars, 60–58, in the closing seconds. The Gophers had three black players, all sophomores: future NBA All-Star Lou Hudson from Greensboro, North Carolina; Archie Clark from Ecorse, Michigan (a Detroit suburb), who went on to play ten NBA seasons; and Donald Yates from Donora, Pennsylvania.

Coming to Houston for their first varsity game was their only trip into the South in the three years they played varsity ball. They were also the first black basketball players to ever play for Minnesota. The football team had been integrated several years earlier with players from the South. The quarterback of the Gophers's 1960 national championship team was Sandy Stephens, an African American who helped recruit Hudson, Clark, and Yates, along with Minnesota coaching legend John Kundla. Kundla coached his alma mater from 1959 until 1968, having earlier coached the George Mikan–led Minneapolis Lakers to NBA titles in 1950, 1952, 1953, and 1954.

Kundla and his three black players and reserve teammate Donald Dvoracek recalled their Houston experiences. "I was on the bench," Dvoracek said. "I can remember the racial slurs being cast at all three players. I played a little bit. I do remember we did all stay in the same hotel. What's always stuck in my mind when I think of Houston is how things changed so quickly down there after they integrated."

While Clark failed to recall any significant events, Yates said, "We were so young. We just couldn't envision stuff like that. I was from

Pennsylvania and I had never been treated like that before. At Minnesota, the fans had always treated us with open arms."

Hudson remembered an incident regarding the Gophers's accommodations: "I remember we went to go check into a hotel by the airport. We [the black players] were always the last players off the bus because we would sit in the back and play cards. When we walked up to the counter, the clerk stopped registering the team and said we had to leave."

"We ended up having to stay in a black hotel," Coach Kundla said. "I also remember going to a restaurant and being refused service there. At the game, I recall some Houston fans calling Lou 'nigger.'

"Lou eventually on one play dunked the ball so hard that the ball hit the floor and bounced back up through the basket. It was a good thing no one was under the basket. The ball came through there so hard—I never saw a dunk like that in my life.

"It hushed up the crowd. I did recruit the first three black players to Minnesota. I got lots of nasty letters and phone calls from fans. The first couple of years were rough."

So less than a year before Elvin Hayes and Don Chaney set foot on the campus of the University of Houston, African American basketball players from visiting colleges were still being treated shoddily when they came to Houston to play the Cougars. However, after the game, they were able to return to their integrated college campuses and not face further abuse. As will be examined later, black players growing up in Houston did not have that luxury of leaving until they got ready to go to college. Once old enough, they, too, left the South for further educational and athletic opportunities, not by choice, but by necessity.

3 BLACKOUTS AND JCC HARDWOODS

It was hard to get praise from Marvin, though. The best I got when I was at UH was, "You might be OK kid." After I made the pros, I came back one day and he said, "You might be a player now." He was a basketball player's friend.
— ELVIN HAYES ("THE BIG E") ON
MARVIN BLUMENTHAL

The desegregation of Houston is generally believed to have begun with actions taken by Texas Southern University students, led by student activist Eldrewey Stearns under the guidance of their Civil Rights movement mentor Quentin Mease. The South Central YMCA, just across the street from the TSU campus, served as the meeting place for students involved in an organization called the Progressive Youth Association (PYA), and Mease was the YMCA director. The PYA studied the tactics used by students at North Carolina A&T. On February 1, 1960, these students had held the first of their sit-ins aimed at desegregating the Woolworth's lunch counter in Greensboro, North Carolina. Lunch counter protests like this one swept through the South over the next month in cities like Nashville and Chattanooga in Tennessee; Montgomery, Alabama; Little Rock, Arkansas; Raleigh, North Carolina; and Portsmouth and Richmond in Virginia.

On March 4, 1960, Eldrewey Stearns and 13 other Texas Southern students staged the first Civil Rights sit-in west of the Mississippi River when they walked from the TSU campus to 4110 Almeda Road and entered a local Weingarten's supermarket to sit at the lunch counter. Store management promptly closed the counter as the group waited to be served. The next day, the students walked to the nearby Mading's Drug Store on the corner of Almeda Road and Oakdale—also within close proximity to the TSU campus—only to face the same closure tactic.

Thwarted in these first two attempts to integrate, the students eventually set their sights on comingling the downtown Houston lunch counters at Foley's Department Store and F. W. Woolworth. Both black and white business owners saw the potential for a possible Houston race riot like those that had become too commonplace in other Southern cities. They began working behind the scenes to bring about the orderly desegregation of downtown Houston stores.

The resulting plan was developed and led by three individuals: Hobart Taylor, a black entrepreneur; Bob Dundas, vice president and head of publicity for Foley's Department Store; and John T. Jones, publisher of the *Houston Chronicle*. They convinced all downtown stores to integrate quickly and in unison. Dundas assured the managers of downtown lunch counters and businesses that there would be no negative publicity if they integrated. In fact, the business leaders took steps to make sure there would be no publicity at all. Dundas convinced every newspaper, television, and radio station in Houston not to report on the downtown integration for a week. Dundas termed the tactic "the Blackout." The news media agreed to it for the good of the city and to ease into integration without the adverse publicity that could very well set off protests and even riots.

Thus on August 25, 1960, 70 downtown lunch counters, department stores, drugstores, and supermarkets desegregated. True to their word, the news media made no mention of the policy change for one week. The September 12, 1960, edition of *Time* magazine questioned the media suppression of the story, even though the blackout used in America's largest segregated city had obviously thwarted the threat of the racial turmoil experienced in other cities throughout the South. Houston business leaders used the media blackout tactic twice more when Houston integrated. In April 1962, the Houston Colt .45s would begin their inaugural baseball season in the National League, the state of Texas' first Major League team, amid another potential race-related controversy. The city's hotels were not integrated. "National League stars like Willie Mays and Hank Aaron would soon be coming to Houston on road trips, and they would not tolerate staying in a segregated hotel," Quentin Mease reasoned at the time.

On April 1, 1962—ten days before the Houston Colt .45s played their first home game in history—the Rice Hotel in downtown, the Shamrock Hilton Hotel (where National League teams were booked to stay), and several other hostelries accepted their first black guests. The news media made no mention of the changes.

The African American individual who drew the task of integrating Houston hotels was Arthur Gaines. He believed in the job he had to do. "White business leaders decided they didn't want all the violence other Southern cities had when they integrated," Gaines explained many years later. "They met with a group of black members of the YMCA board of directors, with Quentin Mease being the leader for the black community. Since I was the youngest member of the board, they chose me to be the one to integrate Houston hotels. The older guys on the board said, 'You're a young guy, you can handle it better than we could.'

"When it became time to integrate, I was told to go down to the Rice Hotel, go check in, and I would stay in a room on the second floor. I got there, checked in, and as I went to get on the elevator to go to the second floor, I passed the in-house detective. He was a white guy with a cowboy hat and boots on. He really didn't notice me at first, and it looked like he was dozing. A white person passing by said, 'Mr. Detective, see that Negro boy coming into the hotel?'

"The detective called out to me, 'Hey boy, where you goin'?' as I was getting on the elevator. When he came up on the next elevator and the detective asked me what I was doing there, I said, 'Check with the hotel manager.' The detective then said, 'How long you stayin' here, boy?' I told him, 'Just one night.' And that's what I did. I stayed there one night and I was on my way."

The media blackout worked a third time in 1963. In May, Astronaut Gordon Cooper conducted the last spaceflight of Project Mercury. Since NASA's Mission Control had just been established in Houston in 1962, Cooper was scheduled to take part in a downtown parade on May 25, 1963. The Progressive Youth Association threatened to disrupt the event unless Houston's movie theaters and restaurants were integrated. Hobart Taylor, John T. Jones, and George Dentler, the president of the Houston Restaurant Association, averted the disruption by agreeing to an immediate integration plan. With the blackout in place a third time, these businesses were opened to blacks without incident in June 1963.

Once again, Arthur Gaines was chosen to undertake the task of integrating Houston restaurants. "You're a young guy, you can handle it," the YMCA board members repeated. "I went to the Pier 21 Restaurant on South Main Street, which was owned by George Dentler, to eat," Gaines recalled. "When my wife and I walked in, the young lady who was the hostess said to me, 'What do you want? Do you want a job?' When I said we were there to eat, she said, 'We don't serve colored here.' Another guy working there said to her, 'It's OK, let them in.'

"My wife and I went into the restaurant, and they seated us in the back in the corner so people coming in couldn't see us when they came through the door. I ordered a lobster. I had always wanted one and so I got one.

"You have to give the black and white community leaders a lot of credit for integrating Houston without incident. People in the Houston Restaurant Association and black leaders like Quentin Mease knew integration was inevitable and so they got it done."

The end result was that—unlike other cities in the South that went through rioting and protests when the time came for integration—the city of Houston experienced few of these problems, in large part because of the news blackout. In all probability, this is why the largest segregated city in the post–World War II South hardly gets mentioned in the histories written about the Civil Rights movement. Although they opened themselves up to criticism because of the news blackouts, the news media operated for the good of the city. And the blackouts worked.

* * * * * * *

The integration of a much smaller venue than places like downtown theaters and major hotels happened in 1958, two years before the TSU students became determined to integrate lunch counters. This widely unheralded event took place on the basketball courts at the old Jewish Community Center at 2020 Hermann Drive, next to Hermann Park Golf Course and Zoo. Ironically, this tree-laden location was just a few blocks from Weingarten's and Mading's Drug Store and only three miles from the campus of the University of Houston.

The person responsible for this noteworthy move toward integration was not a native Texan but rather a man from the eastern United States with ties to many of the famous names and teams from college and professional basketball's early years. Marvin Blumenthal was born in 1924, a native of Trenton, New Jersey, and graduate of Trenton Central High School. After graduation, Blumenthal went off to Temple University in Philadelphia and played basketball and soccer from 1942 until 1945. Blumenthal was captain of the basketball team and was named honorable-mention All-American in his senior year. After graduating from Temple with a degree in physical education, Blumenthal played a year of professional basketball in the Eastern League, the forerunner of the NBA, in 1945–46 for the Philadelphia SPHAs, an acronym standing for South Philadelphia Hebrew Association. He played under legendary Coach Eddie Gottlieb.

In September 1946, Blumenthal accepted the position of director of health and physical education at the Jewish Community Center in Troy, New York. He also continued his basketball-playing career, first for the Cohoes Mastadons of the New York State Professional

Basketball League and then the Troy Celtics of the American Basketball League. Considered one of the nation's finest teachers of basketball, Blumenthal had long relationships with some of the pioneers of early East Coast basketball. While at Troy, Blumenthal started the tradition of holding basketball-coaching clinics.

One friend and coaching colleague of Blumenthal who traveled to Troy every year for the clinics was legendary Long Island University coach Clair Bee, the namesake of the Clair Bee Coach of the Year Award, which is given to the NCAA Division I basketball coach who has made the most positive contributions to the sport the preceding year. Coach Bee is also the renowned author of the Chip Hilton sports-fiction books for juveniles as well as other books on coaching. Bee's career winning percentage of .826 is still the highest of any Division I basketball coach in NCAA history. His teams won the NIT in both 1939 and 1941.

Bee also helped implement the three-second rule and was known by his contemporaries as the game's greatest defensive strategist for his development of the 1-3-1 zone defense, which is still in use today. Bee wrote many technical books on basketball and conducted coaching clinics around the world. In 1968, he started Kutsher's Sports Academy in the Catskill Mountains in New York.

Blumenthal was also friends with Boston Celtics legend Red Auerbach, who was instrumental in the integration of the National Basketball Association. In 1950, Auerbach drafted Chuck Cooper, the first African American player in NBA history. In the early 1960s, he was the first NBA coach to have an all-black starting five: Bill Russell, K. C. Jones, Sam Jones, Willie Naulls, and Tom "Satch" Sanders. After he stepped down as head coach in 1966 to become general manager of the Celtics, Auerbach hired Bill Russell as the first black head coach in NBA and major professional sports history.

In September 1951, after five years in Troy, Blumenthal accepted the position of director of Health and Physical Education at the Jewish Community Center in Houston, familiarly known as the "JCC." He took the job because, in the words of his wife Carol, "he wanted a change."

Once Blumenthal got to Texas—historically a hotbed for football but lagging behind in basketball coaching expertise, level of interest, and quality of players—Blumenthal spent the next few years trying to change attitudes and advance the game of basketball in the Lone Star State. Steady as he went in his new home state, Blumenthal resumed his practice of bringing Clair Bee in for coaching clinics. In the late 1950s and 1960s, Bee conducted clinics in San Antonio, Houston, El Paso, and the South Texas town of Edinburg, home of Pan American University, which soon became part of the Blumenthal success story.

Blumenthal also quickly became a person that high school, college, and professional players turned to for help and advice. It wasn't just basketball players, either. Blumenthal helped people from all levels of social strata and served as a mentor to many young people. Doris Blumenthal, wife of Marvin's younger brother, Bernard, told the story of how Marvin helped her husband after bringing him to Houston. She said, "Bernard ended up owning his own chemical company. Marvin was also a huge influence on our son. Marvin used to take Bernard to the JCC to introduce him to all the players."

While the elder Blumenthal primarily assisted basketball players, he also helped other sports figures in the Houston area. In Mickey Herskowitz's description, "Marvin was like a God to the players. He would help negotiate the pro players's contracts. He was a great person. Marvin was decades ahead of his time. He didn't have self-interests. He always did what was best for the player. It wasn't just basketball players Marvin helped, either. For example, Solly Hemus [Houston Buffs minor leaguer who graduated to the St. Louis Cardinals and later made Houston his home] would go see Marvin for advice on financial things and even which doctors he should see."

Yet Marvin's greatest interest and influence centered around basketball players—black or white—from Houston high schools and nearby colleges and even the professional players who passed through the Jewish Community Center in the late 1950s and 1960s.

Donnie Schverak, who played and coached at the University of Houston, went to the JCC when it was in its old location near Hermann Park. He said, "I practically grew up there. I used to take Ken

Spain over there and we used to play. I knew Marvin really well. He was a great guy." Others, like Luke Jackson, played in the JCC summer league and got to know Marvin well for his kindness and toughness, saying, "He wanted to see athletes play ball. He really helped."

Jack Thompson became the captain of the 1962 Cougar team that compiled a 21–6 record and went to the NIT in New York. Thompson himself hailed from the Bronx and was automatically attracted to the Blumenthal approach to basketball at the JCC. "Marvin used to work with us," Thompson remembered. "He was very hard-nosed and did not praise us much. He was very special, though. He was like a dad to me. I used to go over to his house. In fact, when my wife and I were planning on getting married, Marvin took us to get our engagement rings. He was that kind of person."

Gary Phillips had the distinction of having had Blumenthal help him at the JCC while still a UH student. Later Phillips would come back to those same hardwoods after his first NBA season to get assistance with the fundamentals of his game. He wound up working with Blumenthal in the late 1960s in an effort to get an NBA franchise to Houston. "Marvin was my mentor," Phillips said. "He played in the old NBA. He was an East Coast guy. He knew more basketball than anyone. He was good friends with Coach Lewis, and not many people know that for the Houston–UCLA game in the Astrodome, Marvin helped Coach Lewis devise the defense for that game. I came back to Houston many times in my pro career when I was in a slump and I would spend hours with Marvin working on the finer points of the game. Other NBA players used to come to the JCC to play ball and get help from Marvin."

Ronnie Arrow went on to become the head basketball coach of the University of South Alabama after winning three NJCAA championships while coaching San Jacinto College in Pasadena, a southeastern suburb of Houston. Arrow later started the basketball program at Texas A&M–Corpus Christi. Arrow grew up at the JCC.

"My mom was the secretary to the executive director," he said. "I was there every day from at least 8 to 5. High school, college, the pros—Marvin would have them working out there. Bernie Kapner,

Ricky Kaminski, McCoy McLemore. I would work out with the older guys. Marvin and Guy Lewis were close. If you were a player passing through town, you played there. Elvin, Gary Phillips, Ted Luckenbill—they played there while they were in college and then they came back after they went to the NBA."

"One guy who really helped me when I first got to Houston was Marvin Blumenthal," Elvin Hayes said. "He was probably one of the two or three best influences in my life. I would go over to the JCC to play pick-up games. It was hard to get praise from Marvin, though. The best I got when I was at UH was, 'You might be OK, kid.' After I made the pros, I came back one day and he said, 'You might be a player now.' He was a basketball player's friend."

* * * * * * *

Unquestionably, Blumenthal's biggest contribution to the advancement of basketball in Houston and the South was his leadership in the quiet integration of the Jewish Community Center in the summer of 1958. "Marvin brought the black players to the JCC because he just thought it was the right thing to do," his wife, Carol, stated more than 50 years after that policy change.

For the majority of the black players, it was the first time they had played against whites, and vice versa. David Lattin was a native Houstonian and graduate of Worthing High School. In 1966, Lattin was the starting center on Texas Western University's all-black starting lineup that won a national championship against all-white Kentucky.

"The summer before my senior year in high school," Lattin said, "Marvin Blumenthal, the athletic director of the JCC, asked me to play there. This was an opportunity that a select few players received, and I knew it. Players such as Luke Jackson played because the JCC served as a conduit for basketball players going to Pan Am University. It was there, in the summer of 1962, that I first played against white athletes. It was a first for a lot of them as well. I believe part of what Blumenthal was doing had nothing to do with finding players for integrated Pan Am U. He had a greater agenda, and we were part of it."

Guy V. Lewis developed a very close friendship with Blumenthal and would say, years later, "I used to go over to the JCC before integration and watch and wish. I wanted McCoy McLemore, but I couldn't have him, because we weren't integrated."

Bernie Kapner was another Houston native who played for Coach Lewis's first three teams at UH from 1957 through 1959, serving as team captain his senior year. Kapner well remembered those first days of integration at the JCC and the actions of his mentor, Marvin Blumenthal. "He was way ahead of his time," Kapner said. "I started going to the JCC when I was in junior high. I remember he would have afternoon camps. We'd get about 60 kids in the gym.

"Marv didn't see color. The first two black guys I remember coming to the gym were Earnest Martin from Wheatley High and McCoy McLemore from Yates. McCoy's nickname was 'Tree' because he was so tall and thin. Bennie Swain, who was at TSU, started coming to the gym, too. Later, Marvin helped other black players like Walter Sampson, Howard Montgomery, and Otto Moore to go play at Pan American University, and later he helped get them into the pros.

"After my freshman year at UH, he would work with me one on one. He would say, 'I want to show you this move'—for example, a crossover dribble. He'd teach people the pick-and-roll and the give-and-go, just way ahead of his time. He was always four or five steps ahead of others. He was such a good teacher.

"He also became friends with Guy V., and they would talk a lot. Marvin also got me a summer job at Kutsher's Country Club up in the Catskills of New York. He was friends with Red Auerbach—who would live at Kutsher's in the summertime and coach teams in the summer league there—and he brought me, Bennie Swain, and Jack Thompson up there.

"We would be bellhops during the day, and at night we would play basketball. Red also came to Houston several times to see Marv. They were both students of Clair Bee."

McCoy McLemore is remembered as one of the first blacks to play at the Jewish Community Center, starting in 1958 while he was still a student at Houston's Yates High School. He recalled how Blumenthal helped him eventually reach the NBA. "Marvin was a friend of Red Auerbach. He opened the JCC two nights a week. UH followed a couple of years later," McLemore said.

"Guy Lewis wanted me to come to UH, but they hadn't integrated yet. I was going to go to Prairie View A&M University, but Marvin and Guy convinced me to go off to a community college first—Moberly Community College in Kansas—and then come back when UH was integrated. Marvin convinced me at the time that if I wanted to play in the NBA, I had to end up at the right white college." McLemore eventually transferred to Drake. Influenced by Marvin and Guy V., McLemore researched the NBA and learned that of the 108 players on contract, only 12 came from all-black colleges. "That convinced me not to go to Prairie View," he said.

It won't be surprising to note that Blumenthal also had a role in the integration of college basketball in Texas. Starting in 1959, Blumenthal began to send black players from Houston and its surrounding area to play under Coach Sam Williams of the tiny Pan American University in the Rio Grande Valley town of Edinburg. Pan Am had experienced little basketball success until Williams took over the program in the 1958–59 season. In the three previous seasons, the Broncos only won 13 games, 8 of them coming against a Mexican college known as Monterey Tech.

Williams got the infusion of talent he needed with players like Howard Montgomery, Walter Sampson, Walter Yates, Mitchell Edwards, and Luke Jackson. The plan hatched by Blumenthal and Williams worked. Led by Jackson, Edwards, and Yates, the 1963 Broncos captured the National Association of Intercollegiate Athletics (NAIA) championship, and in 1964 they were semifinalists. Jackson went to the Philadelphia 76ers as the fourth pick of the 1964 NBA draft and played on the gold-medal 1964 US Olympic Team.

"I came to the Valley in 1950," Williams said. "We weren't winning very many games. We needed help. I got a lot of players from Houston and the Jewish Community Center. I don't know why they wanted to come down here. We didn't even have our own gym. I took a chance on a lot of kids that other coaches wouldn't.

"I got to know Marvin at the JCC. Everyone would go there to play basketball. Marvin was also very influential in getting Clair Bee to come to Edinburg for a basketball clinic. Mind you, this was a poor area for basketball. After the clinic, though, Clair said, 'I'm coming back next year,' and the next year's clinic was much more successful.

"Marvin helped everyone if you were honest and sincere. The JCC was known throughout the country as a place where blacks could come to play. I think Marvin kind of liked the underdog school and would try to help them out. I had a lot of good players come through here thanks to Marvin."

Howard Montgomery, a Houston Wheatley graduate, was the first black from the JCC to head to Pan Am, and he played there from 1959 through 1962. He eventually was the first Pan Am player to play in the NBA, appearing in 20 games for the San Francisco Warriors in the 1962–63 season. "I had gone to TSU at first and I met Marvin," Montgomery said. "Guy Lewis used to play there. Marvin eventually got me to go to Pan Am. He knew Sam Williams, the coach there.

"When I got there, I was the only black guy on campus. I later helped recruit Walter Sampson, Walter Yates, and Luke Jackson to come there. Without Marvin, I wouldn't have stayed in college and I wouldn't have played pro basketball. I even worked at the JCC some. He would work us out until midnight sometimes.

"Marvin would even take me home occasionally. He would put me on a cot in his house. Marvin knew Red Auerbach, and so he got me a job at Kutsher's. I would be a bellhop during the day and play in the games at night. I met Wilt Chamberlain there. Oscar Robertson and Elgin Baylor played there, too.

"In the four years I was at the JCC, we never had any racial problem. I remember there was some white guy there one time who was not a regular and he was in the shower. Marvin asked him, 'What are you doing?' The guy said, 'Looking for soap.' Marvin said, 'There's some.' The guy said, 'It's been used.' Marvin knew what the guy was implying, and he ate that guy up pretty good and told him to never come back. The JCC was a great experience."

Walter Yates was another Wheatley graduate who made it to Pan Am via the JCC. He played on the 1963 championship team and later was a longtime basketball coach in the Houston Independent School District. Yates said, "Marvin was close friends with Collin Briggs, my high school coach at Wheatley. Marvin had a summer league at the JCC. The University Interscholastic League (UIL), the white governing body for high school athletics in Texas, and the Prairie View Interscholastic League (PVIL), which was the governing body for black high school athletics in Texas, had rules against summer leagues. But Marvin just called it 'open gym.' It was by invitation only, though, and the players were handpicked. Howard Montgomery was there, McCoy McLemore was, too.

"Marvin was also influential about getting us in school. He stressed conduct and character—just like my high school coaches, Collin Briggs and Jackie Carr. Marvin was so far ahead of his time. He was assimilating white kids and black kids. Whites hadn't played ball against blacks, and vice versa. Guy Lewis would come and watch. The next summer [1960], he started to open his gym to blacks and whites. It improved Houston basketball. We went from segregated to integrated."

Marvin Blumenthal continued to advance the cause of college and professional basketball in Houston into the late 1960s. After the success of the Houston–UCLA basketball game in the Astrodome on January 20, 1968, Blumenthal arranged for an NBA doubleheader on February 4, 1969, also in the Dome. The Detroit Pistons played the Cincinnati Royals in the early game and the Boston Celtics—with Don Chaney on their roster—played the San Diego Rockets, which featured rookie Elvin Hayes in the second game. The two-game set was first promoted at a news conference in Houston on June 27, 1968. Atlanta Hawks owner Ben Kerner was there along with fellow promoters Marvin Blumenthal and Gary Phillips.

The news conference also served notice to the public that Blumenthal and Phillips wanted to bring an NBA franchise to Houston by the start of the 1969 season. "Marvin was the only person that I knew of who could get things done on a large scale," Phillips said. "He helped bring the doubleheader to the Dome in February 1969, and that drew

41,000 fans. Marvin was also trying to buy the Atlanta Hawks from Ben Kerner. He was trying to get a group of about 20 buyers."

Blumenthal developed his ideas and implemented them. Early in 1969, he was ironing out the details needed to open the new Jewish Community Center in Southwest Houston. Still active after all these years, he was in the process of trying out one of the new handball courts just a few days before the scheduled opening.

He never gave up exercising. He knew he had a bad heart, having had his first heart attack at age 38. As his sister-in-law, Doris Blumenthal, would later recall, "Marvin knew it was going to kill him. He said he didn't care; he would rather go out being active rather than being an invalid."

Alas, he never saw the new JCC officially open. On March 18, 1969, Marvin Blumenthal died of a massive heart attack. He was only 44 years old.

Marvin had been around long enough to open the door to integration, and once that door became more than just slightly ajar, coaches in two sports at the University of Houston were ready to kick it in.

4 BLACK PLAYERS LEAVE JIM CROW TEXAS

San Francisco will always have a warm place in my heart. The woes of Texas seemed to fall away. I knew we were in a different world. It seemed a world where everyone got a chance. There were Mexicans, Chinese, Blacks, Irish—imagine!—all in the same school.
—BASKETBALL STAR K. C. JONES

The cases of McCoy McLemore and David Lattin were not unique. Typically, black athletes in Texas and throughout the South played for nearby all-black colleges or went out of state to a Big Ten school. On occasion, they might be recruited to the West Coast to play at Southern Cal or UCLA if they could play major college football or basketball.

Sometimes, sensing better opportunities and less racial problems elsewhere, black families moved from Texas before the players reached high school or college in order to provide more options for the future. In some cases, a family would send just the individual athlete somewhere to find more opportunity. The most common place these families and their athletes ended up was California, which had been integrated for years and was more tolerant of blacks.

One such player who moved with his family to California before he reached college was future NFL Hall of Fame member and Olympic silver medalist Ollie Matson. Many know Matson starred at the University of San Francisco and led them to an undefeated season in 1951—ironically, the last year the school had a football program. Despite this glowing record, the team was turned down for a bowl game in the South because of Matson and his black teammate, Burl Toler. It is not well known that Matson spent his early years in the East Texas town of Trinity, and when he was 11, his family moved to Houston.

He eventually attended Jack Yates High School, where he played football his freshman and sophomore years. Matson played left end on offense and defense and even scored a touchdown in 1945 against the Temple Lions in an 87–7 Yates victory. Unfortunately, as a sophomore that same year, Matson's football season ended at the halfway point when he suffered a broken ankle. Ollie Matson's sons, Bruce and Ollie Jr., and his twin sister, Ocie, have vivid recollections of why the Matson family left Houston for San Francisco in 1945.

Bruce Matson, who became a Houston dentist, said, "My grandmother decided to go to California to teach and get married. Another reason she went was she wanted my dad to be a dentist, and she figured it would be easier for him in California. From what I understand, when the family moved to California, my dad was only about 150 pounds. It took him a little while to fill out, and that's one reason he went to San Francisco Junior College before he went to the University of San Francisco."

Ollie Matson Jr. said, "My dad wanted to be a boxer. He went to Yates High School his first couple of years. My grandmother sent him to San Francisco. She did not want him to go to an all-black college. Some of my dad's sisters and brothers were already in California. He had broken his ankle and had missed half of the 1945 season at Yates High. They left Houston and Dad ended up going to Washington High School in San Francisco his last two years.

"The family left Houston because of segregation. Back then there were two Houstons—the black part and the white part—and the races rarely mixed. The family had come down from the family farm in Trinity. We used to have dairy cows. We did OK during the Great Depression, but my grandfather got a job with the railroad in Houston.

"My grandmother had wanted to be a funeral home director in Texas, but she couldn't be. In California, she could be anything. She ended up teaching school and marrying a dentist. People didn't get along in Texas like they did in California."

Ocie Thompson, Ollie Matson's twin sister, recalled, "We went to California in 1946. My mother thought there were more opportunities there than in Houston. Ollie was tall but thin. Most of his best football days were ahead of him in California. At the time in Houston, we didn't go to school with the white kids. We pretty much had very little contact with whites at all."

Another black who started in Texas and ended up in California because there were more opportunities out there was basketball legend K. C. Jones, whose family also went to San Francisco, where he eventually played basketball at the University of San Francisco. Besides being on the 1955 and 1956 NCAA championship teams with Bill Russell, Jones also briefly crossed paths with Ollie Matson, the football player.

K. C. Jones recalled his early days: "I was born in Taylor, Texas, in the Jim Crow South. As far as my home went, I realized that what we were doing was surviving. We were a black family struggling to live in a white man's world. Nothing was easy for us. Early on, I realized white folks made the rules, *all* the rules. We wandered through the heart of Texas during the Great Depression. When I was two, we left Taylor for Corpus Christi. When I was four, we went to Dallas.

"When I hit the ripe old age of nine, we were in McGregor, Texas. In McGregor, my mom and dad separated between my ninth and tenth birthday. One day without any discussion, my mom put us five kids on a train with her. She told us we were going to San Francisco to start a new life. How right she was.

"San Francisco will always have a warm place in my heart. The woes of Texas seemed to fall away. I knew we were in a different world. It seemed a world where everyone got a chance. There were Mexicans, Chinese, Blacks, Irish—imagine!—in the same school. When you got on the bus, you sat wherever you wanted. There was no sign for a colored section in the movie theater. You could drink from any water bubbler you saw.

"At the University of San Francisco, we had football teams that made the pro scouts's mouths water—people like Ollie Matson. In the fall of my freshman year of 1951, those fellows had an awesome team and went through the entire season undefeated. As I was walking to class one day with the great Ollie Matson, he said to me, 'Well, we've done it. Now you guys go ahead and do it.'

"I looked at him and said, 'What do you mean?' He said, 'Go undefeated. The football team was undefeated. Now let's have that basketball team go undefeated.' Ollie Matson was a wise man. Or a prophet. My last two years, our record was 57–1. We set an NCAA record of winning 56 straight games, and we won back-to-back national titles."

One player who moved to California for better opportunities without his whole family was basketball player Joe Caldwell, who left Texas City to attend high school in Los Angeles. He eventually went on to play at Arizona State and won an Olympic gold medal in 1964 when he was teammates with Walt Hazzard, George Wilson, and Lucious Jackson. Later, he was one of just a handful of pro basketball players to be an all-star in both the NBA and the ABA.

Caldwell explained his situation: "My older sister convinced my mom and dad to send me to California with her. I was the ninth of 13 kids. There were more opportunities for me out there. I was actually better at baseball than basketball. My dad had played baseball, and coming from Texas that was a no-no for a black. He was denied the opportunity to play. If I hadn't gone to California, I probably would have ended up at Texas Southern University. My brother Eddie played there from 1950–52.

"Going to California was one of the best moves I could have made. I ended up going to Fremont High School, which was all-black. When I went to Arizona State, where it was integrated, it was a bit of a culture shock at first. The other thing I remember was my dad telling me that if I messed up, he would whip me all the way back to Texas."

Then there was the case of Lucious "Luke" Jackson. Growing up in the Central Texas town of San Marcos, he explained his unique circumstance: "In 1955, schools integrated in San Marcos. We were one of the first schools in Texas to integrate after *Brown v. Board of Education*. I couldn't play basketball, though. I was able to practice with Coach [Sam] Stovall's team, but the school board always came up with an excuse as to why I couldn't play in games.

"I also never had a coach or teammate say how much they would like to have me on the team in the two years I practiced with them. All I wanted was a chance to play, and I never got it. Our other black students—I think there were about 30 of us—couldn't play football or be in the marching band or other school activities. We couldn't even eat in the school cafeteria. I had to walk home about a half mile to eat.

"My break finally came when I started on weekends playing in some basketball tournaments for some of my old coaches from my old school. I was noticed at a tournament in Round Rock by Texas Southern Coach Ed Adams." Adams's father, Charles P. Adams, had been sent by Booker T. Washington from Tuskegee Institute in 1901 to establish Grambling University in Louisiana.

Jackson continued, "Coach Adams convinced me after watching me play that I could play in college, but only if I got to play high school ball. So I left San Marcos High School to go live my senior year with Coach Adams's brother, Henry, who was principal at Morehouse High in Bastrop, Louisiana. We won state my senior year." Two of Jackson's teammates were Bob Brown, who later played defensive tackle for 11 years in the NFL (including as a member of the Green Bay Packers in their first two Super Bowl championship years in 1966 and 1967), and future NBA All-Star Bob Love, who was a junior on the team and the sixth man.

Unfortunately, Coach Adams died not long before Jackson graduated. "Out of respect for Coach Adams and for all he and his brother did for me," Jackson said, "I went to Texas Southern for my freshman year. No Southern white colleges looked at me. What's interesting is that Grambling football coach Eddie Robinson wanted me to go there and play football. Southwest Texas State University in San Marcos never even took a look at me.

"After I transferred to Pan American University, we played and beat them three times, which was nice. Those were just the times. I benefited from it. It made me tougher both physically and mentally. The reason I went to Pan Am is I was playing in a summer league at the Jewish Community Center when Walter Yates and Howard Montgomery were already there, and they convinced me to go there.

"It worked out well. We won the NAIA title in 1963, and I ended up being the number-two pick in the 1964 NBA draft, and I got to play on the Olympic gold-medal team in 1964."

If a black player didn't have the chance to leave before he graduated from high school, and he had to play sports in Texas, his options were limited to playing football or basketball for Texas Southern, Prairie View A&M, or Southern University in Louisiana. If good enough to attract the right scouts, he could wind up at a Big Ten school like Minnesota or Michigan State or a western university like USC or UCLA. These schools outside of Texas were all integrated.

The list of Texas high school football players attending historically black colleges included future NFL and American Football League (AFL) All-Stars such as Otis Taylor, Jim Kearney, and Kenny Houston from Prairie View; and Warren Wells, Ernie Holmes, and Winston Hill from Texas Southern.

By the late 1950s and early 1960s, many black football players made the trek to play college ball at integrated schools. This practice was not quite as common with black high school basketball players in Texas, since basketball had not reached the popularity of football. Even the historically black colleges had only a few players that reached the NBA. Prairie View has had only two, Zelmo Beaty and Guy Manning, and Texas Southern that same number, Bennie Swain and Woody Sauldsberry.

In comparison, Prairie View had 11 players reach the AFL or NFL in the 1950s and 1960s, and Texas Southern had 16. There were some black high school basketball players from Texas who went

North or West, but the only two who played in the NBA were McCoy McLemore from Yates High School in Houston (Drake) and Dave Stallworth from Dallas Madison High School (Wichita State).

There are several examples of blacks heading north or west to attend college. One such player was A. Z. Drones, whose younger brother, Jerry, started at defensive end for the University of Houston from 1967–69. Drones was an all-state offensive and defensive tackle who came out of San Angelo Central High School in 1964, the same year Warren McVea graduated. Drones helped lead the Bobcats to the state quarterfinals in 1963 under the direction of legendary Texas high school coach Emory Bellard, who later implemented the famous wishbone offense as an assistant coach at the University of Texas before serving as head coach at both Texas A&M University and Mississippi State University.

In 1964, McVea and Drones became the first two blacks to be chosen to play in the Texas High School Coaches Association All-Star game, McVea on the south team and Drones on the north. Drones was also an all-district selection in basketball when in 1963 he helped the Bobcats win their only state basketball championship. Drones was highly sought after by recruiters, even drawing interest from some white Texas colleges. But he chose to go out of state. "I ended up going to Missouri at first," he explained. "I visited some other Big Eight schools like Nebraska and Oklahoma State. Going to Missouri probably had the most to do with the fact that Johnny Roland had gone there." Roland was a running back from the integrated Corpus Christi Miller High School who had helped them win the state championship in 1960. He later played and coached in the NFL for many years.

"I admired him a lot," Drones pointed out. "I wouldn't have minded playing close to home. Arkansas showed some interest. I got somewhat of an offer from the University of Texas. They wanted me to play there, but their dorms were not integrated yet, so I would have to walk on and live off campus. I never talked to Houston, but Coach John Bridgers from Baylor came to talk to me. My parents wanted me to go there and I got an offer, but I decided not to go to Baylor. I did leave Missouri after my freshman year and went to a juco, and I ended up at West Texas State University.

"I could've gone to Houston by then, but I just didn't care for the Houston area. West Texas State was a good place. I eventually got drafted by the Rams in the sixth round in 1969."

Like A. Z. Drones, another African American who left Texas to play college football was both a football and a basketball star. Junior Coffey was from the West Texas town of Dimmitt, and he became the first black to play for an all-white team in the Texas Panhandle. Coffey also helped Dimmitt reach the state basketball tournament in 1960 and 1961, becoming the first black to appear in a state tournament.

After Coffey went all the way to Washington to play football, Guy V. Lewis said, "Take that Junior Coffey, the Washington halfback who was injured at the Rose Bowl the other day. He's a Texas boy, and he was as good in basketball as he was in football." One of Coffey's high school teammates was Kent Hance, a one-time West Texas congressman who later became the chancellor of Texas Tech University in Lubbock. "He was an amazing player," Hance said. "I was always surprised he didn't play basketball at Washington as well as football. On our Dimmitt basketball team, my job was to get the ball to Junior."

Coffey led the Huskies to the Rose Bowl in his junior year. He went on to the NFL and was a member of the 1965 NFL champion Green Bay Packers and later played for the Atlanta Falcons. Coffey described his recruitment and why he chose Washington.

"When I graduated in 1961, Texas was on the breach of integrating," Coffey said. "I talked with my coaches, J. D. Covington in football and John Ethridge in basketball. We talked about possibly going to West Texas State, but they thought it would be better at the time to go to a different environment. Texas Tech was interested, too. However, they didn't think the Southwest Conference would integrate for a couple more years, so I ended up not going there. I would have wanted to stay home if I had the chance.

"I always root for Tech. I wanted to go to Tech so they could beat Texas and bring Tech some notoriety. I visited Minnesota, Illinois, Oklahoma, Kansas, and several other schools. When I went to

Washington to visit, Seattle seemed to be pretty well integrated. On my visit, I went to the Olympic Hotel. Everyone was Caucasian—the car people, the maître d', and the waiters. I was able to go into the restaurant there without being asked to leave.

"That's when I decided to go to the University of Washington. Another reason I went was that one of their assistant coaches was Chesty Walker, who had coached high school ball at Phillips, Texas. He remembered me from a scrimmage Phillips had with Dimmitt while he was coaching there. He saw some film on me and convinced me to go there. I actually did play basketball my freshman year at Washington, but after that I decided to stick with football.

"Before I went to Dimmitt, I lived in Maxwell, Texas, which is south of Austin between Luling and Lockhart. They closed our black school, so I went to school in San Marcos for a while. I went to school with Lucious Jackson. I then went to Dimmitt in 1956. My first year there I went to an all-black school. My teacher in eighth grade, Mrs. Garrett, helped me study to take the exam to get into the high school when it integrated in 1957."

Another black who left the Houston area to play college football out of state was Ben Wilson from Aldine Carver High School. Wilson ended up going to the University of Southern California and became the starting fullback and team captain of USC's 1962 national championship team. From there, Wilson went on to play four NFL seasons and was the Green Bay Packers's leading rusher in their Super Bowl II victory over the Oakland Raiders.

Wilson described his experience: "I went to Carver High School in Aldine. I was the state champ in the shot put and I also played football. I made very good grades. I was a Jones scholar, and I could have gone to the University of Cincinnati on an academic scholarship. No white schools in Texas contacted me about playing football, not UH or UT. There was a junior college in Corpus Christi that showed some interest in me.

"Grambling, TSU, Prairie View, and Southern University all showed interest in me. I ended up at USC because our superintendent of schools had some contacts at USC. After I went to USC, we did come to Texas once to play Baylor in 1960. The hotel we were to stay at in Waco tried to put us out of the hotel, but Coach [John] McKay said no. Waco was the first time someone called me the N-word on the football field. And to top it off, Baylor beat us."

Beaumont, in far Southeast Texas near the Louisiana border, was a hotbed for African American football talent in the late 1950s and early 1960s. There was all-black Hebert High School, which featured Warren Wells, a future AFL All-Pro wide receiver with the Oakland Raiders, as well as brothers Miller and Mel Farr and their cousin Jerry LeVias, who in 1966 became the first black scholarship player in the Southwest Conference for the Southern Methodist University Mustangs. There was also future Houston Cougar Don Bean, who played football and baseball at UH. Hebert High's all-black rival, Charlton-Pollard High School, featured legendary coach Willie Ray Smith. His sons Bubba and Tody played for Charlton-Pollard, as did Jess Phillips, who later joined the Smith brothers at Michigan State.

Miller Farr, the older of the two Farr brothers, came out of Beaumont in 1961 and went to Wichita State University. After college, he became a three-time All-Pro defensive back in 1967–69 with the Houston Oilers as part of his nine-year professional career. He was eventually named to the all-time AFL second team. Miller Farr said, "I probably would have considered the University of Houston if they had contacted me. It was close to home and I had a lot of relatives who could've seen me play. Lamar Tech in Beaumont tried to recruit me some.

"I looked at Arizona and Arizona State. I considered going to Missouri because Johnny Roland was there. I ended up deciding on Wichita State. I was happy I went there. There was a Texas guy, Dave Stallworth, on the basketball team, and Bill Parcells was my teammate."

Younger brother Mel Farr graduated from Hebert High School in 1963. He ended up deciding to go west as a running back for UCLA, where he earned All-America honors in 1966. From there, Farr was a first-round pick of the Detroit Lions, the 1967 NFL Offensive Rookie of the Year, and a two-time Pro Bowl selection.

Mel Farr spoke of his days in Beaumont and his recruitment by tennis great Arthur Ashe: "We had a heckuva backfield my senior year at Hebert in 1962. I was the biggest and slowest, that's how much talent we had. Jerry LeVias was only a sophomore on that team, but he was the fastest. He ran a 9.5 hundred. Jerry Ball ran a 9.6, Don Bean ran a 9.7, and I ran a 9.8. In track, we never lost a race in the 4×100 yards, and we held the national record for a while.

"After high school, I probably would have considered white Texas colleges if they would have offered, but none did. I was recruited just about everywhere in the North and West—Wichita State, Michigan State, Iowa—just about every major college. In fact, Bud Wilkinson of Oklahoma came to my school to visit.

"I eventually decided on UCLA. I was very happy there. I went there because of its history. When I visited UCLA, I got to meet Jackie Robinson; Woody Strode, the first famous black actor; and gold-medal-winner Rafer Johnson."

Rafer Johnson had been born in Hillsboro, Texas, in 1935 and later lived in poverty in the black section of Dallas. Years later, Johnson said, "I don't care if I ever see Texas again. There's nothing about it I like. If my family had stayed in Texas, I not only would not have represented the United States in the Olympic Games, I wouldn't even have gone to college." In the mid-1940s, Johnson's family had moved to Central California in search of a better life.

"Later, after I had been at UCLA for a while," Farr continued, "I helped recruit Kareem Abdul Jabbar [Lew Alcindor] to come to UCLA. Oh yes, when I went on my recruiting visit, I got to sit in the Dodger dugout, and I got to meet Sandy Koufax."

Ironically, one of the main universities in the North that recruited black athletes in the 1950s and 1960s was Michigan State, where Bill Yeoman was an assistant coach before he took the University of Houston head coaching job in 1962. At that time, the Spartans made recruiting inroads in Southeast Texas in 1963 when they recruited defensive end Bubba Smith and running back Jess Phillips out of Beaumont's Charlton-Pollard High School and wide receiver Gene Washington out of Baytown's Carver High School, just east of Houston.

Michigan State used these three and other black players, including quarterback Jimmy Raye and linebacker George Webster, from the South to lead the Spartans to a 19–1–1 record in 1965–66 and a share of the 1965 national championship. Bubba Smith was the number-one pick of the 1967 NFL draft, going to the Baltimore Colts, while Washington was the number-eight pick by the Minnesota Vikings in the first round, and Phillips was a fourth-round pick and played ten NFL seasons.

Jess Phillips recalled, "I don't know if I would have considered any all-white colleges in Texas like the University of Houston. I was never contacted by any of them. I was also not contacted by any of the black colleges, either. Pac 8 schools like USC and UCLA contacted me, as did Wisconsin and Michigan State, among others.

"Dan Boisture recruited me to Michigan State. Duffy Daugherty came down to Beaumont and convinced my parents into letting me go to Michigan State. Michigan State was cool. The folks in Michigan were great. They bent over backwards for us."

Bubba Smith said, "When I got out of school in 1963, the University of Texas hadn't integrated yet but they wanted me to come there. The coach there said they could give me a scholarship, but I couldn't play right away. I turned that down. I knew Coach Yeoman well at Houston. I would have considered going to Houston, but I wanted to get away. In the end, I didn't have a choice. My daddy made the deal for me to go to Michigan State. He was trying to break down barriers."

Gene Washington came to Michigan State along with Bubba Smith in the fall of 1962. In fact, it was Smith who got Washington to become a Spartan. After playing football and basketball against Washington in high school, Bubba Smith put in a good word about him to Michigan State head coach Duffy Daugherty. Washington was initially put on a track scholarship, and he eventually became a two-time first-team All-America wide receiver and also won an NCAA hurdles title in his track career.

Years later, Washington compared his days in Texas and Michigan State. "I'm actually from La Porte, Texas, which is east of Houston on Galveston Bay. I was bussed to Baytown because we did not have a black high school there. It was on that bus, though, that I did meet my wife, Claudith.

"Michigan State knew nothing about my background in athletics. I got to East Lansing solely on Bubba's recommendation. His dad may have had something to with it, too."

Willie Ray Smith Sr. was a legendary high school football coach at all-black Charlton-Pollard in Beaumont and amassed 235 wins in his career in the Prairie View Interscholastic League (PVIL), the league for black schools up until the late 1960s. Over the years, he sent many of his football players to schools in the North and the West.

Smith Sr. also had a reputation for being a tough taskmaster. Legend has it that during the halftime of a game in which Charlton-Pollard was behind, Coach Smith pulled out a belt and gave each of his players a whack. Legendary Texas high school coach Bum Phillips, who was coaching in the Beaumont area at the time, remarked, "I'll tell you what, business sure picked up in the second half."

When Washington made it to Michigan State, it was different from anything he had experienced back in the Houston area. Houston had separate water fountains and restrooms for African Americans. Its hotels were closed to black people. "I had never played against white players," he said. "The races didn't mix in Houston, so I had barely interacted with any. Now all of a sudden I'm sharing a room with two white swimmers. Everything was segregated in Texas, both on the field and in everyday life, but now all of a sudden, I'm in an open, friendly atmosphere. It was great.

"About the only thing different I ran into at Michigan State was I never had white teachers before. The chemistry was different. I was used to black teachers and the small classes where we were given a lot of individual attention. I had these huge classes at Michigan State and very little interaction and personal attention from the white professors. I eventually adjusted, though."

After an All-Pro career with the Minnesota Vikings, Gene Washington worked many years for 3M Corporation in Minnesota before retiring in 2011. Education was very important to him, as he explained, "After coming out of that segregated situation in Texas, I was driven to get my education so I would never have to go back to Texas. I made sure I kept my grades up so I could have a career."

Washington then summed up what many of the black players from Texas that had to go play college football in the North and West must have felt: "All of the black players from the South that went to Michigan State weren't wanted by the white colleges. We had players from the Carolinas, Louisiana, Virginia, and, of course, Texas. We did form a bond at Michigan State, since we were outcasts from our home states. We had something to prove."

It would not be much longer that black players from Texas and other Southern states would be outcasts. Two coaches from the University of Houston, Guy V. Lewis and Bill Yeoman, were getting ready to make sure that African American players would receive the same opportunities that their white counterparts had to play their respective sports in their home states if they chose to.

5 BILL'S VEER AND GUY V.'S DUNKS

*In Glendale, we had Poles, Russians, and we had a fair amount of
Japanese around that helped with the nearby farms. I never cared
what people were. My parents instilled that in me from an early age.*
—BILL YEOMAN

*Coach Lewis taught me that all the prejudice that I had been
taught was false. It was nothing but a bunch of junk.*
—ELVIN HAYES ON GUY V. LEWIS

After Marvin Blumenthal integrated the Jewish Community
Center in 1958, Houston Cougar basketball coach Guy V.
Lewis would watch the action in the gym there and get frustrated. Lewis took over the reins of the Cougars's program
in the 1956–57 season from Alden Pasche, and the team
struggled to 10–16 and 9–16 records in his first two seasons
with mostly Texan players and a few from the Midwest on
the roster.

Because of the popularity of football in Texas, basketball was lagging behind in interest and quality of players. Lewis and Assistant Coach Harvey Pate decided to scour the Midwest for more recruits because of its quality basketball reputation. Recruiting players from this region brought better results, such as NCAA appearances in 1961 and 1965 along with an NIT invitation in 1962. But it wasn't everything that Lewis had hoped for. On a daily basis at the JCC, Coach Lewis saw players that could take his program to the next level. He was certain of it, but he couldn't recruit them because of the color of their skin. His goal was to eventually get some of these players on the Houston campus, because as he himself put it, "We wanted to win basketball games, and it was also the right thing to do."

Guy V. Lewis was born on March 19, 1922, in the small East Texas town of Arp. He began his athletic career at Arp High School, where he quarterbacked the football team for three years and played on three district championship basketball teams. After graduation, Lewis attended Rice Institute in Houston and played on the varsity basketball team in 1942. Lewis married Dena Nelson of Troup, Texas, in 1942 and had three children. One son, Vern, played on the 1968 Lewis-coached UH Final Four team.

After serving in the US Army Air Force for three years in World War II, Lewis came to UH in 1946 because Bill Swanson, his half-brother, was trying to put together the school's first basketball team, and he convinced Lewis to suit up. Guy V. Lewis is generally regarded as UH's first great athlete. He was cocaptain of the 1946 and 1947 Cougar teams, leading them in scoring both seasons and becoming the first UH athlete to earn all-conference honors in the Lone Star Conference. UH was also conference champion both of these seasons.

After graduation in 1947, Lewis returned to East Texas and was in private business until coming back to UH in 1953 to become Alden Pasche's assistant for three seasons. When Pasche retired after the Cougars's first NCAA appearance in 1956, Lewis took the helm, revolutionized UH basketball, and kept it going for 30 years before his retirement in 1986. He amassed 592 wins and 279 losses, for a winning percentage of .680. His teams advanced to the NCAA Tournament

14 times, five of them advancing to the Final Four in the years 1967, 1968, 1982, 1983, and 1984. The last two advanced to the NCAA title game. He was National Coach of the Year in 1968 and 1983, both years finishing the regular season ranked No. 1 in the nation. He is the only NCAA coach with three of his players on the NBA's 1997 list of the top 50 all-time players. The mere mention of these three men is like waving a magic wand over the UH campus. They are Elvin Hayes, Hakeem Olajuwon, and Clyde Drexler.

Guy V. Lewis was an innovator. He helped put together the Houston–UCLA basketball game in the Astrodome in 1968 that helped push college basketball popularity to the forefront. He stands out as one of the first coaches to emphasize the dunk as a high-percentage play.

"The dunk," he explained, "was an important part of our game, and we worked on it. It's a high-percentage shot. It wasn't for show. I would tell other coaches, 'You can't dunk without hustling.' We were dunking before Elvin and Don and Phi Slama Jama. Lyle Harger [team captain and leading scorer in the 1962–63 season] once had 15 dunks in a half. I don't remember who we were playing, but he had had only two points before the half.

"I told him not to do anything but dunk the second half, and he ended up with something like 41 points. Most people think the dunk was outlawed in the late 1960s because of Lew Alcindor at UCLA. I read once where John Wooden had said to Alcindor, 'It wasn't you that caused them to outlaw the dunk. It was that crazy bunch from Houston.'"

Even though the dunk was outlawed in college basketball from 1968 to 1978, UH's Phi Slama Jama later changed how the game was played. In the Cougars's Final Four run from 1982 through 1984, the team—along with the University of Louisville's Doctors of Dunk—changed basketball into a game that is played above the rim.

Lewis had gotten a reputation over the years as a "roll out the balls" type of practice coach. Larry Cooper is a native Houstonian who attended Waltrip High School and became a reserve on the 1968 Final Four team. He also later became a successful high school coach at Jones and Humble high schools, compiling a 464–194 record over 20 seasons. Cooper disputed the claims about Lewis's practice philosophy. "The word was for years that Coach Lewis just rolled out the balls at practice," Coach Cooper said. "That's a lie. His practices were long, intense, and organized. He was a master motivator. I learned so much from him and Coach Pate on practice organization, which later helped me in my coaching career.

"Coach Lewis was one of the best. He was flamboyant, and he was good for basketball. I think a lot of other coaches were jealous of him. It's unjust that he's not in the basketball Hall of Fame. He also cared about me as a person. I was just a reserve who didn't play a lot, but when Coach Lewis found out I was thinking about transferring, he drove me around campus for about an hour one night trying to convince me to stay."

(Although not a hall of famer at the time Cooper was interviewed, Coach Lewis was enshrined in the Naismith Memorial Basketball Hall of Fame in Springfield, Massachusetts, in September 2013).

Jack Thompson, who was a guard and team captain for the 1962 NIT Houston team, echoed Cooper's sentiments. "I don't know how he got the reputation as a 'roll out the balls' type of practice coach," Thompson said. "You should have come to one. The practices were hardnosed. There were not many whistles blown. It was always defense first. It was a war every day."

Gary Phillips said, "Coach Lewis gave me a lot of freedom. That's not to mean we were a helter-skelter team. Being a bunch of kids from the Midwest, we knew how to run a fast break, but we could run an offense, too. We also knew how to play defense, thanks to Coach Lewis and assistant coach Harvey Pate, who played for defensive wizard Hank Iba at Oklahoma A&M. What Coach Lewis really taught me was about not quitting, about being tenacious and hardnosed. He displayed all of those same characteristics."

Jack Margenthaler, the Cougars's 1965 team captain, said, "Coach Lewis liked competitive practices every day. He was a players's coach. Everything was structured to where you end up playing to the best of your ability. Houston was a phenomenal experience. It made me what I am today."

Gary Grider, cocaptain of the Cougars's first Final Four team in 1967, said, "Coach Lewis was a good coach—a disciplinarian when he started out. He had average players and he got them to play above their heads. They were always in good shape and they were tough. Elvin and Don coming in were a big adjustment for Coach Lewis. He had never had that kind of talent. He made a few errors at first with them, but to his credit, he adjusted and eventually got the most out of their talent."

Don Chaney said, "You have to give Coach Lewis a lot of credit for bringing in two black athletes at the same time. It was a bold move, especially in Texas. I admire Guy Lewis. Before Elvin and I got there, he was more of a half court coach. To his credit, he changed his style and let us run."

Howie Lorch, team manager from 1962 to 1968, said, "Guy V. was charming and engaging. Players were attracted to him—parents, too. He was very honest. What Coach Lewis would say, he would do."

Bill Bane, a junior reserve on the 1968 Final Four team, said, "Guy V. recruited me. He needed a shooting guard, and his son Vern and I became best friends. In fact, sometimes he used to call me Vern by mistake. Coach Lewis used to say, 'If you take care of me on the court, I'll take care of you off the court.' We stayed first-class everywhere we traveled."

John Egan, the only white starter on Loyola of Chicago's 1963 NCAA championship team, almost came to UH. Egan said, "I was recruited by Guy Lewis. I went to Houston and I met two other Midwest guys, Gary Phillips and Ted Luckenbill. I loved it. I came very close to coming to UH. I always liked Guy Lewis and his approach to recruiting. He was very honest and straightforward."

The most important piece of the legacy of Guy Lewis is that he changed who got to play the game of basketball. Lewis had known for years that he had been missing out on the black athletes. He knew this by watching the games at the Jewish Community Center in the late 1950s. He eventually set into motion a plan to recruit blacks. But the first UH recruits, Elvin Hayes and Don Chaney, were not the first black athletes he had wanted on his teams.

Hayes said, "I never would have gotten where I was today if it hadn't been for Coach Lewis. He's like a father to me. My father died when I was in the eighth grade. I went through a tough period when I came to UH.

"When I first got here, it wasn't long before I went back to Rayville. My brother eventually came back here with me to keep an eye on me. There was a lot of hate in me, 18 years's worth. Coach Lewis taught me that all the prejudice that I had been taught was false. It was nothing but a bunch of junk.

"People of both races did it to keep us from getting into trouble. They did not want the races to mix for our safety. All that does is create prisons for people. One time, Coach Lewis called me into his office and asked me, 'Why do you hate me so much? What have I done to you?'

"Coach Lewis was right. He had treated me great, and all I had been giving him back was hate. Eventually I had a great relationship with Coach Lewis and his family. His son Vern was my teammate and his two other kids, Terry and Sherry, were like my brother and sister.

"I eventually wore down a path from Baldwin House (the athletic dorm) to Guy's house. He is a tremendous man. All that I achieved in basketball and as a person has been through what I learned from Coach Lewis."

After the three losing seasons to start his UH head coaching career, Lewis experienced 27 consecutive *winning* seasons before he retired. As often proclaimed, Lewis knew he had to get better players than what Houston and the state of Texas were producing if he was to be successful. Recruiting players from the Midwest in the late 1950s and early 1960s helped. Lewis's first NCAA Tournament team in 1961 featured the Cougars's first All-America player, guard Gary Phillips from Quincy, Illinois, the Boston Celtics's first-round pick in 1961, and forward Ted Luckenbill from Elkhart, Indiana, the number-15 pick in the same draft.

Other key players from the Midwest in the early to mid-1960s were guard Jack Margenthaler of Pinckneyville, Illinois, the team captain in 1965 who later became a college coach for 25 years at Western Illinois and at Southern Illinois–Edwardsville; guard and 1966 team captain Joe Hamood of Detroit, Michigan, who originally came to Houston as a quarterback; and the 1967 cocaptains—guard

Gary Grider from Washington, Indiana, and forward Leary Lentz of Cahokia, Illinois.

Ironically, several of those white players, including Phillips, Luckenbill, and Grider, had no idea that Houston and its namesake university were still segregated. Phillips said, "I had always played against black kids back home in Illinois. I didn't think anything of it."

Luckenbill said, "I was shocked. It took me a while to realize there were no blacks on campus. I thought to myself, 'Where are all the brothers?' I just didn't realize that kind of stuff still went on. I remember going to places in Houston and seeing things like the separate drinking fountains. I didn't experience anything like that back in Indiana."

Grider added, "Back in Indiana, our schools were integrated. In fact, all of my Northern teammates at the University of Houston had grown up playing with and against blacks. I remember when Guy Lewis was at my house recruiting me. My mom asked, 'Is your school integrated? Do you have any blacks?' Coach Lewis said, 'Why Mrs. Grider, no.' My mom and I couldn't believe our ears."

The Cougars achieved a measure of success with these players, reaching the NCAA Tournament in 1961 and 1965 and the NIT in 1962. The Lewis-coached UH record from 1961 through 1965 was a quite respectable 88–48. The Cougars were often recognized as one of the best all-white college basketball teams in the country, but Lewis wanted more. For years, he had been missing out on the talent he had seen at the JCC and later when he opened the Jeppesen Field House gym to blacks in 1960. "It was ridiculous these kids couldn't play at UH," the coach said. "It was very frustrating. I couldn't stand it."

There were at least two black players Lewis hoped to get to come to UH before he got Elvin Hayes and Don Chaney in 1964.

Six-foot-eight forward McCoy McLemore was a star at Jack Yates High School, which was located right across the street from the University of Houston. McLemore would go on to play eight NBA seasons, including one as a member of the 1970–71 champion Milwaukee Bucks. To this day, he tells of Lewis's plan to get him to UH.

"I graduated in 1960, and Coach Lewis wanted to offer me a scholarship," McLemore said. "Houston wasn't integrated yet, but Coach

Lewis felt it would be coming soon. His proposal was for me to go away to a junior college, and then he felt Houston would be integrated by 1962. I went to Moberly Junior College for two years. When the time came to go to the University of Houston in the spring of 1962, the school had not quite integrated yet. I was a Juco All-American, so I decided to go to Drake instead. Things worked out well there, but I still wish I could have gone to Houston."

Finally, in the summer of 1962, UH integrated its student body. Dr. Philip G. Hoffman, the UH president from 1961 to 1977, explained, "Integrating was the right thing to do. However, we did not want a Mississippi or Alabama on our hands. We decided to integrate in the summer of 1962 when there weren't as many students on campus. We also had a local media blackout for a week so as not to publicize the event. My resolution was to get the best possible students on campus regardless of their color. The later recruiting of black athletes was a byproduct of our integrating the school."

The integration process was accomplished without incident.

By 1963, however, the athletic department had not yet integrated. Coach Lewis made basically the same proposal he had made to McCoy McLemore a couple years earlier to another Houston product who would attend a junior college for a year with hopes of integrating UH the year after that. David Lattin graduated in the spring of 1963 from Worthing High School as the top recruit in the state of Texas. "My dream was to play basketball at the University of Houston," he said. "Guy Lewis probably came to half of my games. We became very close.

"The reality, though, was that UH was still segregated. I figured UH would make an exception for me. 'Change is coming,' Coach Lewis would tell me. As I was getting ready to graduate, Coach Lewis started talking to me about attending a junior college first and then going to UH.

"Coach Lewis said, 'Go to a junior college first for a year. Then I can bring you here. It's going to happen.'" As it turned out, Lattin missed the integration of UH athletics by a year. He went on to fame as the star player on Texas Western University's 1966 NCAA championship

Philip G. Hoffman, circa 1960s
(Courtesy of Special Collections, University of Houston
Libraries)

team, where the team's all-black starting five defeated Adolf Rupp's all-white Kentucky squad, 72–65.

*   *   *   *   *   *   *

In the midst of Guy Lewis getting basketball integrated in the early 1960s, another man came to UH in December 1961 to change the face of the school's college football program.

Like the UH basketball team of the late 1950s and early 1960s, football was mired in mediocrity. In 1961, the team ended up with a 5–4–1 record. Cougar head coach Harold Lahar had resigned earlier in the schedule over a contract dispute that was not made public until season's end. In five seasons under Lahar, the Cougars compiled an unremarkable 24–23–1 record. Out of Michigan State University came an assistant coach who accepted the head coaching job because, as he explained, "It was a warm spot in the South, and I wanted to be a head coach."

Bill Yeoman was born December 26, 1927, in Elnora, Indiana. He eventually graduated from Glendale High School in Arizona, where he was all-state in football and basketball. Growing up in Glendale, Yeoman said, "I never paid attention to what people were. In Glendale, we had Poles, Russians, and we had a fair amount of Japanese around that helped with the nearby farms. I never cared what people were. My parents instilled that in me from an early age."

Yeoman spent his freshman year of 1945 at Texas A&M, lettering in both football and basketball. In 1946, he received an appointment to the United States Military Academy at West Point, New York. He played under legendary coach Harold "Red" Blaik and was a teammate of the famous Army backfield duo of "Mr. Inside" and "Mr. Outside," Glenn Davis and Doc Blanchard, respectively. By his senior season in 1948, Yeoman was the starting center, team captain, and second team All-America.

In 1949 and 1950, Yeoman served as a graduate assistant coach under Coach Blaik and had the opportunity to learn football from future football coaching legends Vince Lombardi, Sid Gillman, Murray Warmath, Paul Dietzel, and Allie Sherman.

"I got to listen to and then talk football with them," Yeoman recalled. "I learned how to organize practices from Colonel Blaik. His practices were short and timed to the minute, usually about an hour and 37 or 38 minutes, and a lot was crammed into those practices. When I played and coached there, no team was better prepared than us. No one. I learned technique and how to teach from Gillman, Lombardi, and Warmath. Murray Warmath was a great teacher. He stuck with the basics, and he taught them over and over until it was mastered."

Ironically, although he grew up in Tennessee and played for the University of Tennessee Volunteers and later coached at Mississippi State, Warmath eventually embraced integration when he coached at

Minnesota from 1954 to 1971, winning the 1960 national championship for the Golden Gophers. His 1960 team included Sandy Stephens, the first black starting quarterback at a Division I school, and
two future NFL Hall of Fame members: defensive end Carl Eller of
the Minnesota Vikings and linebacker Bobby Bell of the Kansas City
Chiefs.

From 1951 to 1953, Yeoman was sent to Europe, originally with
the intention of serving as an artillery communications officer. Instead,
he was chosen to coach one of the Army football teams in Europe. It
was there Yeoman had his first experience coaching African American
players.

"We were going to play another Army base and they had a pretty
good team," Yeoman said. "I ended up going with an all-black backfield. We had Ira Judge at quarterback, John Wilson at fullback, and
Morris Brown and Hosea Alexander at running back. At the end of
the first half, we were down 21–20. But in the second half, Hosea
Alexander ran wild for four touchdowns, and we ended up winning,
50–21. I saw then how skilled the black athlete was. It left a lasting
impression on me."

When Yeoman returned to the United States, he joined the Michigan State football staff under Duffy Daugherty in 1954. Yeoman
coached defensive backs with future Nebraska coaching legend Bob
Devaney before switching to offensive backs in 1959. When Yeoman
took the Houston job in December 1961, he was Daugherty's top assistant. "I learned how to deal with people from Duffy," the coach said.
"He was the greatest at the social side of things. Duffy handled bad
situations and resolved them better than anyone I had ever seen. I
learned so much from him.

"Another thing I learned from Duffy was how to recruit. I didn't
know a thing about it. Duffy was the best in the United States at
recruiting. Working with Duffy on the social side of things and working with those other coaches technique and teaching-wise, I could not
have had better teachers to help prepare me to be a head coach."

Not long after taking the Houston job, Yeoman made a bold prediction to groups of boosters he encountered. Following the advice of golf

coach Dave Williams, Yeoman proceeded to tell whoever would listen that his goal was to "win a national championship." Considering UH had only fielded a football program since 1946 and had a percentage just over .500 (81–75–4) during that time period, this seemed like a rather lofty and unrealistic goal. But as Williams had told Yeoman, "If you want people to take you seriously, you have to have serious goals."

Yeoman later said, "I believe my saying that and having that attitude helped us in recruiting in the long run, with both white and black players. Great players want to win, and they knew we took things seriously at Houston."

Yeoman was wise to take the advice of Williams, the UH golf coach from 1951 to 1987. Over those 36 years, his teams won 16 national championships, more than any other coach in NCAA history in any sport. Known as the "Father of College Golf," Williams had delivered more or less the same speech after his first season as golf coach. When he took over the program in 1951, the Cougars golf team had lost 25 matches in a row and had only two scholarships, and the golf coach didn't even draw a salary.

After his team won its last match of the season, beating Lamar Tech, Williams was asked to get up and speak at the end-of-season banquet. "I was choking up and didn't know what to say," Williams recalled. "They announced me, and I said, 'We're going to win the national championship.' Everybody laughed. Boy, that was the biggest joke of the year. The school was new in athletics then.

"We'd never gone for a national championship in anything. I was choking and I just blurted it out. The golf team wasn't even playing in the NCAA. They started calling me 'National Championship Williams.'"

But Coach Williams got the last laugh. By 1956, the Cougars won the first of five consecutive NCAA titles, winning ten over the next 12 years.

*   *   *   *   *   *   *

After a 7–4 1962 first season that culminated with a 26–21 Tangerine Bowl victory over Miami of Ohio, the Cougars struggled in 1963 and 1964 with 2–8 and 2–6–1 records, respectively.

Bill Yeoman, circa 1962
(Courtesy of Special Collections, University of Houston
Libraries)

Yeoman realized during the 1963 season that he had to change his
approach to personnel. He also had to change the X's and O's in his play-
book. He changed the landscape of college football in 1963 by becoming
the first coach to recruit a black player at a major Southern university,
and in 1964, he invented and implemented the innovative Veer offense.

When Yeoman was planning to recruit black athletes in the fall
of 1963, he met with local black community leaders at a dinner at
the Shamrock Hilton Hotel. The leader of the black community
was Quentin Mease, still the director of the South Central YMCA,
and there were also in attendance prominent doctors, lawyers, and

businessmen. Mease said, "Bill got up to speak to the crowd and said, 'I'm prejudiced, all right.'"

"All their eyes lit up," Yeoman said, "and they showed concern until I said, 'I'm prejudiced against bad football players.'"

Mease continued, "After Bill's statement, everyone laughed and it broke the ice."

Once Yeoman started to recruit black athletes and install the Veer offense, the University of Houston football program was headed in the right direction.

The Veer was a result of a lack of quality personnel. The coach credited with inventing it explained, "Our offensive line was a major problem. The University of Mississippi had trounced us in 1962 and 1963, and a lot of the reason was we couldn't block their tackles. They were all over us."

Thus came the idea for the Veer offense. The offense was created so that the Houston backs could avoid defensive tackles who were not blocked by the Cougars's offensive line. Yeoman's theory was "If you can't block them, get away from them." At spring practice in 1964, the team worked on a power sweep with a split backfield and a tight end formation, and the offensive line was having a difficult time blocking the defensive tackles.

Yeoman said, "I finally told the quarterback to run the handoff into the line." The Veer offense was born. "We tried it against Ole Miss that fall of 1964 with mixed results and then tried it against Penn State towards the end of the season. We lost, 24–7, but we moved the ball up and down the field against them."

Houston started dismally again in 1965—Warren McVea's first varsity season—with a 1–4 record at the midpoint in the season. Yeoman had still not fully committed to the Veer, and the Cougars were struggling with morale. Yeoman made two key decisions that would decide his and the University of Houston's football fate: he decided on his starting quarterback and committed to running the Veer offense full time. The quarterback in this exciting scenario was junior Bo Burris, described by Warren McVea as a "magician with the football." Burris in 1965 was struggling to keep his starting job. The Cougars started

1–3, and then Burris had been benched in favor of Dick Woodall when UH played Miami and were trounced, 44–12.

The team now had a 1–4 record, and Yeoman was fighting for his job. Dummies of Yeoman and Burris were hung in effigy on campus, prompting Yeoman to later remark, "It just showed that someone cared about football at Houston."

Burris described the decisive moments. "It was the night before we played Tennessee," he said. "We had gotten up there a little late, and the stadium gates were closed and we ran around the stadium. It was misty out and I was feeling down about the whole situation, when Coach Yeoman pulled us all together and said, 'I'm not going to give into this. Tomorrow we're going to run the Veer, and Bo Burris is my quarterback.'

"We went out and played Tennessee a good game (a 17–8 loss), and a couple of weeks later, we beat Mississippi for the first time, 17–3, and the next week we defeated 10th-ranked Kentucky, 38–21. The Veer was on its way." So was McVea, who in one game caught 80- and 84-yard touchdown passes from the new full-time quarterback. By 1968, the Cougar football team averaged a NCAA-record 562 yards a game on offense. Included in its victories was a 100–6 rout of Tulsa. The Cougars remained among the nation's total offense leaders for the duration of Yeoman's career.

Besides being an innovator with offensive football, Yeoman also was considered a master motivator, a status verified by members of his staff and former players. The head coach assembled a top-notch staff during the 1960s that included future NFL head coaches J. D. Roberts, Chuck Fairbanks, and Bum Phillips. The original staff also included Tom Boisture, who ended up becoming the New York Giants head of player personnel from 1980 to 2000.

Former Houston Oilers head coach Bum Phillips was a member of Yeoman's defensive staff in 1965–66 when his son, Wade, another future NFL head coach, was a starting linebacker. Bum said, "I loved my time at the University of Houston. I was a very happy coach. Yeoman was a great coach. Not many people can come up with an offense like he did."

Wade Phillips added, "Coach Yeoman, he was definitely an innova-tor. Although he was an offensive coach, he was still able to motivate the whole team. One thing about him, too, was that he treated his players with respect, so his players liked him and played hard for him. Those things I learned from him, and I applied his method of how you treat players when I coached."

Melvin Robertson, UH defensive coordinator from 1965 to 1971, said, "Working for Bill Yeoman was a great experience. I had more fun coaching at Houston than anywhere. It was exciting being an inde-pendent, playing games all over the country. Opening the Astrodome in 1965, going up to Michigan State in 1967, in 1968 going to Aus-tin to take on Darrell Royal and having Texas unveil the wishbone offense on us. Coach Yeoman doesn't get near enough credit for what he accomplished."

Former San Francisco 49ers defensive back and kick returner Joe Arenas was part-time receivers coach under Yeoman from 1963 to 1986. "Coach Yeoman gave me an opportunity and I was grateful for it," Arenas said. "I would work in real estate during the day and then go to practice in the afternoons during football season. Coach Yeo-man had a way of getting his point across to an individual. He could explain to a player, 'Do it this way and this will happen.' He could also get the most out of a player that you were supposed to."

Chuck Fairbanks, a member of Yeoman's staff from 1962 to 1965 and later head coach at the University of Oklahoma and for the New England Patriots, said, "I had a positive experience at Houston. I was great friends with Bill Yeoman, and I learned a tremendous amount from him. During his era, he probably did the best coaching job of anyone. He took a program that was in shambles and eventually got the University of Houston accepted into the Southwest Conference. He also integrated the program with Warren McVea and was innova-tive as a forerunner of triple-option football by coming up with the Veer offense."

Barry Sides was with Yeoman as center and tackle from 1964 to 1966 and later as an assistant coach of the offensive line / defensive ends from 1969 to 1978. Sides said, "Coach Yeoman was a great person to play for and was also the best person to work for. He was a family man, and he wanted you to spend time with your family."

Other Cougar players recalled their experiences with Yeoman. Tom Paciorek came to Houston from the University of Detroit after the school disbanded football in 1964. He played defensive back and returned punts for the football team and played baseball on the Cougar team that made it to the College World Series in 1967. He later had an 18-year Major League Baseball career for the Los Angeles Dodgers, Atlanta Braves, Seattle Mariners, and the Chicago White Sox. "I really loved my days at U of H—very enjoyable," Paciorek said. "The two greatest motivators I have seen in my athletic career are Tommy Lasorda and Bill Yeoman—two completely different personalities, though, but they both got their point across, in very different ways."

Tom Beer also came to UH after Detroit dropped football. "Tom Boisture, my old high school coach, was on Bill Yeoman's staff," Beer recounted. "Coach Yeoman was a very decent man. He was a great motivator. The man revolutionized football with the Veer offense. In fact, a lot of the read-option football you see today has its foundations in the Veer offense. Once Coach Yeoman committed to the Veer before the Tennessee game in 1965, our program took off. In 1966, we had the best offense in the nation."

Wide receiver Ken Hebert played for Yeoman from 1965 to 1967 and was the nation's leading scorer in 1966 with 113 points. In addition to being a receiver, Hebert also handled the place-kicking duties: "I felt blessed to have a coach like Bill Yeoman. I was around him for four years, and I never heard one foul comment come out of his mouth."

Although Yeoman suspended him for part of the 1966 season for a curfew violation, defensive end Royce Berry—who went on to play seven NFL seasons with the Bengals and Bears—said, "I never regretted going to Houston. I got caught on a curfew violation before the Ole Miss game and I was kicked off for the rest of the season. I had a date on a Tuesday night and I had to go to La Marque (45 miles south of the campus) to her house, and I got caught. Coach Yeoman did what he had to do. Overall he did a great job. He is one of the finest people I have ever met."

Jim Pat Berger played safety from 1965 to 1967. He eventually became Warren McVea's closest friend on the team. "Coach Yeoman is one of the greatest guys I have ever met. He taught me how to get along with people," Berger said.

Linebacker Greg Brezina (1965–67) followed up his UH career with a 13-year stay in the NFL with the Atlanta Falcons. He said, "I was really happy at UH. Bill Yeoman is one of the great coaches. He doesn't get near the credit he should. He's just a great guy."

The 1967 All-America guard Rich Stotter said, "I enjoyed being with Coach Yeoman. He and Coach Lewis were able to get 110 percent out of their players. Coach Yeoman liked finding diamonds in the rough—a lot of kids from small towns—and then teach them how to play and to play hard."

The quarterback on the 1967 team was Dick Woodall, who said, "I have great memories of Coach Yeoman. I think when you leave home for the first time, you have to find someone to help you mature and show you the way. Coach Yeoman was that person to me. I look upon Coach Yeoman as family."

A freshman teammate of McVea, Jody Powers, said, "A lot of credit should go to Coach Yeoman and Coach Lewis. They created a positive environment for Warren, Elvin, and Don. I've always said leadership determines the environment. We were told Warren was one of us and he was to be treated as an equal. I was injured my freshman year. Coach Yeoman could have cut me, but he kept me around. After I got my degree, I eventually became president of Halliburton."

Unknown to most, future Dallas Cowboys defensive tackle Larry Cole spent about three weeks as a Houston Cougar at two-a-days in August 1967. Cole had played his first three seasons at the Air Force Academy, including a game against the UH freshman team, the only full game Warren McVea played that season. Cole had to leave Air Force because of an honor code violation. He indirectly knew that cheating was going on but did not report it. He had to find a new college to play for as a senior. After leaving Houston, Cole ended up at the University of Hawaii with several other former Air Force teammates.

Cole said, "I wanted to play one good year of major college football. I looked at a couple of schools and decided to give the University of Houston and Bill Yeoman a try. It was culture shock. It was very Southern. And the heat—it was August two-a-days—I didn't know people could survive in that kind of heat. I remember we did 25 minutes each practice doing warm-up exercises to help us with the heat. Those exercises helped me later when I went to the Cowboys's training camp.

"Even though I didn't stay long at Houston, I found out from Gil Brandt, the Cowboys's personnel director, that Coach Yeoman had called and put in a good word for me. I think he may have done that because he had been at West Point in the early 1950s when they had the honor code violations, and I think he maybe could relate to what I had gone through at the Air Force Academy with the honor code violation."

Now that the University of Houston had integrated in the summer of 1962 and they had their basketball and football coaches in place, all that remained was to decide which players would be the ones to integrate their respective sports.

6 WONDROUS WARREN AND THE JUDGE

*I think the reason we had so little backlash is that people
around here wanted to win, and if they thought Warren
could help us, they didn't care what color he was.*
—BILL YEOMAN ON PRIZE RECRUIT WARREN McVEA

Once the University of Houston student body was integrated
in the summer of 1962, the stage was set for Bill Yeoman and
Guy V. Lewis to integrate their respective sports. When Yeoman came to Houston in December 1961, integration wasn't
a priority. "I didn't talk about integration when I interviewed
for the job," he said in reflection. "When I got here, though, I
saw how fast our players were, and I realized we needed help.
All I wanted were the best players available."

Yeoman's assistant coaches on the staff in the early 1960s
felt the very same way, each echoing the "best available"
approach. Melvin Robertson, a member of the defensive staff
from 1965 to 1971, said, "We didn't think about it. A lot of

us grew up around blacks. We recruited the best players, period, white or black."

Another member of the defensive staff was future Houston Oilers head coach Bum Phillips. He said, "Recruiting black players was the natural thing to do. We were all for it. We wanted to win."

Former Cougar quarterback and offensive assistant from 1962 to 1965, Jim Dickey, who later became head coach at Kansas State University from 1978 to 1985 and led them to their first bowl appearance in school history in 1982, added, "I don't remember any discussion between Coach Yeoman and the other coaches about whether we should recruit blacks—we just looked at the film and recruited the best players. Yeoman was a great guy to work with. He didn't care what color they were. When we looked at film, we looked for the best player. There was never a discussion as to whether we should recruit black players. We just did it."

Future NFL coach Chuck Fairbanks, another member of Yeoman's early staff, said, "I don't know if integration was a priority with Coach Yeoman. He just wanted the best player available. We all knew the skill of the black athlete. With our Michigan State backgrounds where the school was very progressive in having black students and black student athletes, it was natural for us to recruit blacks at Houston."

"Yeoman set the stage, coming from Michigan State," offensive assistant coach Bobby Gill said. "We just followed him. We changed the face of college football."

The question was who the African American player was going to be that would change the face of college athletics, not only at the University of Houston, but also throughout the South. When it came time for Yeoman to recruit his first black player, he said, "I was too stupid to realize people had a problem down here. I wish I could say it was a conscious decision and I mulled it over and contemplated doing it, but I just didn't pay any attention to it. I went to Athletic Director Harry Fouke and President Hoffman and I told them I was going to recruit Warren McVea. We looked at a couple of other black players, but we decided against them because we thought they couldn't handle it. Warren was a magnificent athlete who could roll with the punches."

Years later, Warren McVea himself said, "When they were looking to integrate the University of Houston, they were looking for the
total package. They wanted someone from a two-parent family. They
wanted a back to integrate, not a lineman. Coach Yeoman was a speed
guy, and I could run like the wind. I also had a strong Christian background. I had also been through integration before with Brackenridge
High School."

There was no better known high school running back than "Wondrous Warren" McVea, as he was known. He was unquestionably the
most-sought-after recruit in the nation by the spring of 1964. A native
of San Antonio, McVea attended Brackenridge High School, which
he helped integrate in the early 1960s. Playing halfback, McVea led
the Eagles to an 11–3 record and a Class 4A state championship in
1962, the largest high school classification at the time, with a 30–26
victory over Borger High School.

In McVea's senior season, Brackenridge compiled an 8–3 record and
lost in a bidistrict playoff game to San Antonio Lee High School
and their star halfback Linus Baer. In what many consider the greatest high school football game ever played in Texas, Lee squeaked
out a 55–48 victory. This being McVea's final high school game, in
which he was inserted into the quarterback position for the first time,
he ran 215 yards on 21 carries, scored six touchdowns, and scored 38
of Brackenridge's 48 points. That season, McVea totaled 1,332 yards
rushing on only 127 carries, an astounding 10.4 yards per carry, scoring
46 touchdowns and 39 extra points. His 315 single-season point total
and 591 total for his career were Class 4A records at the time.

At the end of the 1960s, Dave Campbell's prestigious *Texas Football*
magazine named McVea as the best runner of the 1960s after he was
chosen by a panel of 600 coaches, writers, and observers. In later interviews in 2004, Campbell himself and Dan Cook, a 50-plus-year sports
editor and television journalist from San Antonio, both said McVea
was the best high school football player they ever saw.

Every major college in the country wanted McVea. During the
1963 season, Oklahoma coach Bud Wilkinson came in person to watch
McVea play. Apparently McVea ran wild in the game, and Wilkinson

said afterward, "I'd lock him in the trunk of my car and head for Oklahoma, but, from what I saw tonight, I'm sure he'd get out."

McVea was also a sideline guest of the Texas Longhorns on January 1, 1964, when the Horns won their first national championship with a 28–6 rout of Navy.

Other schools used famous alumni, such as when UCLA sent 1960 gold-medal decathlete Rafer Johnson and baseball pioneer Jackie Robinson to try to convince McVea to attend their alma mater.

The University of Missouri, which was a school high on McVea's list, got former president Harry Truman to write McVea a letter trying to convince him to become a Tiger. In fact, Dan Devine, the Missouri coach, said of recruiting McVea, "I've never seen anything like it. Every place I go I hear of this kid. It seems like everyone has heard of him."

When Bill Yeoman decided to recruit McVea, he realized he would need help from Houston's African American community leaders. One person that Yeoman turned to was Quentin Mease. "Yeoman said if he could get Warren, a star, on his team, it would impact the whole collegiate system," Mease said years later. "As it turned out, my wife's parents lived in San Antonio, right across the street from the McVeas, and they all attended the local Baptist church where Mr. McVea was a deacon. I guess we had some influence on getting Warren to come to Houston."

Yeoman also got help from another person who was considered to be a giant to young men in the black community. In Houston's black community in the 1950s and 1960s, there was no bigger figure among athletes than Lloyd C. A. Wells, also known as "The Judge." A native Houstonian from the Fifth Ward neighborhood, Wells graduated from Pickett High School in nearby Brenham and went to Southern University in Baton Rouge on an athletic scholarship. After two years in college, Wells joined the Marine Corps to fight in World War II.

He returned to Houston after the war to attend Houston College for Negroes, which later became Texas Southern University. He played football and basketball and ran track there before returning to the military again to fight in the Korean War. Once a civilian again, Wells went to work as a photographer. He also spent a number of years writing an influential sports column for a couple of Houston's black newspapers, the *Forward Times* and the *Informer*. Wells used his column to bring about the elimination of segregated seating at the minor league Houston Buffs games and in Jeppesen Stadium at Houston Oilers games.

Later, in the 1960s, Wells became a part-time and then full-time scout for the Kansas City Chiefs, responsible for bringing as many as eight players to the team who were part of the Chiefs's Super Bowl IV victory over the Minnesota Vikings on January 11, 1970. Former Chiefs owner Lamar Hunt said, "The success we had on the field as a franchise came from our ability to find and develop talent, and Lloyd was a big part of that."

Hank Stram, the head coach of the Chiefs's Super Bowl team, was the man who hired Wells. He called Wells "an excellent scout. He was terrific, a lot of fun, but very serious about his work. And he got a lot of talent for us." The Wells-scouted players who became Chiefs were Mack Lee Hill, Otis Taylor, Jim Kearney, Warren McVea, Buck Buchanan, Robert Holmes, Aaron Brown, Noland Smith, Jim Marsalis, and Curley Culp.

When his stint with the Chiefs was over by the mid-1970s, Wells became part of Muhammad Ali's entourage, serving as an advisor for eight years. Gene Kilroy, who served as Muhammad Ali's business manager for 15 years, said of Wells, "After Lloyd lost his scouting job with the Chiefs, I brought him into Muhammad Ali's camp. We ended up being good friends. When I stayed with him one time in Houston at his house on Chew Street, Lloyd said that was the first time a white person had stayed in his neighborhood.

"Lloyd was just a great guy, a remarkable individual. He had a lot of athletic ability. He helped integrate press boxes at Houston sporting events in the 1960s. Hank Stram said he was the best scout in pro football. Most people don't know that Lloyd's mother was an elementary school teacher in Houston, and one of her students was heavyweight champ George Foreman."

What Wells was best known for in the Houston area was serving as an advisor and many times a surrogate father to young black athletes at the high school, college, and pro levels. Jim Kearney, who was from

Wharton, a small town south of Houston, went to Prairie View A&M, where he played quarterback. Eventually he played defensive back for the Chiefs because of Wells. "Oh, he was the man," Kearney said. "In Houston, nobody was bigger than Lloyd. *Nobody.* He was quite the man. He became a person we could go to and talk about problems. He had seen the world; he knew the score."

Walter Yates, a 6-foot-8 forward, was a Wheatley High School graduate who eventually went to play basketball at Pan American University and was part of their 1963 NAIA championship squad. He later returned to Houston and was a very successful high school basketball coach. He said, "Lloyd was such a motivator. He taught us confidence. He had a certain way of talking to people. He was also the kind of guy who could get the black athlete exposed at the next level—in other words, helping young blacks get college scholarships."

One young man who probably knew Wells better than anyone was Eddie Hall, who first met Wells as a young boy and eventually starred as a 5-foot-11 guard at Wheatley High School before attending TSU in the early 1960s. "I was a little athlete, around seven years old or so," Wells said. "Lloyd was a lifeguard at the Julius C. Hester House in the Fifth Ward. I was a basket boy at the pool. I had only one parent. He took me under his wing. He was like a father figure to me.

"Lloyd helped me in all areas of my life. He looked at me as a whole person. Lloyd was a pioneer. He was instrumental in young men's careers. He didn't smoke or drink. He was a true role model. He was very instrumental in my life. He taught me to do the right thing. Lloyd was my swimming coach first. He taught me as an athlete to stay focused. After a while, no one beat me at swimming. He was a one-of-a-kind gentleman."

Former Kansas City Chiefs All-Pro wide receiver Otis Taylor was a native Houstonian who also benefited from Wells's guidance and interest in young black men. Taylor recalled that "Lloyd Wells followed my career since junior high school, to Worthing High School and eventually to Prairie View A&M University, where he knew the coach, Billy Nicks. The number of schools I could attend was very limited.

"The University of Houston was very close to my house, and I could have virtually walked two blocks to the left and been on their campus.

But the University of Houston was still segregated in 1960. Eventually, during my senior season at Prairie View, Lloyd started coming to campus more and more, bringing pro football scouts with him to watch our practices. Lloyd was very positive about my making it in the pros, but he said it was all up to me."

Taylor concluded by saying, "The best way to describe Lloyd Wells is to say he's an extravagant extrovert. When he's around, you know it. Always the center of attention, Lloyd was a ladies man—by his own admission—and was also crazy about sports and athletics. One thing, more than anything else about Lloyd that has always stuck with me, is that if something was said and plans were made or promises pledged, he made it happen and always followed through. That's the kind of guy he was."

Another Worthing High School graduate under Wells's wing was David Lattin. "From the time I was playing at Worthing, a local newspaper reporter and photographer, Lloyd Wells, took an interest in me," Lattin said. "Later I learned his interest wasn't just in black athletes. He lent a hand to young black teens who went on to become doctors, lawyers, and university academics as well.

"Lloyd was the hardest-working man I knew. He was a cheerleader and a one-man public-relations operation for the entire black community. He took us under his wing, nurtured us, showed us the value of hard work, and turned us into men.

"Lloyd was very flamboyant, a great dresser. He was a trailblazer, a man ahead of his time. Not one to follow, he always took a new path. He was a great talker, and you couldn't *not* listen. But he wasn't just a talker, he was a doer. I never knew a man who worked harder. 'If you want something done, give it to a busy man,' he would say. He told me over and over that for all my talent and size, I'd never make it if I didn't apply myself.

"I had to work hard. I had to study, too, because I might get injured. I had to expect failure along the way, because that's how life could be. He walked tall and taught us to do the same. He was that kind of man."

Over at UH, Donnie Schverak knew Lloyd Wells very well. "I played for Lloyd in the basketball leagues over at Texas Southern," he said. "Later, when I was an assistant at Houston, Lloyd was my contact in the black community. In fact, Lloyd Wells opened every door for me in the black community as far as getting players to come to UH.

"We used to have a courtside seat reserved for Lloyd at every home game. He used to always call me on game days and ask, 'Donnie, you have my pass for me?' Of course, we always did. Lloyd was just a super guy."

Apparently it was UH sports information director Ted Nance who brought Lloyd Wells to Bill Yeoman's attention. "Ted Nance was very important in getting me recruited," McVea recounted. "He's the best that's ever done his job. Apparently Ted went to Coach Yeoman and said. 'You don't have a chance to get Warren. He's never even heard of the University of Houston.' I was planning on going to USC—all the tailbacks and the Heismans.

"Coach Yeoman didn't know what was going on in the black community in Houston. He knew Ted did, so he got leaders in the black community to recruit me. He got Lloyd Wells, of course, and other business leaders. I already knew a little about Lloyd Wells. A lot of people thought the only way I would go to UH would be through Lloyd. I guess that's somewhat true."

Nance underscored that belief. "I told Coach Yeoman about Lloyd Wells," Nance said. "I had gotten to know Lloyd because he was a columnist for one of the black newspapers in town, and we were the first college in the South to admit black media to our games. Once Coach Yeoman met with Wells, he introduced him to the black leaders of Houston."

It was not just Wells who convinced McVea to attend UH. While Wells was a catalyst, it was a collaborative effort of many people in and around the UH football program. On Yeoman's staff, Chuck Fairbanks was one of the coaches involved in McVea's recruitment. "Warren was a great young man to be recruited to U of H," Fairbanks said. "He was a phenomenal player. To this day he is probably the greatest instinctive runner I have ever seen or coached.

"Tom Boisture was another member of the Cougar coaching staff that was instrumental in recruiting Warren. We both helped recruit

Warren. Before Warren came, we were struggling for recognition as a college and as a football program. When Warren decided to come to the University of Houston, he made it acceptable and popular for blacks and whites to come to UH. I have a great appreciation for what Warren went through being our first black football player. He was the right person to do it, though. He was very outgoing and wouldn't let little things bother him."

Boisture was the assistant coach most responsible for the historic signing. He eventually became head coach at Holy Cross in the late 1960s and was director of player personnel for the New York Giants from 1980 to 2000. In the latter capacity, he had a hand in drafting players like Lawrence Taylor, Mark Bavaro, Carl Banks, Michael Strahan, and Amani Toomer for four Giants Super Bowl teams.

"Chuck Fairbanks and I recruited Warren," Boisture said. "I did most of the chasing around, and Chuck handled the other parts. Bill would visit with Warren, too, from time to time. Lloyd Wells also helped a lot.

"To us, the biggest stumbling block was Missouri and Dan Devine. Warren had a lot of schools chasing him. We figured out that he wanted to stay close to home. Being close to his mom was a big factor. He spent a lot of time in Houston. Warren eventually accepted the challenge to help build the program at U of H. Things exploded at Houston after that. We all liked Warren. He was a good kid."

The feeling was mutual. "Coach Boisture was the main assistant on Yeoman's staff who recruited me," McVea said. "He was a good coach. He kept us loose. I ended up being very close to him."

In hindsight, the role of Ted Nance can't be emphasized enough. Besides connecting Coach Yeoman with the black community, Nance made sure McVea was comfortable when he visited the Cougar athletic offices. "Recruiting Warren was nothing too special," Nance said. "I knew he liked sports a lot. He used to come by my office on his visits here to get sports magazines I had saved for him. He used to hang around, and we would talk sports, too."

Another person, who on the surface would appear highly unlikely to have a stake in McVea's recruitment, was Cougar basketball

Ted Nance, circa 1960s
(Courtesy of Ted Nance)

player Donnie Schverak. A native Houstonian, Schverak had just finished his basketball career in the fall semester of 1963 and held a rare distinction—he was the UH's first four-year letterman. He was injured in the second semester of his sophomore year, thus enabling him to play the fall semester of his final season. He also ranked near the top in UH career scoring and rebounding.

In 1967, Schverak became an assistant on Guy V. Lewis's staff and would continue in that capacity for 19 years. "Warren and I became close because of Lloyd Wells," Schverak said. "When Warren would come to Houston to visit, he would call Coach Yeoman and tell him ahead of time that Don better be there to show him around.

Don Schverak, circa late 1960s
(Courtesy of Don Schverak)

"Yeoman would say, 'Donnie, Warren's coming into town, and he said he wasn't coming unless you were going to be there.' When Warren came, he always wanted me to be with him to get some pie a la mode. At the time, he wasn't real big about going out to these parties they had for recruits with a couple of hundred people there. Warren was just really down to earth. There was one time, though, we were at a club in Houston, and James Brown was playing there. Before one of his songs, he said, 'This one's for you, Warren.'"

McVea readily acknowledged the importance of Schverak in his recruitment: "When I came to Houston, Lloyd Wells introduced me to Donnie. He helped out a lot in my recruitment. He used to take me around when I came to Houston. We became good friends. It was kind of unique recruiting me with a white guy. It made me feel good, though, like I was being included."

McVea went on to say, "Another person who helped in my recruitment was David Lattin. He was friends with Lloyd Wells, but I had actually gotten to know David a little bit the year before when his school, Houston Worthing, came to San Antonio to play Wheatley High School. I was a big sports fan and I went up to him before the game and introduced myself to him. He was very well known.

"So later when I came to Houston to visit, I would hang out some with Lloyd and David besides Donnie Schverak. In fact, later on my last day of high school, David and Lloyd came to San Antonio to 'rescue' me. I still hadn't signed and there were eight or nine coaches in San Antonio trying to get me to sign.

"I was looking at Oklahoma. I went to a hotel to meet with Coach Gomer Jones, and we had a nice conversation. The next thing I knew after that meeting, David and Lloyd grabbed me and they snuck me out of town. They said they were scared I was going to sign with Oklahoma, so they ended up taking me to Houston."

The last piece of the McVea recruiting puzzle was, of course, Bill Yeoman. "After I visited with Warren and saw how he acted around his mom," the coach remembered, "I knew we had a chance to get him. We were the closest major college to San Antonio that actually had integrated. I knew he wasn't going to go too far from home. To tell you the truth, my main worry was St. Mary's University in San Antonio. Some were saying that they were going to recruit Warren and resurrect their football program."

"I was a mama's boy," McVea admitted. "We had nine in our family. A lot of times, I would come home from a recruiting trip after only a day or so because I was homesick. Coach Yeoman was the only coach who picked up on this and the loneliness I felt.

"I had never seen a coach like Coach Yeoman. He hardly ever said anything. He would sit back and watch and size up the situation. He was also one of two coaches who picked up on the importance of religion (Dan Devine of Missouri was the other) to our family, and Coach Yeoman really focused on winning over my mother.

"I looked at a lot of schools. A. Z. Drones tried to get me to go to Missouri with him. My mom and Dan Devine had also gotten to be close. In the end, though, Missouri was too small for me. I like the big city.

"If I hadn't chosen U of H, I would have gone to USC, probably. I was a big Mike Garrett fan. I also knew Raymond Johnson from San Antonio, who was out in Los Angeles. I knew his younger brother, Cliff. When I happened to go out there to visit, for whatever reason we were out late and it was really cold, so I decided then and there I didn't want to go to USC. In the end, my mom not wanting me to be too far from her and the fact that Houston was close ended up being the main reason I chose to sign with Houston."

By modern recruiting standards, McVea signed his letter of intent very late. As the recruit said, this "was because I just wasn't ready before that. I had to check out all of the schools." He did not sign the letter of intent until Saturday, July 11, 1964, when Yeoman and Nance drove to San Antonio to get McVea's signature. Legendary sportswriter Dan Cook of the *San Antonio Express News* got the exclusive story. Then McVea's signing made newspapers all over the country as both the Associated Press and United Press International picked up Cook's story.

"When we signed Warren," Yeoman said, "we were driving back to Houston, and when Ted and I got to Seguin (30 miles east of San Antonio), we realized we had taken the wrong papers with us. We had to go back and get the correct papers from Warren."

Once McVea was signed, no one in Houston really knew what to expect in terms of the social ramifications of signing the first black football player in UH history. Would McVea be accepted just like any other player, or would the racism that had been prevalent to opposing players from the early 1950s up until 1963, the previous season, reappear?

Decades later, the coach who got the prized recruit summed up the situation: "I only caught flak from one fan over recruiting Warren. He used to call me drunk and complaining. I knew who it was, though. I think the reason we had so little backlash is that people around here wanted to win, and if they thought Warren could help us, they didn't care what color he was."

In hindsight, McVea's assessment of the coach who recruited him to Houston got straight to the point: "I'd never seen a coach like him. When he was around, he never said a lot. He would sit back and observe the situation. He was the only coach who picked up on my loneliness and homesickness.

"He knew I didn't want to go too far from home. When I got to U of H, he let it be known in his own way that I was to be left alone. I even asked Coach Yeoman a while back if he was nervous about our situation, with me being the first black player. He said no, it never really crossed his mind."

Now, with the nation's top football recruit wrapped up and coming to the University of Houston, the job would be to get Warren McVea acclimated to his new surroundings when he arrived in Houston in the late summer of 1964.

7 ELVIN, DON, AND MATERNAL INFLUENCE

My mother decided where I was going to go to college.
Coach Pate came down and my mom liked him.
He actually recruited my mother, not me.
—ELVIN HAYES SPEAKING OF HIS UH RECRUITMENT

As much hype, publicity, and excitement as the recruitment of Warren McVea brought to the University of Houston, the signing of Elvin Hayes and Don Chaney to the Cougar basketball program in the spring of 1964 brought little fanfare.

Don Chaney came from Baton Rouge's McKinley High School and had led his school to the Class 3A state championship as a junior. Chaney was the better known of the two recruits. He ended up his senior season as a *Parade Magazine* High School All-American as a member of the third team, far down the list of *Parade* honorees such as Lew Alcindor and Wes Unseld. Chaney's future UH teammate, Ken Spain of Houston's Austin High School, was a choice for the fourth team.

Ironically, the least heralded of the three African American recruits was Elvin Hayes. "The Big E" ended up having the more illustrious college and professional career. Hayes came from the small Northeast Louisiana town of Rayville. He stood tall in the background with his record. He led his Eula D. Britton High School team to the Class 2A state championship as a senior in 1964. He scored 45 points and grabbed 20 rebounds in the title game to top off a 54-game winning streak for the school. He was considered a relative unknown when comparing his high school career to that of Warren McVea or Don Chaney.

Guy V. Lewis only found out about Hayes when Isaac Moorehead, the head basketball coach down the street at Texas Southern University, was afraid Hayes was going to sign with nearby Grambling University, which played in the same conference as TSU. Moorehead hoped Lewis might be interested in getting Hayes to visit UH. "I already knew about Don," Lewis said. "I had Harvey drive over to Louisiana to watch Elvin play, and he said Elvin was one of the best players he had ever seen."

It should be noted that the "Harvey" Guy Lewis referred to was his assistant coach from the time Lewis became head coach in 1956 until his retirement in 1980. Harvey Pate came to UH by way of Cameron Junior College in Lawton, Oklahoma, where he had compiled a ten-year won-lost record of 198–57. A native Oklahoman, Pate was born in 1918 in the town of Byars and eventually graduated from Capital City High School in Oklahoma City in 1937. Pate helped his team to the 1935 state championship. After high school, he went to Oklahoma A&M University and lettered for three years under legendary Coach Hank Iba, while getting to play in both the 1940 NCAA Tournament and the NIT. After college, Pate joined the service during World War II and started his career at Cameron when the war ended.

At UH, Pate handled many tasks besides assisting Lewis. Unlike football, where Bill Yeoman usually had about seven assistant coaches in the early days, Pate was the only full-time assistant until former player Donnie Schverak was hired in 1967. Pate also served as the freshman coach from 1956 to 1972 during an era when freshmen were not eligible to play varsity ball. Pate's duties also meant serving as chief

Harvey Pate, Guy Lewis, and Don Schverak, circa late 1960s
(Courtesy of Don Schverak)

recruiter. "Harvey was a great coach and my right arm all of the time and my left arm most of the time," Lewis avowed. "He was the best in the business at scouting opposing teams."

The players of the era attested to the assistant coach's positive attitude in what became UH's family approach to getting the most of every athlete. One of them, Neal Kaspar, said, "Coach Pate was like a father to all of us. I have a very high regard for him. I remember if you had problems with a class, you could get copies of previous tests from a particular class. It was more or less accepted. I always sensed Coach Pate never endorsed that. It was like he was above doing unethical things like that."

Paul Ozug came to Houston from Gary, Indiana, in 1964, the same year as Hayes and Chaney. "Harvey was a tremendous fella," Ozug said. "He took me under his wing. He sold me on UH. I had other Big Ten offers. I wanted to go to Northwestern, but I didn't have the grades. Coach Pate made the difference, though. He was like a dad to me. I was 1,300 miles from home. Ninety percent of schools had classes just to keep players eligible. Coach Pate made sure we took regular classes so we could get an education."

Jack Margenthaler, team captain and starting guard on UH's 1965 NCAA Tournament team, said, "I enjoyed Coach Pate. He was ideal for Coach Lewis. When you were on the freshman team, you dealt mostly with Coach Pate. He was more easygoing than Coach Lewis. He would guide you."

Even football's Warren McVea got to know Coach Pate. "How could you not like him?" McVea said. "He was just an old country boy. He used to try and get me to come out and play basketball. He was the best thing to happen to Hayes and Chaney their freshman year."

"Coach Pate was like a father to me," Elvin Hayes said. "I love him. Sometimes you're closer to your freshman coach. At first, we were all scared of Coach Lewis. Coach Pate, along with Coach Lewis, Dr. Hoffman, and [Athletic Director] Harry Fouke, were all men of high moral character, and they committed themselves to making everything work, and they did."

Guard Bill Bane came to Houston from Charlotte, North Carolina, and was a junior on the 1968 Final Four team. "Harvey was a great guy," Bane said. "He was kind of like the good minister. He would be the go-between a lot of the time, too. He was also a heckuva recruiter." In fact, Coach Lewis himself described Pate as "the best recruiter I have ever seen."

Guy Lewis's son Vern played with both Hayes and Chaney and called Pate "a real character and fantastic recruiter," saying, "He got Otis Birdsong out of Florida to come here. When Harvey really wanted someone to come to UH, he would tell them, 'Young man, do you want to be a star?'"

Ted Luckenbill and Gary Phillips came to UH from the Midwest, both becoming catalysts for the Cougars becoming an NCAA Tournament team by the time they were seniors in 1961. "Coach Pate was the most honest of the coaches that recruited me," Luckenbill recalled. "I had been recruited by several schools, and I was offered cars and other under-the-table stuff.

"Coach Pate said I would get an education. Once Gary Phillips and I got to Houston, we drove Coach Pate crazy. He was used to a set offense where you would pass the ball at least five or six times—the Hank Iba way. Being from the Midwest, where we would fast break a lot, Gary and I would take off down the floor as freshmen and try to score quickly."

"I really liked Coach Pate and Coach Lewis," Phillips said. "They were on a recruiting trip in Illinois, and they suggested I come down to Houston for a visit. There was three feet of snow on the ground at the time in Illinois, and when I got to Houston, it was about 80 and they were having their annual Frontier Fiesta.

"It came down to Kansas or Houston. In fact, Houston didn't have a scholarship available, but Harry Fouke said they would figure something out. The University of Houston turned out to be very good to me. Coach Pate was a tremendous recruiter, and he fit into the coaching staff well. He loved defense—in-your-face defense. Coach Pate got that from Hank Iba. I learned it well because when I went to UH I wasn't a good defensive player. But by the time I went to the pros, I usually guarded the other team's leading scorer, like Jerry West."

Margenthaler also referred to Pate's honesty and the fact that the first time he met him was when the coach came up to Pinckneyville, Illinois, in April 1961 on a recruiting trip. "We hit it off, and he had Coach Lewis come up for a home visit. I had offers from Tulsa, Marquette, St. Louis, among others," Margenthaler said. "Coach Pate was totally honest with me in the recruiting process, and that's a big reason I came to Houston."

Melvin Bell was one of Pate's prize recruits. From Clinton, Oklahoma, Bell was among the second wave of black players who came in 1965, the year after McVea, Hayes, and Chaney. This 6-foot-7 forward was one of the most recruited players in the country. "It seems every week he was up there in Clinton. I had 102 scholarship offers," Bell said. "In fact, when I went to Texas Western to visit, David Lattin showed me around. Harvey, though, was very persistent, and I wound up at the University of Houston. I loved Harvey and Guy."

Joel Williams told a story about Harvey Pate's recruiting persever-
ance that made the rounds at UH over a number of years. Pate was
trying to get 6-foot-9 Louis Dunbar from Minden, Louisiana, to play
at UH in the spring of 1971. "Supposedly, on signing day, a coach from
another school shows up at 7 a.m. to try and sign Louis," Williams
said. "When the coach knocked on the door, who should answer it but
Coach Pate in his pajamas?"

Once with the Cougars, Dunbar went on to average 22.3 points
and 7.7 rebounds over his three-year career. He then went on to a long
career as "Sweet Lou" Dunbar with the Harlem Globetrotters.

Donnie Schverak confirmed the Williams story and added, "Actually, Harvey was in a bathrobe with a towel draped over his arm because
he was getting ready to take a shower. Also, Louis's daddy was a sheriff
in Minden, and Harvey would ride around in Louis's daddy's big four-
door Cadillac squad car while Mr. Dunbar was on patrol."

Six-foot-ten center Dwight Jones—along with Bill Walton and
Tom McMillen—was the country's most highly rated recruit in 1970
after leading Houston's Wheatley High School to three straight state
championships. He was also at the top of Pate's recruiting list. "Coach
Pate was very easygoing," Jones said. "He kind of hung around and
stayed close. I was about to sign with Jacksonville. Coach Pate was persistent, though, and made me feel wanted. He was a natural recruiter.
Color didn't matter to him. As our freshman coach, Harvey let us play,
which was his style. Harvey was real good people."

Schverak remained the person who knew Harvey Pate better than
anyone else. Pate recruited him, and he played at Houston from 1960
to 1964. A 6-foot-4 forward, Schverak averaged 13.4 points and 7.6
rebounds a game for the Cougars. Then he worked alongside Pate as
an assistant coach and recruiter from 1967 to 1980, Pate's last year at
UH. "I wasn't playing for my high school team," Schverak said, "so I
was playing in a league over at TSU. I was the only white kid in the
whole league. Coach Ed Adams of TSU called Harvey and said, 'Come
take a look at this kid.'

"Well, I scored 60 points in the game. Harvey told Guy Lewis,
'You've got to come see this kid play.' So Guy comes and watches me,

and I score 55 points in the championship game. I ended up getting a half scholarship to Houston, books and tuition, which in those days was not much.

"Once I got to UH, Harvey was like my daddy when I was there—very kind, down home, never showed his superiority. Then, when I later started coaching at Houston, Harvey taught me a lot about how to run a practice and recruiting. He was the best there was at recruiting—honest and straightforward. One thing he taught me about recruiting was to never promise a potential recruit playing time or anything else. Harvey would tell the recruit he would have every opportunity to succeed at the University of Houston, nothing more, nothing less. Harvey and I were very close. I was much closer to him than I was with Guy."

In 1973, Pate recruited Otis Birdsong out of Florida, who eventually scored 2,832 points for the second-place all-time record behind Hayes at UH. He was a consensus All-American as a senior in 1977. The number-two overall pick in the 1977 NBA draft, Birdsong was a four-time NBA All-Star with the Kansas City Kings and New Jersey Nets.

"I grew up in Winter Haven, Florida," Birdsong said. "Coach Pate was like a guy from the South—he had that country and grandfather appeal. When he said something, you believed it. My family was crazy about him. I narrowed my choices to Purdue, Western Kentucky, and Houston. Coach Pate, once he started recruiting me, was relentless. He made you feel at ease, though. He got to my mom. She's 93 and she still asks about him. He used to say to me, 'How you doin', Rattler?' Maybe he called me that because I was from Florida, and there were a lot of rattlesnakes there.

"When I was at UH in the seventies, he wasn't at practice much—he was out recruiting. He would be at the games, though. I heard that back when Harvey was coaching, he was a helluva coach. Coach Pate was just a gentleman and a great, great guy."

Pate gave his own opinion of his abilities, saying, "I felt I was a pretty good recruiter. I was able to recruit black, white, rich, poor. I could fit into any situation I needed to. I felt that my recruiting Elvin played a big part in the University of Houston integrating its athletic programs."

When the time came to recruit Hayes and Chaney in the spring of 1964, Guy V. Lewis focused mostly on Chaney and Pate on Hayes. "I found out about Elvin from Isaac Moorehead, the TSU coach," Lewis explained. "I already knew about Don. Harvey drove to watch Elvin play and said he was one of the best players he had ever seen. I mostly recruited Don.

"I remember when they came to Houston to visit, we showed them a mock model of Hofheinz Pavilion," Lewis said, referring to the arena that wasn't completed until 1969. "We used to show it to a lot of the recruits we brought in. We ended up getting two of the best players the University of Houston ever had by showing them a model of an arena they never got to play in.

"As it turned out, we signed Elvin and Don on the same day. Harvey dropped me off in Baton Rouge to sign Don, and he went to Rayville to sign Elvin. Don's mother was probably the biggest factor in him coming to Houston, though. She told him that's where he was going."

Indeed, Chaney's mother had the greatest influence on the venue of her son's college career. "My number-one choice as to where to go to college was Loyola of Chicago," Chaney said. "They had won the NCAA title in 1963, and I really wanted to go there. I was recruited heavily by them. I wanted to go out of state and up north. Guy and Harvey came down on a couple of occasions. They talked to my mother and my high school coach, Carl Stewart. I still knew where I was going to go. In fact, I told everyone in my neighborhood that I was going to Loyola.

"My mom made the decision for me to go to Houston. She was big on the Civil Rights movement and she felt this was an opportunity to be a pioneer. The way she presented it to me, it made sense; it would be a challenge.

"I must say, too, that I admire Guy Lewis for the commitment he made in recruiting black athletes. He never mentioned it, like he had done all of this before. Once we got there to Houston, he didn't treat us any different. Everything was team."

Pate said, "I spent a lot of time in Rayville. Coach Lewis had told me about Chaney. He seemed to know a lot about him. I remember Don's mom worked at Southern University in Baton Rouge, and she was very interested in Don going to college. Texas Southern had told us about Elvin. They didn't want him to go to Grambling to play against them."

Pate also remembered his first encounter with Hayes at a basketball tournament in Bunkie, Louisiana. "I watched him play three or four games, and he really impressed me," the recruiter said. "On one play in particular, Elvin blocked a layup, grabbed the ball while it was still in the air, and threw the ball to the other end of the court to a teammate for a basket before Elvin's feet ever hit the ground.

"There were just a few schools interested in Elvin. Northern schools didn't come to Louisiana much to recruit. I think Elvin considered Wisconsin for a while because that's where his sister went to college. One time when I was in Rayville, I met the (white) owner of the local radio station. I told him, 'You have a kid here in town that will be famous. He'll put Rayville on the map.' He had never heard of Elvin, but I told him, 'You better go interview him.'"

Recruiting success was uncertain. "For a while," Pate said, "I thought we weren't going to get Elvin. Then one day about 6:30 in the evening, Elvin's sister called and said Elvin wanted to go to Houston with Coach Pate. I got in the car with Guy, dropped him off in Baton Rouge, so he could sign Don, and then I drove to Rayville all night to go sign Elvin the next day.

"You know, Elvin is the best player I ever recruited. He's the best player the University of Houston has ever had. He put UH on the map. Some people talk about some of these other players that came along a few years later like Drexler and Olajuwon being the best.

"Believe me, they were great players here, but they both got better after they went to the pros. Elvin was a bit headstrong but a good kid. And trust me, he was the best."

Besides Pate, the biggest influence on Hayes coming to UH was—like both McVea and Chaney—his mother.

"My mother decided where I was going to go to college," the player who would become known as "the Big E" said. "Coach Pate came down and my mom liked him. He actually recruited my mother, not me. When he would come to visit, Coach Pate would start talking with my mom about going fishing.

"She eventually said, 'You're going to UH with Coach Pate.' Once Harvey set his sights on a player, he was the best there was at reeling them in. I was going to go to Wisconsin. My sister was there, and they recruited me hard. I didn't like the cold weather, though."

Unlike Bill Yeoman, who made Warren McVea his only African American recruiting target, Hayes and Chaney were not the only African American players Lewis was looking to bring to Houston. Recall that Lewis tried to bring McCoy McLemore and David Lattin to UH before integration. But *after* integration, in the spring of 1964, the other target was Bob Rule, a 6-foot-9 forward from Riverside Community College in California, where he was coached by future University of Nevada–Las Vegas coaching legend Jerry Tarkanian. Rule eventually became a second-round draft pick of the Seattle Supersonics and was a 1970 NBA All-Star.

Rule recalled the University of Houston's attempt to recruit him. "I remember visiting Houston in the spring of 1964," he said. "I was there on a weekend with several other recruits. I got to meet Coach Lewis, and we stayed at the Shamrock Hilton Hotel. We went and visited the campus. Houston seemed like a first-class place, and the University of Houston seemed first class.

"I actually considered going to Houston, but my mother was dead set against it. She had been raised in Oklahoma and had experienced Jim Crow and racism firsthand, and she didn't want me to deal with it. I ended up going to Colorado State."

Ironically, in the 1966 NCAA Tournament, Colorado State lost, 82–76, in the first round to UH, which was led by sophomores Elvin Hayes and Don Chaney.

Once Warren McVea, Elvin Hayes, and Don Chaney signed their letters of intent, what now remained was arriving in Houston in the summer of 1964 to see what awaited them.

8 COMING TO HOUSTON

The thing you probably don't realize is that I have never been allowed to speak to a white person before without their permission first.
—DON CHANEY TO HIS WHITE
ROOMMATE JOHN TRACY

When Warren McVea, Elvin Hayes, and Don Chaney arrived in the summer of 1964 to attend the University of Houston, the city, the university, and its fans underwent a transformation.

Before this historic entry, the Houston fans's treatment of opposing African American athletes from visiting schools was poor and unsportsmanlike. It started with terribly seg-regated hotel accommodations and continued unmercifully with verbal harassment during the actual games. While not entirely incident-free, UH students appeared to welcome their new fellow Cougars. Interestingly, the acceptance of McVea, Hayes, and Chaney transpired fairly quickly. Years later, some of the coaches, players, and fans close to the ath-letic program provided key insights about this fascinating transformation.

In 1965, when Jerry LeVias became the first African American scholarship football player in the old Southwest Conference, his experience was entirely different from what McVea faced the year before. LeVias was the subject of hate mail, death threats, confrontations at social events, and racism in class. McVea, however, encountered relatively few problems when he arrived on the UH campus. Why was it different for him? SMU was a rich, elitist school, and UH was a working-class, urban institution. UH students, faculty, administration, and—yes—many alumni wanted a winner so badly that skin color was no problem. The three new Cougars looked like a growing number of UH students. Identity was more easily established.

Native Houstonian Bill Worrell experienced the arrival of Warren McVea from a unique perspective. Worrell was a UH cheerleader, a member of the Cougar baseball team, and a resident of Baldwin House, the athletic dormitory. "Warren was well-liked," Worrell remembered. "I had several classes with him. Put yourself in Warren's shoes. What would it be like for me at Grambling?

"The University of Houston, I felt, did an overall excellent job with integration. From Dr. Hoffman to Athletic Director Harry Fouke to the head coaches, they were way ahead of their time. One thing is that the UH campus had become pretty liberal by the mid- to late 1960s. Blacks on campus started to have a voice, led by campus activist Gene Locke. We also elected a black Homecoming queen, Lynn Eusan, in 1968.

"As far as I know, we were the first college in the South to do so. Warren would have been voted most popular student on campus easily. When Warren walks into a room, it's electric. In the classes I had with Warren, he ended up being the teacher's pet."

Before he arrived on campus, McVea showed a little apprehension in a conversation he had with Donnie Schverak, who recalled, "Warren did ask me a couple of times when he came here on recruiting trips, 'What would I face as the first black on campus?' I told him not to worry about it too much because I believed most of the football and basketball players wouldn't see color out there; they wanted to win."

That color blindness gradually became apparent. Defensive back Bill Hollon spoke of the anticipation of being teammates with McVea:

"I was an 18-year-old white kid from the town of Elsa in the Rio Grande Valley. I went to a high school that was 80 percent Hispanic. Being around minorities was first nature, not second nature, for me.

"When Warren came on campus, I didn't see or hear much in the way of bias. I think the coaching staff had prepared everyone for it. Warren, too, handled it pretty well. He was very upbeat, fun, great to be around. I ended up having a locker across from him. I always got along with him. I was tickled to play with him.

"I remember, as recruits, we would get update letters telling us who else UH was recruiting for my class. I remember when I read that we had recruited Warren, I was really excited. Even though Warren did receive some preferential treatment, we accepted it. We all knew he was special, and we wanted to win."

Quarterback Bo Burris was a year ahead of McVea. He said, "As far as I know, Warren didn't have much in the way of problems when he got here. Heck, he was a celebrity. Everyone here already knew who he was."

Tom Paciorek, a defensive back and University of Detroit transfer after the 1964 season, said, "I remember seeing films of Warren before he got here. We had never seen anything like him. He was a great guy, as were the other black players that followed him, like Paul Gipson and Jerry Drones. I think most of us involved were proud of integration. We were for it. I was from Detroit, and I had friends and teammates who were black. We just played. We didn't place any emphasis on color. What helped was that Warren was a great guy. He could get along with anyone."

Gus Hollomon of Beaumont played alongside Paciorek in the defensive backfield. "This was all new territory for us," Hollomon said. "We wanted to make it work, and the coaches worked hard to make Warren feel welcome. It really worked out well. Now, if Warren would have been a jerk, it may have been different. E and Duck were great guys, too. They were just fellow players and athletes to us—comrades."

Wade Phillips said of McVea, "Mac was a fun guy to be around. He was one of the greatest open-field runners ever. He had such a great personality, people just loved being around him. Oh, and he was also a great ping-pong player."

Jody Powers, a freshman teammate of McVea's, said, "We were all excited to have Warren join us. He had gotten a lot of press. At first, Warren was somewhat quiet and shy. We always wondered how it felt to be in his shoes. When he first got there, we did have a couple of rednecks on the team, but we kept them in check. At first, there were some dumb-ass remarks. A lot of the credit for the way Warren, Elvin, and Don were treated had to do with Yeoman and Lewis. They created an environment of acceptance. Leadership determines the environment. It was understood that Warren was to be treated as an equal."

Flanker Ken Hebert, the nation's leading scorer in 1966 with 113 points, recalled, "I came out of Pampa, Texas, in the Panhandle. We integrated my high school my senior year. So, honestly, when I came to Houston, from an integration standpoint it was not a big deal. Warren and I spent a lot of time together at school and practice because we were in the same backfield.

"Socially, though, he had his friends and I had my friends. We ended up being close, though. Honestly, it was an issue that was never really an issue. When you're out there fighting for your lives, you don't think about it."

Linebacker Greg Brezina of Louise, Texas, said, "I didn't know of anyone that didn't like Warren. I didn't really think much about the integration thing. I think I learned about integration and acceptance from my mother.

"I remember in my hometown of Louise in 1961, my brother Gus was a senior and there was a basketball playoff game scheduled against a team with blacks on it. The town of Louise held a public meeting as to whether to play the game or not. I remember my mother got up in front of everyone and said, 'Let the boys play.' Then Gus stood up in front of the crowd and said basically the same thing. My mom took a chance getting up and speaking out. She was the school dietician, and she could have lost her job."

Rich Stotter came to the University of Houston from Ohio and in 1967 became an All-America guard in part because he blocked for McVea. He spoke of UH back then: "I grew up in the Cleveland suburbs, so I was playing with and against blacks. When Warren got here, I don't know if he faced any racism. I know I didn't see it.

"Now, sometimes when Warren wasn't around, some of the other players would say some racial slurs. Turns out most of those kids were small-town kids who had been raised on this racial stuff. To be honest, they were jealous of him, and most of them weren't very good players anyways."

Defensive back Jim Pat Berger of Weimar, west of Houston, eventually became one of McVea's best friends. He said, "We were a special group—very close-knit. No one really thought of Warren as black. Warren was really the first black person I had ever played with or against. He was so outgoing, you couldn't help but like him. He was the perfect person to integrate UH. We ended up being close friends. We just clicked as far as being friends."

This developing chemistry had a natural flow, as confirmed by Bill Yeoman, no less. "Some people thought I met with the team beforehand about how Warren should be treated," the Cougar coach said. "No, heck no. That's the biggest collection of bull. It was my football team, and I was the one in charge. I didn't have to say anything to the players about how Warren should be treated.

"The players knew where I stood. Warren adapted well once he got here. He was perfect to integrate the program. Warren was easygoing, and he also had the gift of being able to go into a crowd and size up the audience. However, if Warren felt he was being pushed, he wouldn't back down, either.

"Warren's recruitment also made it easier to recruit all players, white and black. They saw in Warren coming here that we were serious and now had a chance to win. We had told people when we first came here in 1961 that our goal was to win a national championship. I got that advice from Dave Williams, our golf coach. He advised me that you have to come in and say that to show people you have high expectations. If you didn't make a statement like that, people wouldn't take you seriously or jump on the bandwagon."

Assistant coach Chuck Fairbanks did recall one potentially uncomfortable situation for McVea when he first arrived on campus: "One of the most embarrassing things I experienced was at the beginning of Warren's first night with the team—the night that freshmen report. The varsity had been there for a few days, and of course they were all white.

"When the freshmen reported for the evening meal, a deafening silence came into the room. It had to be uncomfortable for Warren. However, because of his outgoing personality, he appeared to let the incident slide off of him."

McVea remembered this event well: "When I got to campus, Coach Yeoman had let it be known in his own way that I was to be left alone. Coach Yeoman put everything to rest. I asked him a while back if he was nervous about our situation, and Coach Yeoman said no, he hadn't given it much thought, he just did it.

"Once I got started at UH, there were a couple of incidents. One time when I was in line at the bookstore, I could hear some comments. Sometimes if there was a crowd somewhere, I would hear the word 'nigger' come from someone in the crowd. Early on, sometimes my teammates would accidentally say the N-word around me. It was never directed at me, and they would always apologize. That was about it. I must say, pretty much all my classroom instructors were helpful to me."

When Elvin Hayes and Don Chaney arrived in the summer of 1964 before the fall semester started, they, like Warren McVea, faced a few obstacles. But for the most part, the transition was fairly smooth.

One person not in the athletic program but fairly close to the situation was Jimmy Disch, who came to UH from Houston's Lamar High School and became a Cougar cheerleader. "I was a huge basketball fan," Disch said, always relishing the October 15 date—the first day of fall basketball practice. "I would do the shot charts for Coach Lewis. Integration was not that big a deal at UH. When you're living it, you're a part of it, and you don't realize you're making history or that some of these guys will be famous someday.

"It was a special time at UH then. It was the perfect place for me. Elvin and I eventually got to know each other, and we got along well. Later, when I started teaching PE at Rice University, Elvin would come talk to my coaching class."

Bill Worrell, the other cheerleader, whose recollections are prominent in this written account of UH sports integration, remembered that Hayes and Chaney were instant campus stars. "If you were in central casting in Hollywood," Worrell said, "Elvin and Don would have been two of the best you could have picked. I admire the bravery and courage of those two young men. All of the people on campus that I knew were 100 percent behind them.

"It took Elvin a little more time than Don to adjust. He was from the country, and he had a slight speech problem. Both he and Don were kind of quiet at first. Both of them were smart, though. I also think that since the University of Houston is on the fringe of the black community in Houston, that helped them adjust when they first got here."

A couple basketball players already on the UH roster when Hayes and Chaney arrived were guards Jack Margenthaler and Gary Grider. Margenthaler was a senior when the two newcomers were freshmen and not eligible in this era to play with the varsity. Grider was one year ahead of the two and started at guard on the 1967 Final Four team when he was a senior and Hayes and Chaney were juniors.

Margenthaler said, "I didn't know anything about Elvin and Don until they signed. Coach Lewis announced it to the team. I never sensed the older players resented them. I wish they could have played my senior year. At first we didn't hang out with them much, but eventually I got to know them pretty well.

"Don was a class guy. Elvin got better as the year went along. We were upbeat that they decided to come to UH. They came here with a little bit of fanfare. I felt the students and the athletes were appreciative of them. Everyone seemed to be glad they were on campus."

Grider said, "We did a smart thing recruiting Elvin and Don. They were two good ones—outstanding athletes. Integration was great for the University of Houston. When they did get to Houston, though, it was a big adjustment for Coach Lewis. He had never before had that type of talent. He made a lot of errors at first. He didn't know any better. We eventually went from a walk-it-up team to more of a running team."

Two players who came in as freshmen the same time as Hayes and Chaney were Neal Kaspar, a walk-on from Houston Lutheran High School, and guard David Wells, who came all the way from St. Jacob, Illinois. "That first summer before Elvin and Don enrolled," Kaspar said, "I overheard Coach Pate talking to Guy Lewis about a couple of kids from Louisiana coming. Elvin showed up two weeks later. At the scrimmages at the old gym at UH, Elvin quickly squared off with David Lattin. Elvin had to learn quick how to play with the big boys. When I went there that summer, that was my first experience playing against black players.

"I had been raised in a very white Houston community, Lindale Park. That summer was my first experience with black people, period. I would go to work at Finger's Furniture and load trucks. There were 21 blacks in the warehouse and me. After work, I would go to the gym. I got along well with Elvin and Don. Not real close, but we got along fine.

"A lot of the freshmen that came in that year, like David Wells, Tom Stein, and Paul Ozug, were from the North and had played against black players before. I felt our freshman team had great chemistry. Coach Pate helped. I felt he was a master at dealing with black players. I do remember one time Elvin got homesick. I think Paul Ozug talked him into staying. They got into a conversation about Paul learning how to play the guitar, and Elvin seemed interested in that and I guess it got his mind off going home."

Wells recalled how Hayes and Chaney adjusted after they got to campus. "Two times Elvin took off to go home," he said. "I know Harvey went to go get him one time. Don was a great guy. Playing with those guys was a great experience. Elvin and Don were good sports. They took part in freshman initiation and everything, which brought us together more as a team.

"Another thing I remember is Elvin used to throw his roommate, Howie Lorch, out of his room fairly often. Howie would complain about something, like how Elvin wouldn't wash his clothes or socks, and Elvin would throw him out."

Vern Lewis, Guy's son, said, "I never saw any of that racial stuff. I know Elvin had a couple of issues as to how he was treated, but it was all hearsay. I didn't see anything personally. What's interesting is that once they came here, there were no more racial slurs from the home stands. Before that there were a lot of them."

Vern Lewis continued, "We all stayed at Baldwin House on campus. The basketball team all stayed on the same floor, so there was a lot of camaraderie. Don was a quiet guy, one of the nicest guys on the team. I was closer to Elvin than Don. He used to come over to the house to eat dinner a lot.

"Also, that first summer, Elvin and I had a job together at Hobby Airport, and we had to sand an airplane that belonged to John Mecom [Houston oilman and original New Orleans Saints owner]. One thing I remember is that Elvin was always bragging about how he was a drum major at his high school. I guess he thought I kind of doubted him, so one day he said, 'I'll show you!' and he picked up a broom and high stepped like a drum major would all the way across the hangar."

Coach Pate said, "I felt that both Elvin and Don fit in well once they got here. When they first got here, they would go play on their own. Pretty soon, though, they would go down to the Jewish Community Center and play there. Elvin broke his hand there. Elvin was also very competitive."

"As far as I know," Guy V. Lewis said in his reflections of the Louisiana duo, "Elvin and Don didn't encounter much in the way of problems. I didn't know of any problems in the classroom, either. My own players didn't retaliate, as far as I know.

"I do know that after we signed Elvin and Don, I did not receive one threat personally. Most of the people on campus seemed happy to have them there, too. Heck, they wanted to win just like I did."

One person who must have known the importance of prize recruit Elvin Hayes was former UH assistant football coach and physical education instructor Andy Zubel, who had Hayes in a freshman swimming class. Dick Woodall, who eventually became the starting quarterback on the 1967 football team in McVea's senior season, was in the same class as Hayes. Woodall recalled an incident with Coach Zubel and Hayes in the swimming class they had together. "Coach Zubel said to me one day, 'Woody, you see that end of the pool?' He was pointing at the three-foot end. 'If Elvin gets out of that three-foot end, you will fail this course!' So I spent the whole semester at the shallow end of the pool. I got to talk to and really get to know Elvin, who couldn't swim."

Chaney recalled, "The timing for integrating UH was great. The school and the students were ready—they wanted a winner. I remember the summer before I came over to Houston from Baton Rouge, my brother and sister used to walk around our house kidding me about what might be in store for me at UH when I got there. When I got to Houston, there was an adjustment period.

"I used to hear some racial slurs at first. Sometimes we'd be sitting in the lounge at Baldwin House watching television with about 25–30 other guys in the room, and someone would shout out the N-word. That didn't last that long, though. After the people there got used to us, it died down after a couple of months."

Hayes remembered, "When I first got to UH that summer, I stayed on campus. I came a little early, so none of the other players were on campus. To keep me from being by myself, Coach Lewis talked to Texas Southern, and they let me stay there. That really helped me to adjust. I had someone to talk to and people to be around.

"When school was close to starting, I naturally thought Don and I would be roommates. But that was not the case. It was a difficult time for us, especially me. We had been brought up in a totally black environment. I had more problems than Don. I lived in a totally segregated society prior to coming to Houston. People in my life had tried to limit contact with whites as much as possible.

"I went home to Rayville, but I came back the next day. My brother came back to Houston with me for a few days. [Sports writer] Lloyd Wells also spent a whole weekend with me to get me to stay. He had dealt with black athletes. I ended up appreciating him. He kept me from making a really bad decision.

"I also learned that there were a lot of players in the dorms who hadn't ever been around blacks. Early on, I would walk in on conversations they were having. Eventually it worked out. By the time I was a sophomore, I was just one of the team.

"When classes started, I had more problems adjusting. I remember in one class, Don and I were sitting next to this girl, and every day in class she would sit there shaking. I even said, 'Don, did you notice that girl shaking?' Don said, 'Yeah, I did, what do you think is wrong with her?' I finally asked the girl after class one day, 'Is there a reason why you are shaking in class all the time?' She said, 'Yes, *you!*' I didn't want to tell her I felt the same way inside.

"I hadn't wanted to interact with whites when I got to campus, but people like Coach Lewis helped change me. Eventually, his son Vern and I became very close, and I used to go over to Coach Lewis's house all the time to eat. In spite of these early incidents, I ended up being real happy with my decision to go to UH."

Hayes thinking he would not interact with whites turned into his worst fear when he found out who his roommate would be. Hayes had just assumed he would be rooming with Chaney. However, Guy Lewis had another idea that he thought in the long run would make the transition easier for both of his black players. Lewis decided to room Hayes and Chaney with white players from the North, two people who had grown up in a nonsegregated society and been raised around African Americans.

Lewis's choices both came from the state of New York. For Hayes, he picked Howie Lorch of Schenectady, the student manager for the basketball team. For Chaney, he chose John Tracy, a guard from the Flatbush section of Brooklyn in New York City. Both Lorch and Tracy had already been at UH for a year. "I said to myself, if we were going to integrate," Lewis said, "we were going to do it right. I felt rooming them with white guys would help."

He said Lorch and Tracy "just seemed like the two best guys to do it. Tracy knew the streets and knew how to get along with people."

"Being that I didn't want to interact with whites," Hayes said, "this wasn't good. Now I'm sleeping with a white person in my room. Once again, in the end it worked out. Sometimes Howie and I would have a disagreement and I would throw him out of the room. One thing Howie did teach me, though, was the importance of getting up and going to class. After a while, I realized Coach Lewis had made the right decision. It ended up broadening my perspective."

Lorch attended the same Schenectady high school as future Kentucky All-American and NBA Hall of Fame coach Pat Riley. Lewis was in town trying to recruit Riley for UH, and Riley's high school coach asked Lewis if he had any use for a manager and recommended Lorch.

Lorch said, "I eventually became head manager and ended up on full scholarship. In the spring of 1964, Coach Lewis told me he had two players coming in to visit and asked if I would show them around campus. It was Elvin and Don. We had a good time. When Elvin arrived that summer, he had everything in a cardboard suitcase. Everything he owned was in it. He didn't even have a pair of decent shoes that fit him. He needed about a size 16. We went down to Saks on Main and Fannin to get him some shoes. I remember the guy at Saks was about 6-foot-10. He went into the back and brought out a couple of pairs of size 16s.

"Elvin had a big adjustment that first year. He got homesick. He came from a town of about two thousand people to the big city. That's a big adjustment. He went home several times. As his roommate, Elvin needed me that freshman year. I always made sure he got up, and I taught him the importance of going to class. He went through tough times at first. Elvin was immature, trying to adapt. His language and vocabulary was also not very good. He would mumble a lot. He did get much better as he got older, though.

"One interesting thing that happened the fall of his freshman year was when [Cougar guard and New York City native] Reno Lifschutz and I went to Rayville with Elvin for Thanksgiving. Of course, Elvin lived on the black side of town. When we drove through the white side of town, Elvin had to duck down in the backseat. We were worried about that.

"When we got to Elvin's house, we had to cross two 2×12s to get across a ditch. His house was maybe 700 or 800 square feet. There wasn't room there for us to stay, so we stayed at a girlfriend's house; her dad was the principal at the black high school.

"Elvin's mom fixed a great Thanksgiving dinner. We had collard greens, possum, and raccoon—among other things. Everything tasted great, even though there was some stuff where I didn't ask what it was, I just ate it.

"What I learned about Elvin eventually was that he was a very competitive player. He hated to lose. He also had more natural talent than anyone I had seen. When the season was over, he wouldn't pick up a ball again until October.

"The first time I ever saw him play, he was unbelievable. Elvin and I were kind of a Mutt and Jeff—a 6-foot-9 black kid from Louisiana rooming with a 5-foot-7 Jewish kid from New York. We ended up getting along great, and we are still friends today."

Don Chaney was also surprised to find out he would have a white roommate. In hindsight, Chaney said, "I think it made the adjustment period shorter for me, and I'll tell you why: rooming a white kid with a black kid was smart on Coach Lewis's part. He roomed us with guys from the North. They had grown up and been around black guys. It was not that big a deal to them and not important. It helped communication. We had stories to tell each other.

"Not that it happened right away, though. John and I spent about three or four weeks feeling each other out. Remember, I had gone to an all-black school in an all-black neighborhood. I eventually explained to John that there were certain unwritten rules when dealing with whites.

"For example, we couldn't look up at whites if they passed by us, and we also couldn't talk to a white without permission first. I told him about having a car full of whites come up behind me as a kid and someone using a fan belt as a strap to hit me behind the legs as they were passing by.

"I had also had drinks thrown on me. I would try not to walk alone. Probably the worst was the day a policeman started following me as I was dribbling a basketball home when I was around 12. He got out and threw me against the car and put a gun to my head and was calling me 'nigger.' That really scared me."

John Tracy eventually left UH because "once I saw Don Chaney play as a freshman, I knew I would never get to play." Tracy ended up in Hollywood and enjoyed a long career as a director of television sitcoms, most notably popular shows from the 1980s and early 1990s such as *Full House, Family Matters,* and *Growing Pains.*

Tracy said, "First of all, I came to the University of Houston because Coach Lewis knew some of the coaches in New York. He pretty much recruited me, not Harvey Pate. Coach Lewis came to see me at a tournament, and he wanted me to come see the campus.

"I had no idea about Texas. I had always loved cowboys. I really thought there would be horses once I got off the plane in Houston. Also, it was a free weekend, and I had never been on a plane before. I was impressed with the campus, so I decided to go there. I was excited.

"After my freshman year, Coach Lewis set up a meeting with me in New York that summer. He was going to be in Manhattan for a week and said he wanted to meet with me sometime that week. He told me about Elvin and Don and how he didn't want to put them together as roommates, that it would just isolate them again. I didn't know for sure why he chose me for Don. Coach Lewis said he didn't need an answer right away but to think about it.

"I talked to my dad about it. He was a cop and was always honest and straightforward. I had concerns like, what if he doesn't study or drinks a lot? My dad said, 'Don't just base your decision on his being black. If a person's a jerk, they're a jerk; it didn't matter what color they are.' I agreed to do it, and nevertheless I was a nervous wreck when I went back to Houston to start the new school year.

"When I got back to Houston and the dorms, it turned out Don had gotten to the room the night before me, and his stuff was stacked up in a corner of the room. Coach Lewis and Coach Pate came by a little later and brought Don in. The coaches told me Don wanted to give me the choice of which bed and closet I wanted. Later I found out that because of Don's upbringing, he wouldn't have dared pick his bed and closet before a white person.

"For around three to four weeks, it was rough. I would try to say something to Don or ask him something, and all I would get out of him was one word answers like, 'Good,' 'Yes,' or 'OK.' Sometimes 'Yup,' or 'Nope.'

Don Chaney, 1966
(Courtesy of UH Athletic Department)

John Tracy, 1966
(Courtesy of UH Athletic Department)

"I finally called my dad and said I was uncomfortable. He said to look at his point of view. He said, talk to Don. You're both away from home; you're both competing for the same job. Try and talk to him and figure out the ground rules. As usual, my dad was right.

"The next thing I had to figure out was how to go about doing all of this. I didn't want to be too forward or look like a jerk. The moment finally happened on a Sunday night in our dorm room. We had a little radio, and we would play a Louisiana station from 6 to 9 p.m. on Sundays. We would play the music very low. We were lying in our beds about five feet apart from each other.

"We were listening to Nancy Wilson and some other artists. I started asking him about who some of the artists were. I didn't know much about jazz, but I liked the sound. On this Sunday night, the setting was perfect. There was a full moon and the window blinds were half open. Being a television director, all of this created a perfect 'feel.'

"I felt that God was saying, 'Here's your chance.' I just started talking for about five or six minutes straight. I talked about how we were sharing a room together, how we probably had some of the same problems, other personal stuff.

"When I finished, I swear I could hear Don's heart beating. My heart was pounding about 100 miles an hour, too. Finally, Don paused and said, 'You know, John, you're saying a lot of good things. The thing you probably don't realize is that I have never been allowed to speak to a white person before without their permission first.'

"How do I respond to that? I asked Don what he meant, and he said, 'You have to realize what it was like in Baton Rouge. Our family didn't go out at night out of fear. You could get tarred and feathered, or hit with a hose from behind by someone in a car coming up behind you at 50 miles per hour. During the day, you better look straight ahead if you encountered a white person. If you glanced up, they would say, 'What's your problem, boy?'

"Don told me about dribbling a basketball home one night and a policeman pulling a gun on him and threatening him.

"For whatever reason, our talk that night broke the ice. We started talking to each other and became friends and remain so to this day. We started going places together. We went to a Ray Charles concert and a TSU basketball game where I was the only white person there. I was honest with Don that one night, and our relationship grew. I think Don felt comfortable with me after that.

"We also went to the movies, and one time we tried to play miniature golf and the owner wouldn't let Don play. I remember that like it was yesterday. About 12 of us went to go play, including Elvin and Don. I think it was Rich Apolskis who went up to the counter, and the guy there said, 'OK, that's ten admissions.' Rick said, 'But sir, we have 12 people.' Without blinking an eye, the owner said, 'We don't let niggers play here, get them the fuck out of here!' That made you realize there was still a lot of prejudice around in the area.

"Not to say everything was easy, though. I received some death threats and some taunts of 'nigger lover.' I never told Don about them at the time. All in all, was it a good choice rooming with Don? Yes, it was. I did what I thought was the right thing to do, and we are still very close over 40 years later.

"I must say the other pairing, Elvin and Howie, was quite interesting. They were always fighting. Howie was a character. Sometimes he thought he owned the team. Elvin would get mad at him and he would throw Howie out of their room in his underwear. Howie would go to Don and say, 'Help!' and Don would help Howie get back in the dorm room. In the end, though, everything worked out between them."

Warren McVea never encountered any type of roommate controversy because, as he himself admitted, "I always roomed alone my whole time at the University of Houston."

Gradually, the pioneering African Americans adapted to their new integrated social environment thanks to well-laid plans that counteracted as many natural conflicts as possible. McVea, Hayes, and Chaney grew to be accepted by their fellow UH athletes and the vast majority of their fellow collegians. Now what remained was facing the white people in the stands and on the Houston streets with the same courage and dignity.

9 McVEA, BIG CROWDS, AND KITTENS

I never encountered anything racial from opposing players throughout my college career, including late hits, cheap shots, or racial remarks.
—WARREN McVEA

Now that Warren McVea, Elvin Hayes, and Don Chaney were new students at the University of Houston in the fall of 1964, what remained was to officially become "Kittens," as players for the freshman football and basketball teams were called.

Freshmen were not eligible to play varsity sports during this period of American amateur sports history, so these three recruits would have to wait a year to show the college sports world their abilities. Usually freshman teams played without fanfare or game hype; very few people outside of the athletic department paid attention to the games, the statistics, the scores, or the standings. Yet these three potential super-stars generated a newfound interest in the Kittens, especially McVea, the nation's top high school football recruit.

The football Kittens usually played a four-game sched-ule, almost always against junior varsity and freshman squads from other Texas colleges. The basketball Kittens played 20 games by taking on junior college teams from East Texas and the Texas Gulf Coast.

The 1964 UH freshman season sparked unique media interest with two magic words: *Warren McVea*. The McVea hype began to intensify the moment he set foot on campus. His reputation was simply too well known. The preceding May, McVea and A. Z. Drones of San Angelo had become the first African Americans ever chosen to play in the annual Texas High School Coaches Association All-Star football game, traditionally held in conjunction with the coaches school in late July or early August—just before two-a-day high school and college workouts began.

Warren McVea, circa 1965
(Courtesy of UH Athletic Department)

The 1964 coaching school and all-star game was held in Fort Worth only three weeks after the "late-signing" McVea committed to UH. The game was played on Thursday, August 6, before a record crowd of 40,000—although some game officials had higher estimates at, say, 50,000—including at least 8,000 McVea fans from San Antonio who drove the 265 miles to see their hero play his last official high school football game. The South team lost 23–14, but its star player didn't let his fans down, showing the massive crowd his brilliance with a 72-yard kickoff return and fourth-quarter runs of 22 and 15 yards.

Even before this star player suited out in the red and white of the Cougars for his first practice session, the UH Athletic Department became more aggressive with its freshman football scheduling plans. The university contacted the Air Force Academy about coming to Houston, even volunteering to pay the visiting team's traveling expenses. These extraordinary efforts didn't stop with Air Force; UH also wanted to schedule a game against Notre Dame. However, the Fighting Irish had a policy against scheduling freshman football games. The Cougars thought the Irish might make an exception, given the McVea factor, but unfortunately the game never materialized.

Once cast in stone, the 1964 Kittens's schedule amounted to an away game with Lamar Tech in Beaumont on October 8 and home games against Air Force on Saturday, October 17; North Texas State University on October 29; and Arlington State University (now UT-Arlington) on November 6. The special Saturday game was very likely the nation's first for a freshman team and was made possible only because it was the only college game in Houston that weekend, played at Rice Stadium to accommodate the potentially large crowd.

*   *   *   *   *   *   *

As the next act in the ever-growing drama at the University of Houston, white players took the practice field for the first time with a black teammate. Freshman defensive back Bill Hollon of Elsa, Texas, remembered his reaction: "This was back in the day when schools could give out all kinds of scholarships. There had to be 75 freshman players out there. UH didn't get the high school All-America types, but we got a lot of good all-district kids, and hopefully some of them would turn out to be pretty good players.

"Once practice did start, I went up against Warren quite a bit. He was just so quick. I wasn't slow, but he could go faster going sideways than I could go forward. One time I thought I was going to get a good lick in on him in practice, but he was just too quick for me. I never did get in a solid hit on him in practice.

"I do remember one incident very well from our freshman year. It was either a Friday or Saturday afternoon practice. Our freshman coach, Carroll Schultz, put the ball on the 30-yard line and said, 'When the offense scores, practice is over.' Warren said, 'Coach, do you mean that?' Coach Schultz said, 'Yes.' Warren took the ball, scored, and practice was over."

Gus Hollomon and Kenny Hebert were the freshman quarterbacks, although Hollomon later switched to defensive back. Hebert always appreciated McVea's talent and swore "he could stop on a dime."

"Remember," Hollomon said upon reflection, "this was all new territory for us, and the coaches wanted to make it work. Warren was treated different. Luckily, Warren fit in—if he would have been a jerk, the whole thing wouldn't have worked.

"The coaches went overboard to make him feel welcome. We were working out for a week before Warren made it out there to practice. We didn't understand that as freshmen. Eventually, Warren took the freshman initiation and he was one of us."

Roger Cude starred as a runner, receiver, and punter for Houston Reagan High School before coming to UH to do some place kicking for the Kittens. "Warren and I are next to each other in the team picture that year," Cude remembered. "I was number 43 and Warren was number 42. We had to sit numerically in the picture that year. I swear I rarely saw Warren at practice that year. He was an amazing athlete, though. Warren went his own way. I hardly saw him in the off-season, either. In the spring of 1965, we had some spring scrimmages in the Rio Grande Valley. I don't remember seeing him there."

Tom Beer, who was a class ahead of McVea, said, "When I got to Houston in late 1964, the coaches made me Warren's right-hand man. In other words, it was my job to get him up in the morning and get him to class. We ended up being very good friends. Warren was just very likeable and very well-spoken."

Once McVea made it to his first fall practice, he suffered a knee injury during only his third session. The injury limited his practice and playing time the rest of the season. It even caused him to miss the Kittens's Red versus White scrimmage on Monday, September 21. Apparently, there was a question whether the star runner would sit out right on up until game time. The scrimmage drew an impressive crowd in anticipation of seeing the phenomenal football star. "The magic name of Warren McVea drew several hundred Negro fans to Jeppesen Stadium Monday night, and they, along with a few hundred white fans, were disappointed," a story in the *Informer* reported.

"Unfortunately, McVea was injured and did not play, and this was not announced to the crowd until late in the game. As it was, when the announcement was made, hundreds of fans, both white and Negro, got up, booed lustily, and angrily streamed out of the stadium." Even a preseason scrimmage was drawing numerous fans, most of them hoping to catch a glimpse of Warren McVea.

The Kittens's first official game that season was played in Beaumont against Lamar Tech. The game was broadcast on KUHF radio in Houston and KAYC radio in Beaumont. The day before the game, the *Daily Cougar*, UH's student newspaper, said, "Cardinal Stadium seats a capacity of 18,000, and with the Lamar Tech varsity out of action this weekend, a full house is expected."

Without McVea playing, the Kittens scored a 13–7 win. Kenny Hebert threw a 39-yard touchdown pass, and Wayne Rains scored on a 14-yard run. The next day, the *Houston Post* said, "An expected crowd of about 14,000 turned into a mere handful of spectators when it was learned that McVea would not be in attendance."

The next game was the specially scheduled Saturday game with Air Force at Rice Stadium. This time the fans would not be disappointed. It was here that McVea made his debut. The day before the game, the *Daily Cougar* said, "A big crowd is expected for the game on Saturday night since this will be McVea's debut and the game will be the only collegiate game in Houston this weekend." The *San Antonio Express*

News ran a front-page article in the sports section the day of the game titled "McVea in Home Opener." The article said, "A crowd of 15,000 is expected."

McVea's debut garnered so much attention, not just in Texas but nationwide, that local reporter Mickey Herskowitz of the *Post* was dispatched to cover the game for *Sports Illustrated*. The two-page article, titled "Warren McVea Goes Thisaway and Thataway," appeared in the November 9, 1964, edition. It was the first feature article in the magazine's history that was written about a freshman college athlete. It wasn't until 1972 that freshmen were eligible to play in varsity competition.

McVea did not disappoint. He carried the ball 11 times that night for 134 yards, or 12.2 yards per carry, scoring a 55-yard touchdown in the first quarter and a 61-yard touchdown in the fourth to break a 14–14 tie. The final score was UH Kittens 20, Air Force 14.

Opinions varied on the size of the crowd. Roger Cude said, "There must have been 20,000 people there." Air Force coach Jim Bowman guessed, "There were about 10,000 people there." Herskowitz's *Sports Illustrated* article said about the popularity of McVea and the size of the crowds, "As a rule, freshman games are of no interest to the public, but large crowds—8,000 at the Air Force game—have turned out to watch McVea, even in practice. Tickets to freshman games are now in far greater demand than those of the varsity, and those fans who cannot get seats perch themselves atop the scoreboard or simply stand."

McVea's 55-yard touchdown run in the first quarter was highlight reel material. Herskowitz said in his article, "On a recent night Houston's celebrated halfback, Warren McVea, roamed 55 yards to score against the Air Force Academy freshmen, and films of the game clearly show that nine players laid a hand on him. McVea reversed his field so often that one poor fellow was able to miss him at the line of scrimmage and still catch up in time to receive a stiff-arm in the mouth as McVea swept into the end zone."

John Hollis, the *Post* beat writer, described it this way: "Mac the Knife started wide right, eluded a crashing end, spun to his left, wriggled free of three tacklers at about 10-yard intervals and sprinted 55 yards to score."

The game also received so much attention that fans who did not attend could listen to it on Houston radio stations KUHT-AM and KUHF-FM. The following week, Channel 8, UH's public broadcasting channel, showed films of the game, which also was covered by newspapers from all over the state of Texas—especially the *Express* and the *Light* from McVea's hometown, 170 miles to the west.

UH's sports information director was Ted Nance, whose unfailing memory offered this account: "Back when we signed Warren in July 1964, he didn't want a press conference. Since Warren had gotten to know Dan Cook at the *Express-News* pretty well, Warren gave him the scoop on his signing.

"The *Light* was furious when they found out. Harold Sherwood of the *Light* called me up and chewed me out and told me his paper would never cover a University of Houston game again. When it was apparent that Warren was going to play against Air Force as a freshman, you know who was the first paper to call me asking for press credentials? The *San Antonio Light*."

Never before in UH football history had a 55-yard touchdown run gone through so many reruns in the mind's eyes of so many spectators. So many of them could very easily supply minute details.

Cougar basketball player Gary Grider saw the game and said, "I had a friend playing at Air Force also. This was the first time I had seen Warren play. After the game, I got together with him and some others and hit some parties. That 55-yard touchdown run! Wow! He could go sideways and backwards faster than most people could go forwards. I met up with my Air Force friend in the locker room after the game and we started counting, and nine guys said they touched Warren on that run."

Kittens linebacker Greg Brezina put it this way: "I bet 13 guys touched Warren on that run against Air Force."

Quarterback Kenny Hebert recalled, "On one play against Air Force, I gave him the ball off tackle. Everybody must have had a shot at him. Warren must have run 110 yards on that play."

Air Force quarterback Elwood "Sonny" Litz said, "It was a Saturday night and it was my first game at Air Force. There sure were a lot of people out there for a freshman game. I also remember it was about 100 degrees. And of course I remember Warren and his swivel hips running past us."

Jim Bowman was the freshman coach at the time—in the seventh year of what would be a 49-year career at the Air Force Academy, the last few years as associate athletic director. "Cougar assistant coach Chuck Fairbanks and I were high school teammates," Bowman said. "Warren was Mr. Everything in Texas. UH paid our room and board for us to come down there. They also held a nice reception for us while we were there. Warren was the first guy we had ever played against that was as quick and fast as he was. My players had never seen that kind of speed before. We ended up paying for it in the game."

Air Force nose guard and 1967 Academic All-American Ken Zagzebski said, "On that 55-yard run, we missed Warren every time. It was like tackling air. It was a phenomenal thing. I also think I was in the picture in the *Sports Illustrated* article."

Defensive tackle Larry Cole, who went on to play left defensive end for the Dallas Cowboys for 13 seasons, remembered McVea well, saying, "I had never seen anyone with that level of athleticism before. We at Air Force just didn't have that kind of talent. We had no one with anywhere near the kind of speed he had."

Defensive back Tom Zyroll played a large role in the game against the Kittens. On offense, he threw two halfback passes for his team's two touchdowns. On defense, he got to face the McVea-intensive offense. "I think I touched him three times on that touchdown play," Zyroll said. "He literally ran back and forth the length of the field twice. Out of all the backs I ever played against, Mel Farr of UCLA was the only one even close to Warren.

"Warren was faster, though, and he could dance—the fastest player I ever witnessed. He was a beast. I also remember that summer before school started, Neal Starkey and Carl Janssen, two Texas guys, were bragging to me about the quality of high school football in Texas. After facing McVea, I could see why they were able to brag."

Neal Starkey of Dallas, an All-America defensive back for Air Force in 1967, recalled, "I played wide receiver and safety. At the freshman level in 1964, Coach Bowman was just trying to get his best athletes on the field as much as possible. I played against Warren in the first college game for both of us.

"Since I was from Dallas, I knew all about Warren and his capabilities. He was so highly touted. Funny thing, the last game I ever played in, Warren was my teammate at the East-West Shrine All-Star Game after the 1967 season. What I remember best about the freshman game against Houston was that touchdown run. When we looked at the film later, everyone missed him. Today, runs like that would have made Warren a star on *SportsCenter*."

"On the 55-yard run by McVea," defensive end Mike Rangel remembered, "I slipped a block and got into the backfield. Needless to say, I missed him. He reversed his field twice. I think I touched him three times on that run. I knew about Warren and how he was heavily recruited before we played him. At the time, I didn't know anything about the social history about him being the first black at Houston."

Carl Janssen of Fort Worth was a wide receiver and ended up being the Falcons's leading receiver his senior year in 1967. He was in the other defensive halfback position in the UH–Air Force game. "You know that article in *Sports Illustrated* that tells about the hapless Falcon that missed Warren twice on his touchdown run?" Janssen said. "That was me. I went from Fort Worth Arlington Heights High School to the Air Force Academy. Of course, I knew all about Warren from high school. I had great respect for him. We had been warned about Warren before the game.

"The problem was there was no way to practice for his kind of speed and moves. I was dazzled. I had been taught excellent fundamentals growing up. I bet I missed about four tackles my whole career at Air Force, and two of them were on that one play. I missed him coming around and then again on the way back. The other thing I remember is that this was the day when freshmen were not eligible for varsity, and I was surprised at the interest in the game, what with the large crowd and the mentions in the media. I guess we owe all of that to Warren."

Another Texan on defense that night for Air Force was Richard Ellis. He said, "We stayed at Ellington Air Force Base. Freshmen were ineligible for varsity back then. Their coach, Chuck Fairbanks, and our coach, Jim Bowman, knew each other from way back. That's why we played the game. At the time, I was not aware of what was going on as far as the integration thing. Where I came from, Sherman, up in North Texas, we hadn't integrated yet.

"Of course, I knew about Warren McVea being from Texas. During the game, Warren had those two big runs and they beat us. Warren ran right by me on one of those runs like I was standing still. Boy, was he fast! With the integration thing, I don't think people appreciate what happened back then and the sacrifices people made."

When the hoopla from the Air Force game was over, it was time for the Kittens to finish out their freshman schedule. The next game was a home contest against North Texas on October 29. The game was played at the Jeppesen Stadium baseball park, which had an estimated seating capacity of 2,500. About 4,800 fans jammed into the park, hoping McVea would repeat the magic he had displayed in the Air Force game. McVea started well, catching an 18-yard touchdown pass from Gus Hollomon in the first quarter. However, only two minutes into the second period, McVea was injured at the end of a 14-yard run. That was the last time he carried the ball his freshman year, finishing the game with six carries and 24 yards. In his limited freshman season, he gained 158 yards on 17 carries and three touchdowns.

The Kittens went on to shut out North Texas, 21–0, and wrapped up the first undefeated freshman football season in University of Houston history by rounding out the year with a 14–0 win over Arlington State on November 6. The latter game was scheduled to be played at Jeppesen Stadium, but wet conditions forced it to be moved to the Cougar practice field. Naturally there was a standing-room-only crowd to see McVea, but he was held out of the game to protect his sore knee.

In the final analysis, Warren McVea never faced the same prejudices and violent heckling as the black players from the visiting teams of the past few years. His only away game was in Beaumont, and he was treated like a hero during his infrequent yet productive appearances in the home games.

Nor did McVea have to face the problem of staying in a dormitory room instead of a hotel with his teammates. "I never encountered anything racial from opposing players throughout my college career," McVea said, "including late hits, cheap shots, or racial remarks."

McVea also appeared to be accepted almost immediately by the Houston fans. The *Post*'s John Hollis had this to say in his Air Force game story: "When he trotted off the field after his last slashing run, the crowd gave him a standing ovation."

It looked like the budding college football superstar would have to wait until he played varsity ball a year later before he would encounter any potential racism at away games or anywhere else. His freshman season behind him, McVea had been elevated to an almost mythical status as he prepared for the 1965 season—as a Cougar, not a Kitten.

10 FRESHMAN DUNKS

At the UH home games I was able to make that year,
there was no more racial stuff from the stands. Before
Elvin and Don came, there were a lot of slurs.
—VERN LEWIS

The UH basketball Kittens, under Coach Harvey Pate, faced a 21-game schedule with home and away games against such two-year colleges as Jacksonville Baptist, Del Mar College, South Texas Junior College, Wharton County Junior College, and San Jacinto College, as well as Victoria, Temple, Tyler, Henderson, and Kilgore junior colleges. The 21st and final game of the season would pit the Kittens against the UH Alumni All-Stars.

Besides Hayes and Chaney, the Kittens's other scholarship players were guard David Wells from St. Jacob, Illinois; forward Tom Stein of Cahokia, Illinois; and highly recruited 6-foot-5 forward Paul Ozug of Gary, Indiana. The other five players on the roster were all walk-ons from Houston: Belton Byrd, Richard Westbrook, Neal Kaspar, Wayne Hall, and Herbert Jaenecke.

Since the Kittens played several of their away games in East Texas, where racism and Jim Crow laws were still going strong, Hayes and Chaney did in fact encounter problems with hotel accommodations, sit-down meals, and rough fan encounters. "I had problems with the freshman team," Coach Pate said. "For example, when we went to Tyler and Kilgore, there were no restaurants in those towns that would feed the whole team. We knew about this ahead of time, so what we did was we called the cafeteria at Sam Houston State in Huntsville, and they said they would cook for the whole team. So we ate steak dinners there about two o'clock on game days.

"It was also tough in some of those East Texas towns finding a restroom Elvin and Don could use. At the actual games, it was interesting the way Elvin and Don were treated by the fans. I never really heard much in the way of racial remarks. Usually Kilgore and Tyler were tough places to play in general, but our visits there went OK. I think Elvin and Don were the first blacks to play in both gyms. In fact, at road games, the fans in a lot of the gyms seemed fascinated by them and how talented and athletic they were.

"I remember there were a couple of games where the hometown refs tried to foul Elvin out of the game. The fans actually got restless because they wanted to see Elvin play, not foul out. At home games, things went well. There were big crowds for a lot of the freshman games. There were no real problems from the home fans; they were real happy that black athletes could be recruited if it would help us win games."

Guard David Wells said, "I remember taking trips by bus into East Texas. It's funny, but I thought at some of the gyms, they treated Elvin and Don better than us. They'd spit on us and throw water on us at halftime. The fans seemed to be in awe of Don and Elvin. They'd never seen anything like them before. I just remember very few incidents aimed just at Elvin and Don. I think once people recognized them and what they represented, the fans didn't bother them much."

Paul Ozug added, "I remember hearing racial and ethnic slurs at road games. We played in some old barns and some nice places. You know what, though, the slurs were not just directed at the black players.

The fans in some of those places were shouting slurs at Polish players, Mexican players, whoever. They didn't care about what you were, they were equal opportunity hecklers. At home games, I never heard slurs."

Although he did not elaborate on the topic much, Chaney said, "I don't remember any stuff going on as far as opposing players on the court. As a freshman, though, I do remember having food brought out to us on the bus a few times."

Hayes was more forthcoming: "Playing at some of the juco places was unreal. I remember we were playing up in Jacksonville and we were killing them. As I was coming off the court, a kid said, 'Mommy! Look at the niggers!' That was the times we lived in, though. Those junior colleges were still pretty much all-white, with the exception of Wharton."

About the same time Pan American integrated its basketball program in the late 1950s, a junior college about 50 miles south of Houston was doing the same thing. Wharton County Junior College in the town of Wharton was under the direction of basketball coach Johnnie Frankie. Frankie integrated the Texas junior college ranks in the 1957–58 season when he put a Wharton product, Doris "Hank" Allen, on his roster.

For the 1959–60 school year, the Pioneers hired Gene Bahnsen as assistant football coach and head basketball coach. In 2014, Bahnsen was still serving Wharton as its longtime athletic director. Five years after his hiring, the Pioneers faced the UH Kittens with five black players. They were Odis Booker of Kirbyville; Alan Canselo and Eugene Smith of New York; John White of Passaic, New Jersey; and Aaron McKenna of New Orleans. The Pioneers were a challenge for the Kittens, as the teams split their two games that season. Both games saw high scoring. Wharton won, 92–80, at home and lost to the Kittens, 91–85, in Houston.

"The two games we played against Houston were great games," Bahnsen recalled. "Houston came to our place undefeated, and we beat them. The return game was at Delmar Field House. I remember the game was at 6 p.m. and the place was packed. It was a heckuva game. I remember one play where Elvin went up for a rebound and Odis Booker came up behind him and dunked the ball over him.

"The crowd went crazy. Odis was only about 6-foot-4 1/2, but he had the wingspan of a seven-footer. Elvin tried to shoot a few shots from the corners, and Odis blocked Elvin's first two or three shots.

"You know, when we first integrated, we faced a few problems, too. Playing at Kilgore was terrible; Tyler was terrible. They would throw stuff at the players during warm-ups. It wasn't like that at Wharton. There the fans were great. I remember the first time in 1960–61 we went to play Lon Morris College in Jacksonville with Bobby Joe Hill, Major Dennis, and Charlie Banks. We ordered 15 chicken-fried steaks for the players at a restaurant. When they saw we had black players, they hustled us to a side room, and the three black players had to eat in the kitchen.

"The next year when we played there, we ate our postgame meal at the college cafeteria. They didn't want us going downtown to eat. Another incident occurred with one of our first black players, Charlie Banks, the next year. We were on Highway 59 going up to East Texas to play a game, and we stopped in some town north of Houston, like Tarkington or somewhere else like that.

"We stopped at a burger joint, and the waitress opened up the sliding glass window to take their orders. When it came time for Charlie to place his order, though, the waitress used the same pad she used for the white players for their orders, and then she used the same grill to cook all the burgers, but she made Charlie step over to a side window that said 'Colored' to place his order.

"She never had to even get up and move to open either window. I kept thinking to myself, 'This whole thing is so stupid.'"

Several Wharton players from the 1964–65 season recalled playing against Hayes and Chaney. "I was from New Orleans," Aaron McKenna said, "so I had faced Don Chaney in high school. I played for San Augustine High School, which was a powerhouse. I just remember we played some good, tight games against Houston. I don't remember any real issues on the road, either, at places like Kilgore or Tyler. Wharton was the first integrated team I played on. We had three blacks my freshman year and four or five my sophomore year."

Guard Richard Brennan said, "I came to Wharton from New Jersey. I remember before we played them a second time, they had just scored a bunch of points against Victoria College [a 103–70 Kitten victory]. Houston beat us, but it was a good game, and there was a good crowd at Delmar. We watched the Houston varsity play Texas A&M after our game, and I kept thinking the freshman team is better than the varsity. Besides Hayes and Chaney, Houston had another really good player, Paul Ozug. He got thrown out of the game for throwing an elbow."

Odis Booker, who was matched up against Hayes in the two contests, said, "We played at Delmar and the place was full. I remember going up against Hayes and Chaney. The other guy who really impressed me for Houston was this big guy from Indiana, Ozug. He had a good game."

Wharton's Alan Canselo said, "We played a couple of hard-fought games against Houston. We knew about Hayes and Chaney. I felt that their player Ozug was the glue for that team. We beat them the first time in Wharton but not in Houston. That was the first time I had ever had my shot blocked under the basket.

"When we played at Houston, there were a lot of dunks in the game. Booker dunked over Elvin. When I came to Wharton from New York, I didn't realize the subtle reminders that racism was still present. I felt a little isolated in Wharton. The first time I went to a restaurant, the lady was polite but said I had to pick up my meal in the rear. I was not used to this in New York.

"I refused to order. I remember seeing parades in Wharton where the black bands had to march in the rear. At the movie house, we had to sit upstairs. The cemetery even had separate sections for blacks and whites. Even with all of this, it ended up being a good experience. I really appreciated Coach Bahnsen. He was like a second father to me."

The Wharton players were not the only ones to recognize the talent of Houston's other prize freshman recruit, Paul Ozug. Ozug, a rugged 6-foot-5 forward, came to the UH from Gary, Indiana, where he had averaged 26.5 points per game as a high school senior, including 48 in one game. "Ozug is one of the top two forwards I have coached at UH," Pate said. "He is also one of our best rebounders. He's just a complete ballplayer." Ozug ended up as the third-leading scorer on the Kittens behind Hayes and Chaney and the second-leading rebounder behind

Hayes. He played his sophomore season at UH before transferring to Northeast Missouri State, now Truman State University, leading the team in scoring and rebounding in 1968. "My experiences at UH were nothing but positive," Ozug said. "My sophomore year, I started the first three or four games on varsity. I left after that year.

"I was 1,300 miles away from home and my mom got sick, so Northeast Missouri was much closer to Indiana than Houston was. I thought our freshman team had great chemistry. I never had any problems except one time Elvin and I got into it. It was my fault. Elvin and I were at practice, and I said some words to him that I shouldn't have. Elvin pushed me into a wall and I ended up getting about 20 stitches."

Donnie Schverak, who had graduated but remained close to the UH basketball program, said Ozug "was one of the meanest, toughest kids I ever saw. He was an animal. Very talented, too. Let me tell you how tough he was. The guys were screwing around in the dorms one day, and someone kicked a door closed and Paul's hand got caught in it. The pressure from the door slamming on his fingers literally blew the fingernails right off the ends of his fingers. His next game he goes out and scores 25 points.

"I wish Paul would have stayed at UH. When he was a sophomore, we were walking out of Autry Court at Rice after we'd played in the Bluebonnet Tournament there, and Paul told me he was going to transfer at the end of the season. For whatever reason, he thought he wasn't going to get to play that much while he was here. Even though we ended up with some great forwards during this time—Melvin Bell and Theodis Lee—Paul still would have played. He could have been a pro."

"Paul was a super guy on the freshman team," Hayes remembered. "It was strange, though. Paul really changed when he got to be around the varsity players the next year. Guys were mouthing off, and Paul started listening to their mess. The time Paul and I got into it, we were at Jeppesen practicing, and he started taking some shots at me. I said, 'What's the deal?' and he said some things and we got into a fight. I really wish he could have stayed at UH. He could have been a pro by practicing and playing against better competition every day."

* * * * * * * *

The Kittens trounced the Victoria College Pirates twice in the 1964–65 season: 102–70 in Victoria on December 11 and 103–70 at Jeppesen Field House on January 4.

Victoria center Bob Goss said, "Hayes I remember better because I had to guard him. Chaney I remember, too. As freshmen they were just so strong and agile. They didn't seem too interested while they were playing us. Considering how bad they beat us both times, I can see why."

Guard Rick Byars said, "They had an amazing team. Three or four of them could dunk. We stopped during the warm-ups and stared at them tearing down the rims. We were in awe and shock. During the game, we just couldn't stay with them. I had to guard Chaney. Needless to say, I didn't do a very good job.

"I remember my uncle came to the game in Victoria. There was one play where Elvin got a rebound and knocked me out of the way. My uncle got mad and wanted to come out of the stands and fight Elvin. We didn't have any black players on our team. I remember Wharton did, though.

"Victoria was still segregated. If we would have tried to have a black on our team, there would have been an uproar in Victoria. Our best player was our point guard, Johnny Eblen. He was a star."

Eblen came to Victoria College from Henderson, Kentucky. He weighed in on the Pirates games against the Kittens. "They beat us pretty good," he said. "They scored over 100 points both times. The game in Victoria I remember better. Hayes dominated the first half and Chaney the second half.

"One time I was backing up to the goal and as a guard I tried to reach in on defense to knock the ball away from Elvin. He was so strong that when I wrapped my hands around the ball, he literally raised me up off the ground along with the ball."

Eblen had a good memory. Hayes scored 20 of his 24 points in the first half, and Chaney scored 20 of his 27 in the second.

Lowell Watson also came to Victoria from Kentucky. He said, "I got to guard Hayes some. It was my claim to fame. I remember a few years later we were watching the Houston–UCLA Astrodome game on television back in Kentucky, and I got to tell my friends that I got to play against and guard Hayes.

"When we first saw Hayes and Chaney, we were amazed. Back in Kentucky, we were used to fundamental, slowdown basketball. Those two guys were so athletic it was unbelievable. I thought Chaney was great. I used to watch him later with the Celtics. Just an awesome ballplayer.

"One incident that I remember that was kind of funny, the first time we played them, was before the game when our center, Bob Goss, asked who he was guarding. Our coach, Stump Evans [so named because he always chewed on a stump of a cigar], said, 'Oh, he's just a big clumsy kid from Louisiana.' Obviously he was talking about Elvin. Houston killed us both times we played them. At Victoria, our basketball team was not known for our athletic prowess."

Another school the Kittens took on was South Texas Junior College in Houston, a school that was absorbed by UH in 1974 and turned into the UH-Downtown. The Kittens captured two wins over the Seahawks with a 111–86 win at Sam Houston Coliseum on December 7, 1964, and a 98–80 victory at Jeppesen Field House on January 13, 1965.

Ernie Azios of South Texas played against Hayes and Chaney as a sophomore. "Hayes and Chaney were quite the one-two punch," Azios recalled. "I remember Chaney's long arms. I was from Houston, and I used to go over to Finnegan Park in the Fifth Ward and play all day against the black players. When I played against Hayes and Chaney, it wasn't that big of a deal because I was used to it. After South Texas, I went to play ball at Pan American, and of course they had had black players there for a few years already."

The Seahawks's Laury Liles added, "We were mostly white, but we had a couple of Hispanics on the team. We had no one to match up with Elvin or Don. They beat us by over 20. We were also out-rebounded by a bunch. Elvin was kind of throwing his weight around out there.

"Chaney had those long arms. I went to Austin High School in Houston, and Vern Lewis was my teammate. I eventually transferred to UH and was a basketball manager there. Elvin liked to throw his weight around there, too. Sometimes he expected things. Don was great. I had a lot of fun with it, though."

San Jacinto Junior College in Pasadena, just east of Houston, also played the Kittens twice, losing 97–64 at Jeppesen Field House on January 18, 1965, and falling at San Jacinto 92–79 on February 11.

Richard Crowley, who was a 6-foot-6 center for the Ravens, said, "I drew the short straw and got to guard Elvin. It was tough because he was six-foot-eight or six-foot-nine and 225–230 pounds, and strong as hell. I had to try and use my own strength to hold my ground. That just ended up getting me in foul trouble.

"Elvin was one of the best players ever, and I got to face him. I always thought Chaney never got the credit he deserved. I was excited to play them. My goal was to eventually transfer to Houston and play there. I had always wanted to go to UH and play for Guy Lewis. I was a local Pasadena guy. I looked forward to playing them as freshmen. When we played them at San Jac, we had a brand new gym and the place was packed."

The Ravens's Gene Blanton said, "I went to Milby High School in Houston. At the time, we weren't integrated. To me, Elvin was the first big guy who could really get up and down the court quickly. Chaney had those long arms—he was so quick. He'd reach in and the ball would be gone."

The third former San Jacinto player to recall playing against Hayes and Chaney was Leonard Springer. He said, "I came out of Pasadena High School. I was a 6-foot-5 center/forward. It was not a pleasant experience going up against UH. Elvin turned out to be more than I thought he was. At the end of warm-ups, he would take a two-handed dunk that was something else.

"I ended up loving Hayes and following his career. I went to the 1968 Dome game against UCLA. Every once in a while, I have a dream about being at that game. Don Chaney I also remember well. He didn't have much of a shot, but he had that long arm span."

Vern Lewis, Guy V. Lewis's son, played at Tyler Junior College from 1964 to 1966 and was later inducted into the Tyler College Athletic Hall of Fame. He had the unique perspective of befriending Hayes

the summer of 1964 before going to play at Tyler. The younger Lewis
was present when Hayes and Chaney led the Kittens against Kilgore
Junior College. Later, he played against the duo while at Tyler.

"I came down to Kilgore to watch Elvin play there his freshman
year," Vern Lewis said. "They may have been the first blacks to play in
that gym. They may have been the first in Tyler, too. I remember that
Henderson College had a black player around this time, but it may
have been the year after Elvin and Don played.

"You could hear some racial comments from the stands. I heard it.
It got nasty there. Kilgore was still all white. There were a lot of catcalls
aimed mostly at Elvin. Don Kruse was on that team for Kilgore, and
down there in Kilgore, he was chewing Elvin up and the fans let Elvin
know it.

"At the UH home games I was able to make that year, there was no
more racial stuff from the stands. Before Elvin and Don came, there
were a lot of slurs. When I was a little boy in the stands for most of the
home games growing up, I could hear very racial remarks. We were in
the Missouri Valley Conference back then, and schools like Bradley
and Cincinnati came in with a lot of black players. Loyola of Chicago
came in, too.

"When Elvin and Don came up to Tyler to play that season, things
went pretty well. Tyler was still not integrated, but since I had worked
with Elvin the summer before we went off to college, we became good
friends. When he and Don came to Tyler, there were no problems. They
came to the dorm before the game and met a bunch of people. So that
helped.

"During the game, the crowd was good, and I think the reason was
that people knew I was friends with Elvin and Don. The place was pretty
packed, and it was a highly competitive game [an 84–83 Kittens victory]
but good-spirited. This was back in the day when football teams would
sit behind the benches and ride the opposing team.

"Our fans at UH used to do it at Jeppesen Field House, and later
when I was playing at UH my junior year, I remember we went up to
Notre Dame not long after their football team had just won the national

championship, and the football players showed up and they rode us hard while we were playing [UH lost, 87–78, one of only four losses in 1966–67].

"At Tyler that night, the football team was there but they behaved. There's another good story from my sophomore year at Tyler, the year after we played Elvin and Don. We had a good team in 1965–66, and we won our conference. We had to play Wharton County JC, who won their conference, in a three-game series to see who would go to the national tournament.

"Wharton won the first game at their place, and we won the second at our place. Before the third game, which was at Sam Houston State, Coach Bahnsen of Wharton was so sure that his team was going to win that he placed a bet with Floyd Wagstaff, our coach.

"The home team for the first two games got to keep the gate receipts. The third game, since it was at a neutral site, the gate receipts were to be split. Coach Bahnsen said to Coach Wagstaff, 'How about winner-take-all on the gate receipts?' Coach Wagstaff agreed, and we proceeded to kill Wharton. I remember Coach Wagstaff coming into our locker room after the game with all this money from the gate receipts."

The best team the Kittens faced in 1964–65 turned out to be Kilgore Junior College, which finished the regular season undefeated, including two victories over the Kittens: 91–86 in Kilgore on February 2 and 94–91 in overtime at Jeppesen Field House on February 6. The Rangers then went on to the National JUCO Tournament but fell short of the championship round. In 2007, the team was inducted into the Kilgore College Sports Hall of Fame. Ironically, the star of that Kilgore team was 6-foot-8 center Don Kruse, who averaged 25 points and 20 rebounds per game that season. Kruse ended up at the University of Houston to finish out his college career, playing two seasons with Hayes and Chaney, and in his senior season, Kruse was the starting center for the Cougars's 1967 Final Four team.

As with the vast majority of the Kittens's opponents that season, many players had recollections of Hayes and Chaney.

*Don Chaney goes for a layup,
and Don Kruse of Kilgore
defends, February 1965
(Courtesy of Don Schverak)*

"They had a really good team," Kilgore's Terry George said. "We were undefeated when we beat them the two times. In Kilgore, we played well. Down in Houston, we were behind most of the game but came back and won 94–91 in overtime when one of our guys stole the ball a couple of times at the end of the game.

"We couldn't stay with either Hayes or Chaney. Elvin and Don Kruse matched up. Elvin was really good. He scored a bunch of points, and it seemed like he got all of the rebounds. Don was the first real big guard anyone had seen. His wingspan was something else. They were both great guys."

Terry Stembridge added, "They had a great team, but so did we. I remember walking into their gym in Houston. What an impressive looking group of athletes! We had heard rumors about how good Hayes and Chaney were. It was a miraculous deal what Hayes and Chaney accomplished in Houston with integration."

Gene Roderick later became the head coach at Alaska-Fairbanks. Roderick is credited with starting the famous Great Alaska Shootout tournament played every year in Alaska. He backed up Stembridge's recollections, saying, "Hayes and Chaney were the first two blacks to play in Kilgore's gym. I had been recruited out of Baltimore, and we had integrated teams there.

"When I went to Kilgore for the first time as a 17-year-old after a three-day train trip from Baltimore, I noticed there were segregation signs everywhere in Kilgore—on drinking fountains, bathrooms, etc. At the movie theater, blacks had to sit in the balcony. When Hayes and Chaney visited, I don't recall any uproar over them playing in our gym. Actually, at the time, their coming to our gym was secondary to the excitement of our undefeated season.

"One thing I remember from the game was one time I had the ball inside against Elvin. I used three pump fakes. I faked once, then twice, then a third time. I was worried about a three-second call, so I tried to shoot the ball. That ball is still in orbit somewhere. Elvin knocked it up into the stands. Really though, Hayes and Chaney were just players to us. I did enjoy watching what those two guys eventually became down the road."

Temple Junior College, between Austin and Waco in Central Texas, was one school that proved to be no match for the Kittens in the two games they played against each other. The Kittens won 114–76 in Temple on December 15, 1964, and scored their biggest win of the season, 139–75, on January 28, 1965.

Five-foot-ten guard Billy Engleke of the Leopards said, "They beat us by more than 50 in Houston. I don't remember them rubbing it in or anything. I did steal the ball one time, and as I was going in for a layup,

Chaney put his arms down and let me shoot and make the basket. He could have killed me if he had wanted to. One of the Houston guys, a big white guy [Paul Ozug], dunked the ball so hard one time that the ball came back up through the goal."

One interesting event happened the next season when the 1965–66 Kittens went up to Temple to play the Leopards. Larry Cooper, a 6-foot-6 forward, was a member of that team, which featured two high school All-Americans: center Ken Spain and forward Melvin Bell. Spain was the starting center on the Cougars's second Final Four team in 1968, and Bell broke Elvin Hayes's freshman scoring record.

Cooper, a native Houstonian from Waltrip High School, told the following story: "I swear this is true. My freshman year we go up to Temple to play. We took a couple of station wagons. We had nine players, a trainer, and Coach Pate. We got to Temple about 5:30 and got out of the cars. There was no one at the gym.

"We go inside and there was a guy sweeping the floor. Coach Pate said to him, 'Hey, young fella, where do we dress at?' The guy said, 'I'm supposed to give you a message from Coach so-and-so. Coach wanted me to tell you how much you cheated us in Houston last year when Elvin Hayes goaltended so much and you beat us by 80 [actually 64] points. Coach cancelled the game and he didn't call you on purpose.'"

Cooper's story appears to have some validity. The 1965–66 Kittens were supposed to play Temple on December 10, 1965, in Temple. The game was never played. Newspaper reports said the game was cancelled, but the reason was never given.

Joel Williams, son of Cougar golf Coach Dave Williams, was on the Kittens team with Cooper. Williams said, "When we got there, we pretty much just turned around and came back to Houston. I didn't know why we didn't play. I didn't know the reason until I heard the story by Larry Cooper.

"I figured Coach Pate may have messed up the date or time. I remember we had a sack lunch we had brought with us, and that was all we had to eat going up there and back. I was also thinking that we weren't going to get to eat out after the game."

Like the freshman football team, the 1964–65 basketball Kittens set a school record for wins with a 17–4 mark for the season. Elvin Hayes's 521 points set a new record, as did his 500 rebounds. Don Chaney and Paul Ozug also shattered the previous freshman scoring record. They, like Cougar fans everywhere, couldn't wait for this mighty group's first varsity season.

11 VARSITY COUGAR

*To us, Warren was just another player on the other
team. I remember no one, players or coaches, said
anything racial about Warren before the game.*
  —OLE MISS DEFENSIVE TACKLE JIM URBANEK

The buildup to Warren McVea finally taking the field as a
member of the University of Houston varsity football team
rivaled the hype around his recruitment and freshman season
as the school's first African American player. Despite his lack
of playing time due to an injury, McVea's flashes of highly
touted brilliance on the football field whetted the growing
appetite of Cougar fans as they visualized what the star running back could do when healthy and on a larger stage.

The upcoming 1965 football season had another apparent
tinge of excitement—the Cougars's new home field was set
to open, the Harris County Domed Stadium, where indoor
football would be played for the first time in history. What
would become known as the Astrodome was set to open in
April for Houston Astros National League baseball. The first
football game was scheduled for the fall.

The exalted and possibly unrealistic expectations for what McVea could do began even before his freshman season ended. The *Houston Post*'s John Hollis wrote a story on October 26 with the headline "Dome May Put UH on '65 Network TV." Hollis discussed the possibility of the first football game in the Astrodome being televised along with the extra added bonus that it would be McVea's first varsity game. The original plan called for Houston opening with Mississippi State University. "Television people are keenly aware of the immense national interest in the Domed Stadium," Hollis wrote. The article also stated that some cities had sent emissaries to examine the stadium for themselves. Memphis sent Early Maxwell, that city's most noted sports promoter. "This plant will put Houston in the top three sports capitals of the nation by 1968," Maxwell said. "New York and Chicago will fall behind." He also predicted that games in the Astrodome would play to full houses, not just because of the venue, but because Houston "has a back like we haven't seen since Red Grange."

Maxwell obviously was referring to McVea. He had witnessed McVea's abilities in a scrimmage against the varsity the previous season. "He runs the 100 in 9.5 and with his speed he combines a change of pace like Grange's. He'll be a senior when the Cougars come here in 1967 to play Memphis State, and thousands will pack our new stadium [the Liberty Bowl, which also opened in 1965] to see this guy carry the ball. If he doesn't break a leg or run into unexpected trouble, I believe he'll be a superstar in college and then with the pros." As it turned out, the Cougars did not play in Memphis in 1967; they played in the Astrodome. In the article, Maxwell also referred to the Astrodome as "the Eighth Wonder of the World."

Mississippi State head coach Paul Davis was also quoted in Hollis's story: "I talked to Mike Campbell [the Texas assistant coach] about McVea, and Mike said he's never seen anything like him. We're looking forward to playing in the Dome."

Right as the 1964 Kitten football season concluded, Mickey Herskowitz of the *Houston Post* wrote a column extolling the virtue of the Cougars's freshman class. The varsity Cougars were in the midst of a 2–6–1 campaign on the heels of a 2–8 mark the year before. The column head stated, "There's a Team of Tomorrow in University of Houston's Future."

"Only a glimpse of tomorrow enables Bill Yeoman to keep his sense of humor," the always-clever, good-natured Herskowitz wrote. "The finest freshman specimens in the school's history will become next year's sophomore class, led by a halfback who played in only half their games. His name is Warren McVea, and he runs like an electrocardiogram. Perhaps one night the University of Houston will attach a tracking pencil to the toe of his shoe, and record all of those remarkable zigs and zags and jiggles."

On McVea's elusiveness, the columnist said, "Warren rarely moves in a straight line, but when he does, he gets there quickest . . . he has the speed and instinct and the ability to shift gears, plus a nice flair for the dramatic gesture."

Then Herskowitz referred to the now-famous 55-yard run against Air Force, saying, "He practically shook hands with the entire Air Force team along the way." He continued writing superlatives about McVea: "Cougar fans had waited a month; in fact, waited all their lives, for great running backs come along about as often as Halley's Comet. And Warren McVea can be a great one."

In order to prepare for the upcoming season, the Cougars decided to hold three of their four spring scrimmage games away from Houston in order to ignite interest in the team for fans all around the state of Texas. This was unprecedented. Practice began Monday, March 8, with the squad traveling to Galveston for its first scrimmage on March 20, followed by another session in San Antonio—McVea's hometown—on March 27. Then it would be back to Houston for an April 3 game, concluding with a final intersquad game in Edinburg on April 9.

Obviously, with the prospect of McVea playing in his hometown, the March 27 scrimmage generated the most interest and excitement. The *San Antonio Light* carried an article on March 7 titled, "McVea Says Knee Okay," referring to the knee that was injured in his freshman season. The knee, he said, "is giving me no trouble at all." The article listed the Cougars's returning starters and expectations for the season. It mentioned other key players like running back Dickie Post, quarterback Bo Burris, defensive lineman and team captain Cotton Guerrant, and center Barry Sides.

Two days before the San Antonio scrimmage, the *Light* printed another article that said, "Warren McVea will see action at either tailback or wingback, or both as he did in last week's scrimmage in Galveston." Advanced ticket sales soared over the 4,500 mark, which the newspaper said was "a figure which is four-fold the 1,100 they drew in Galveston."

On the Saturday of the San Antonio scrimmage, the *Light* ran a front-page story headlined "McVea, Houston Cougars Catch Fancy of S.A. Football Fans." The game was to be played at Northeast Stadium, capacity 10,000, and the paper added, "The stadium is expected to be crammed with the curious." The article listed the lineups for the Red and White squads. The game would be broadcast by radio station KSAT.

"We played at a high school stadium in San Antonio where the capacity was 8,000 to 10,000," Yeoman recalled. "There were a lot more there that night. Fans were standing all around the track surrounding the field."

McVea's popularity led to the scrimmage being mentioned in the September 20, 1965, issue of *Sports Illustrated*. The Dan Jenkins article, titled "Look Out Man, He Went Thataway," said, "Last spring in San Antonio, for a mere intra-squad game, McVea put 7,971 in the seats, then scored twice on runs of 11 and 33 yards." Jenkins's account also fed the McVea publicity machine by including a quote by legendary Coach Darrell Tully of Spring Branch High School in Houston. It so happened that Tully's No. 1–ranked Bears lost a state semifinal game to McVea's San Antonio Brackenridge squad in 1962 by a 30–23 score. "He's the greatest broken-field runner in Texas history," Tully said. "He's the only guy I've seen sidestep a tackle without being touched on a dive play!"

The *Sports Illustrated* article also said McVea "has received more publicity that any schoolboy star since Bill DeCorrevont went to Northwestern." Jenkins was referring to a high school running back from Austin High School in Chicago, who in 1937 was the most

hotly recruited prospect ever. Surprisingly, DeCorrevont stayed close
to home and attended Northwestern University, a school that had not
made much of a name for itself in Big Ten football over the years. The
similarities were profound. Like DeCorrevont, McVea stayed close to
home and chose an unlikely school. And like McVea, DeCorrevont's
recruitment and subsequent college choice made national news. In his
final high school game, played before an estimated 120,000 fans at
Soldier Field in Chicago on the Saturday after Thanksgiving in 1937,
DeCorrevont led his Austin High team to the Chicago City championship by running for three touchdowns and passing for a fourth in a
26–0 victory. Also, like McVea, DeCorrevont was compared to legendary Illinois running back Red Grange.

The allure of the upcoming 1965 football season was heightened
by the Astrodome. The brainchild of Houston Astros owner Roy Hofheinz, the $36 million stadium was the first of its kind and would
remain so for ten years. Configured for the two major sports at the
time, the Dome seated 46,000 for baseball and 55,000 for football.
Built mostly to keep Houstonians from the sultry heat and humidity
of the local summers, not to mention attacks from mosquitoes in the
evening, the Astrodome offered cushioned seats and air conditioning. The climate-controlled indoor environment also eliminated the
weather factor from any game played there.

Dick Woodall was backup quarterback to Bo Burris in 1965 and
1966 but started for the Cougars in 1967. He grew up in the Westbury section of Southwest Houston in the late 1950s and early 1960s.
Woodall described the excitement and interest: "I saw the Dome being
built. We lived pretty close to the construction site, and my dad would
take me over to there every couple of weeks to see what progress was
being made. It was exciting. Then, when the Dome opened, I got to
see the Astros play the Yankees there in the first game. I got to see
Mickey Mantle hit the first homer in the Astrodome." That stirring
moment was tailor-made for the Dome's history book, what with the
low-ranking Astros pitted against the likes of Mantle, Roger Maris,
and the other famous members of the Yankee dynasty in a memorable
exhibition game.

An added bonus for the Houston Cougars was the recruiting factor. The new stadium caught the interest of high school players throughout the state of Texas. In the spring of 1965, legendary Amarillo sportswriter Putt Powell wrote in a column, "Don't ever underestimate the power of the domed stadium of Houston." Powell then quoted former Amarillo High School and newly hired UH assistant coach Bum Phillips, who said that because of the Astrodome, "recruiting is going very well."

Bum Phillips's son Wade was in the process of being recruited to UH, and he was impressed with the Astrodome. He said in a 2014 interview, "Everything was exciting about going to UH. They had put a lot of money into the program. We had 55 freshmen in our recruiting class. It was a really talented group of players. And then there was the Astrodome—the Eighth Wonder of the World—it was a great recruiting tool. Everybody who saw it went 'Wow!'"

As one would expect, the current Houston players were in awe of the building. Running back Dickie Post said, "Whenever I walk into that place, I get chills up and down my back."

Defensive lineman Royce Berry said, "I could have followed my brother to TCU, where he was playing. I came to UH because I liked the Dome."

And Dick Woodall added, "It was unbelievable when I found out we were going to be playing our games in the Astrodome. It was like a dream come true."

Another former player who spoke of the recruiting advantage of the Astrodome was Harold Smith, who, along with Jerry Drones, was among the second wave of black athletes to come to UH in 1966. Smith and Drones took a recruiting trip to Houston from their hometown of San Angelo, where they had played at integrated San Angelo Central High School under Coach Emory Bellard.

Smith said of his trip to Houston, "Wow, the Astrodome, when you think of the impact of that stadium. Jerry Drones and I were going on every recruiting trip in the world. We came to Houston together, and while we were there, Coach Yeoman said, 'Come take a ride with me.'

"He took us to the Dome. We parked there and he took us through a door, and the next thing you know, he was taking us out onto the middle of the field. You can imagine what that meant to two country boys from San Angelo. Coach Yeoman stopped and said, 'We play all of our home games here.'

"After our trip to the Astrodome, Jerry and I were saying to ourselves, 'Where do we sign?' And the next week we did indeed sign with Houston."

The debut of both the Astrodome and Warren McVea led NBC television to televise the first-ever indoor football game to a national audience—also the first time the Houston Cougars appeared on national television. Televised college football was much different in the days before cable television and ESPN—usually there was only one nationally televised game each week, and college teams were limited to just two games per season on television.

The Cougars had to settle on their opening-day opponent. Mississippi State had been discussed, but eventually Tulsa University got the nod. Glenn Dobbs, the Tulsa head coach, had seen the Astrodome firsthand when his Hurricane team came to Houston the previous December to play Ole Miss in the Bluebonnet Bowl at Rice Stadium. Dobbs figured the game would be the national opener for the NCAA television schedule, so he was happy to schedule the UH game. Tulsa was figured to be a tough opening-game assignment, with a defense led by Willie Townes and offense led by record-setting pass receiver Howard Twilley.

As the season approached, the excitement in Houston reached a fever pitch. Upon reflection, Sonny Yates, sports editor for the UH campus newspaper, the *Daily Cougar*, said, "Warren was the most exciting player I had ever seen. He stirred things up. He got everyone on campus excited before the season started. I felt our student body was completely supportive of Warren. I remember that *Sports Illustrated* sent someone to follow him around campus with the hopes of writing a feature article about him. As far as I know, they had never done that before."

On August 31, columnist Emil Tagliabue of the *Corpus Christi Caller Times* wrote about the upcoming Houston–Tulsa game under the headline "Heavy Pressure on Wondrous Warren" 11 days before the official kickoff. "It is doubtful any sophomore ever stood poised for the leap into varsity waters carrying more pressure on his broad, young shoulders," Tagliabue wrote. "So dazzling was he as a high schooler, those who saw him on several occasions have about convinced themselves he'll go straight to the Hall of Fame before his sophomore year at U of H is completed."

Even 1,550 miles away from Houston, much was being written about the Tulsa game on September 11, 1965. Dave Lewis, sports editor for the *Long Beach Independent*, wrote a column titled "Opening TV Game Is a Prize Package." Lewis wrote, "Houston, which will play all of its home games in the Astrodome, will be presenting in his first varsity appearance, Warren McVea, the Texas schoolboy phenom virtually every college in the country made a pitch for and who is expected by many observers to develop into one of the most exciting football personalities to come along in many years."

Finally, before 37,138 fans and a national television audience, the Tulsa Hurricane pulled off a mildly surprising upset with their 14–0 season-opening victory over the Houston Cougars in history's first indoor football game. Even more surprising was the fact that the Cougars's offense and Warren McVea were shut down by the Willie Townes–led Tulsa defense. Howard Twilley led the Tulsa offense with 11 catches for 111 yards, including the first-ever touchdown scored indoors—a 6-yard pass from quarterback Bill Anderson in the second quarter.

McVea experienced a nightmarish first college varsity game, carrying 11 times for a mere 21 yards. In addition, he fumbled the ball away four times. He was benched for much of the second half, and when he did return late in the game, he was booed lustily by the Cougar faithful.

The would-be superstar had big problems with the rock-hard Astrodome grass playing field. The field consisted of real grass the first year of the Dome's operation. The conversion from real to artificial grass rewrote both the baseball and the football history books. During baseball day games, players had kept losing balls hit in the air in the sun shining off the clear panels in the Astrodome roof. The panels had been eventually painted over, solving the sun problem, but then the grass on the field died because of the lack of sunlight. By the time football season came about, the field was almost barren of grass. What grass remained had to be spray-painted for the benefit of the television audience.

Almost every time McVea touched the ball that afternoon, he slipped, many times when no opposing player was even near him. Allen Gilbert of the *Northwest Arkansas Times* in Fayetteville described what happened: "The occasional cheering for Tulsa players by the Houston fans was in marked contrast to the jeers that were bestowed on the Cougars's Wonderous Warren McVea, the most highly touted Texas high schooler in history. In the press box no one could remember a highly publicized star who got off to a worse start.

"Ironically, Houston University has moved to the Astrodome for all of its home games this season. Then, in the very first game, it turns out that Wondrous Warren McVea, the Houston meal ticket, can't run on the home turf." Gilbert couldn't resist commenting on the advent of indoor football. "It is unusual, for instance, to play at lunchtime under artificial lights. It is also unreal to me to play football indoors on a field covered by artificially colored grass and sawdust. I imagine night games will have more charm. Aside from the fried chicken dinner and the air-conditioning that are served to pressmen in the Dome, I don't quite dig it."

One item that received nary a mention by the media was the fact that McVea became the first African American to play football for UH and the first in the South to play major college football. Many times throughout the season, McVea was the only black player on the field, the first to play against several colleges from the South, and therefore the first to officially integrate their stadiums.

Several people who broadcast, watched, coached, or played in the historic game have never forgotten what happened. The voices of that day's game were future Baseball Hall of Fame broadcasters Harry Kalas and Gene Elston. Their regular job was broadcasting Astros games, but as soon as football season started, they also voiced Cougar football games. Kalas said, "Nineteen sixty-five was my first year broadcasting in the Major Leagues. I remember Warren. He was a special player. To be honest, I really don't remember much from that first Astrodome game. In fact, I didn't know the Cougars weren't integrated until that game with Tulsa."

Elston said, "I recall the Tulsa game. We really didn't say anything on the air about Warren being the first black player. To a lot of people, though, it was a big thing. That whole time period in the mid- to late sixties, when I was calling Cougar games, was a great era for them. They used to play some really tough teams back then."

What is somewhat lost in the distant memory of the Tulsa game is the fact the game almost started on a positive note for the home team. McVea took the opening kickoff and—just as he was breaking free to go for an apparent touchdown—a Tulsa player who had already fallen to the ground reached up and tripped the runner. Cougar cheerleader Jimmy Disch recalled, "On the opening kickoff, Warren almost scored. Some Tulsa guy reached up at the last second and tripped him up. If Warren had scored, who knows if things would have been different that day? Maybe he wouldn't have had the bad day with the four fumbles."

Frank Schultz, sports columnist for the *Cougar*, echoed what Disch said in a column on October 28, right as the Cougars lost to Tennessee to go to 1–5 on the season. "In his opening varsity game against Tulsa," Schultz said, "it looked like he would go all the way with the first kickoff. However, a defender who had already been knocked down reached up and tripped the 180-pound speedster off his feet. If McVea could have gone all the way for six on that play, things could have been different this season.

"First, they would have been leading in the game, which is something they have not been able to do all year. UH has been forced to play catch-up all season long. And the pressure would have been off Mac right away. Besides, being tabbed as 'Mr. Football' in high school is quite a reputation to live up to. It is a long fall from the pedestal."

Many conversations were devoted to McVea's dismal opening game on a terrible playing field. Charlie Miller, assistant to Ted Nance in the

Sports Information Office, said, "The field was terrible for the Tulsa game. I remember John Hollis of the *Post* said, 'It was three yards and a cloud of Astrodome.'"

Cougar baseball player and cheerleader Bill Worrell commented, "The Tulsa game in the Dome—a huge day. Everyone knew what a big day it was. Tulsa had a good team. Problem was, there was not really any grass on the field. They watered the dead grass and rolled the field. Eventually they painted the field green so it would look good for the crowd and TV. The players had trouble, especially Warren, with him slipping all the time. He also fumbled four times. The bad field eventually led to Judge Hofheinz getting Astroturf the next season."

Cougar safety Tom Paciorek said, "Warren and I roomed together the night before our first game against Tulsa. I got to run back punts that day. I couldn't see the football off the ceiling of the Dome. I remember trying to fair catch balls and trying to shield my eyes. I was nervous.

"Nobody did well in the Tulsa game. The grass was dead, and there were only a few blades of grass on the field. It was like concrete, and players were slipping all over the place. I made a joke that someone must have gotten Earl Scheib to paint the field before the game." He was referring to the oft-advertised car-painting service with a cut rate at facilities in about 23 states, including Texas. Scheib's advertising slogan was "I'll paint any car, any color, for only $39.95!"

"Playing on that Astrodome grass field in 1965 was like playing on the parking lot outside," quipped Dick Woodall. "Some of the players really did injure themselves badly by falling on the field, tearing open their skin and then letting the wound get a bad infection."

Cougar assistant coach Chuck Fairbanks said, "That opening game against Tulsa, the playing conditions were terrible. Warren kept slipping and fumbling. It was the coming-out party for the black athlete at U of H, and the game was on national TV. I talked with Warren's mom after the game and tried to comfort her. It took Warren a while, but he eventually overcame that game. The whole thing had to be tough on him. He had to have a lot of stuff built up inside him. He ended up having a good career, though, and got drafted by the pros."

McVea himself told it like it was many decades after the fact. "I never liked the Dome," he said, "the field, that is—most especially the first year when there wasn't any grass. I kept slipping all the time, especially in the Tulsa game. I thought I could go out and take the ball and score when I got ready, like when I was a freshman. I just didn't take it seriously."

After the disappointing start, the Cougars's next game was also played in the Astrodome on September 18 against Mississippi State. The Cougars's woeful scoreless streak continued as they were dominated in a 36–0 shutout. The only real event of note for UH and McVea was that he became the first African American to play against the Bulldogs. He played the entire game without incident. He even commented later, "Mississippi State was the cleanest team we played all year. They talked to me during the game and were nice."

However, after the Mississippi State game, there were grumblings coming from the Cougars locker room. The *Daily Cougar* reporter Frank Schultz spoke with a couple unnamed players about the debacle after the game. He quoted one UH player as saying, "We're through. We'll be lucky if we finish 1–9." Another player opined, "None of the players have the respect of the coaches." The player asserted that Head Coach Bill Yeoman "has our best safetyman playing quarterback and me at a position I have never played."

Schultz then added his own commentary: "A writer is supposed to cover football and not tell the coach how to run his team. However, after viewing the Cougars's two stale performances like the Tulsa and Mississippi State games, you realize something is wrong. The parts are there, but Coach Yeoman is having a hard time making them fit."

The Cougars righted the ship momentarily in their next game on September 24, a rare Friday night game, again in the Astrodome, against the Cincinnati Bearcats. The Cougars broke their ongoing 11-quarter scoreless skid by scoring 21 fourth-quarter points in a 21–6 win before 27,576 patrons. McVea scored his first touchdown on a six-yard pass from quarterback Bo Burris.

The next week, McVea became only the second African American football player to take the field in College Station against Texas A&M

University. Rollie West of Villanova had been the first one in 1956. Besides that, the Cougars lost their first road contest, 10–7. Yeoman chose to go for the win on fourth-and-goal from the Aggie nine-yard line late in the game rather than settle for a field goal and possible tie. Burris underthrew a wide open Tom Beer in the end zone and the pass was intercepted. Yeoman offered no excuses. "You never go for the tie, always the win," he said.

The next week, on October 16, McVea again made history as the first African American to play against the University of Miami Hurricanes in Miami. The game itself was forgettable; the Hurricanes blasted the Cougars, 44–12. The low point was when McVea failed to cover a second-quarter Miami kickoff that had sailed into the end zone. The Hurricanes recovered the ball for a touchdown to extend their lead to 17–6. McVea then had a crucial fumble on the Cougar 31-yard line in the third quarter, which the Hurricanes converted into a touchdown to go up to 31–6.

Besides the difficult night on the field, McVea experienced some rough treatment from some of the Miami faithful. Barry Sides, the Cougars's starting center in 1964 and 1966 and left tackle in 1965, said, "I remember Miami my junior year in 1965. It was a bit of a hostile environment for us and Warren. Even their cheerleaders, who were behind our bench, were getting on our case."

Royce Berry said, "I always felt whenever we went on the road in the South to places like Knoxville or Jackson, we always had an extra heavy police force. Other than that, I didn't think about the integration thing that much."

Team captain and defensive tackle Cotton Guerrant said, "Warren and I ended up being good friends. I remember when we went down to Miami my senior year, they gave us a hard time. I guess being down there, you could expect it. You know, in those years, we played some good ball clubs—Georgia, Tennessee, Ole Miss—that was one good thing about being an independent."

It was after the Miami game that the heat was applied to Bill Yeoman, who was hung along with quarterback Bo Burris in effigy on the UH campus.

With the next game against Tennessee in Knoxville, Yeoman found himself at the proverbial crossroads. It was here that the coach decided to go with the Veer offense full-time, committing to Burris as his starting quarterback. Although the Cougars lost to the Volunteers, 17–8, to bring their record to 1–5, there seemed to be a transformation taking place. The Cougars stayed with Tennessee the whole ball game, losing after a scoreless first half.

Again, McVea established yet another first, becoming the first African American to play a game against the Volunteers in Knoxville. "I was up there by myself," he later recalled. "I met some of the Tennessee guys like Dewey Warren and Bob Johnson later in the pros when I was with the Bengals. They said that in their team meetings before they played us, they said nice things about me, like how I could run like the wind. At the game in 1965, the Tennessee players were great. They would help me up after a play."

Off the field, however, the Tennessee fans were a different matter.

Tight end Tom Beer said, "Warren didn't have a good game against Tennessee. I think the way the fans treated him may have had something to do with it. You could just feel the animosity from the stands. It was quite an experience. The crowd in back of our bench was leaning over the railings calling Warren 'nigger' and us 'nigger lovers,' among other things. It was an eye-opener for me. I was shocked. I had grown up around Detroit and had never experienced what I saw in Knoxville."

With Burris entrenched as the starting quarterback, the Cougars started back on the road to respectability on October 30 with a much-needed 40–7 victory over Chattanooga before 32,731 fans back in the friendly confines of the Astrodome. Burris set a single-game passing-yards record with 223 yards on 9 of 18 passes. His three touchdown passes, 39- and 60-yarders to Mike Spratt and a 69-yarder to Ken Hebert, tied a school record for touchdown passes in a game. McVea also contributed to the victory with a 21-yard punt return and the delivery of a key block on Dick Post's 32-yard touchdown run in the fourth quarter.

The next game was Homecoming in the Astrodome against Ole Miss. The Rebels came to town with an uncustomary 4–3 record but

remained a formidable opponent. At this juncture, Ole Miss dominated its series against the Cougars, having won each of the 12 games,
often by lopsided margins. This Dome game drew 38,197.

The game was significant because it marked the first time Houston
defeated Ole Miss, and more important, it was the first time Ole Miss
took the same football field as an African American player. What made
the game even more special for McVea was the fact that he finally
broke out of his season-long doldrums. He caught two long touchdown
passes from Burris: an 80-yarder in the third quarter and a school
record 84-yarder in the fourth.

Burris broke his own school passing-yardage record with 284 yards.
McVea also set a single-game receiving-yardage record with his six
catches for 201 yards. After the game, ecstatic UH fans carried their

Warren McVea,
circa 1965
(Courtesy of UH
Athletic Department)

hero McVea off the field. It appeared McVea could now begin to erase the bad memories of his first seven varsity games. McVea's two touchdown catches were also significant because he beat Rebel All-America safety Billy Clay, a 9.6 speedster, for both scores. Clay tried to intercept the first pass that McVea took in for his first score of the game by cutting in front of him. McVea hauled the pass in at his own 42-yard line and sprinted to the end zone all alone.

On the 84-yard fourth-quarter touchdown, McVea faked out his man, caught the ball on his fingertips at midfield, and outran the speedy Clay to pay dirt.

Royce Berry, the Cougars's defensive end, summed up the victory: "Ole Miss in 1965 was my best memory. They were a good team. We had never beaten them. Our defense played well, and Warren caught those two long passes. After that game, I knew we could beat anybody."

Sophomore Bruce Newell, who would later become Ole Miss's starting quarterback, was the other Rebel safety that day. "That game," Newell said, "was before they had turf in the Dome. It was painted green. Billy Clay, our other safety, was a real fast kid. McVea got one step on him and beat him for a touchdown. On the other long pass, Clay went for the interception but missed. The ball went right through his hands."

McVea reported no incidents with any of the Rebel players concerning the fact that he was a different color than everybody else on the field. One player who did comment was Jim Urbanek, who was born in Oxford, Mississippi, but moved to Houston and spent 11 years there, up through his junior year at Waltrip High School, earning all-district honors his junior year at fullback and defensive tackle. He returned to Oxford for his senior year and ended up being a two-time All-America defensive tackle for Ole Miss in 1966 and 1967. "They beat us 17–3 when Warren caught those two long passes," Urbanek said. "I knew about Warren pretty well because I had played in Texas. I knew he was fast. To us, Warren was just another player on the other team. I remember no one, players or coaches, said anything racial about Warren before the game."

The day before the Ole Miss game, there was one incident off the field that summed up the racial attitudes of some of the Rebel faithful. Charlie Miller, who had come to UH as an assistant trainer under Tom Wilson and who eventually lent a hand to Ted Nance in the Sports Information Department, had a story to tell: "The Friday before the Mississippi game in the Dome in 1965, we met with some Ole Miss people—their sports information director, the assistant athletic director. We were at the Shamrock Hilton Hotel, and we had had a few drinks. The Mississippi guys were bragging about Billy Clay, their All-America defensive back.

"Then they started in on Warren. Every other word out of their mouth was the N-word. They kept saying sarcastically, 'Why did you get him?' I stayed diplomatic, not trying to get into an argument with them. Obviously, Warren had a good night. He slipped behind Billy Clay for those two long touchdown catches. It was the first time we had beaten Ole Miss. After the game, I saw the assistant athletic director with his head slumped over. I said to him, 'You doin' all right? Did you get a good look at Warren? That's why we got him.' I just laughed and walked away. It's funny, when we played Mississippi State earlier in the year, their guys didn't act like that. They were nice guys."

With the thrill of the Cougars's victory over Ole Miss still on their minds, one might have expected a letdown the next week against 10th-ranked Kentucky, once again in the Astrodome. The Wildcats came into the game with a 6–2 record and a three-game winning streak, but they left 37,248 Cougar fans happy after falling to Houston, 38–21. Probably the key play in the game was a fake punt by Ken Hebert, who raced 61 yards from deep in his own territory to the Kentucky 19-yard line with the Cougars down 8–0 in the second quarter. UH proceeded to score shortly thereafter and were on their way to their second upset victory in as many weeks.

Hebert explained the fake punt: "I did it on my own. I looked up, and on the right side, nobody for Kentucky was rushing. Everybody had turned their backs and was heading downfield. So I took off. Coach Yeoman didn't say a word. Then the next day, he told me to never do it again."

Burris said, "Pound for pound, Hebert was the guy. That fake punt against Kentucky—I'm standing next to Yeoman, and he hollers, 'What in the devil is Hebert doing?' Lucky for Kenny, it worked."

McVea continued to contribute. After Kentucky went up 15–6 in the second quarter, he raced 41 yards on a kickoff and shortly thereafter scored on a 19-yard pass from Burris. However, the budding star suffered a bruised thigh late in the second quarter and did not play in the second half.

McVea was the second African American to take the field against the Kentucky Wildcats. In their 1965 opener, Kentucky had gone to Columbia, Missouri, to take on the Tigers, who had several African American players on their roster, including All-America defensive back Johnny Roland. Ironically, the reason Roland was at Missouri was because when he graduated from Corpus Christi Miller High School in 1961 after leading Miller to the 1960 state championship, Texas colleges had not yet integrated.

Although the Cougars were down 21–16 to Kentucky at the half, Bo Burris threw three second-half touchdown passes, two to Mike Spratt and one to Ken Hebert, as the Cougars scored their third straight victory. All that now remained was their season finale in Tallahassee against Florida State University on November 20.

There was talk from Bluebonnet Bowl officials in Houston that if the Cougars beat the Seminoles, they might get a bowl bid. A final game victory eluded the Cougars, though, as they had to settle for a 16–16 tie.

McVea became the first African American player to play in Tallahassee, and it didn't take him long to get the home crowd's attention when he returned a kickoff 92 yards for a touchdown after Florida State had gone up 6–0. The Seminoles, who had an 11-game home winning streak, were able to salvage the tie when Ken Hebert missed a tough 38-yard field goal attempt from the left hash mark with just two seconds left in the season.

Florida native Sonny Yates, the *Cougar* sportswriter, recalled a story his parents told him about McVea's kickoff return touchdown. "My mom and dad were at the game," Yates said, "and they told me about this Florida State fan who kept shouting, 'Kick the ball to Calhoun! Kick the ball to Calhoun!'"

The fan was referring to Algonquin J. Calhoun, the black lawyer on the old Amos and Andy radio and television shows of the 1940s and 1950s.

"The Calhoun reference was obviously aimed at Warren. Well, the ball was kicked to Warren, and he raced 92 yards for the touchdown. After that, my parents said the fan started shouting, 'Don't kick the ball to Calhoun! Don't kick the ball to Calhoun!'"

As it turned out, even if the Cougars had won their last game, they were not in serious consideration for the Bluebonnet Bowl. Earlier that day, Tennessee—the last team to defeat the Cougars in 1965—got the official nod. Nonetheless, the 1965 Cougar season ended on a positive note after starting the season 1–5, as the Cougars went 3–0–1 down the stretch in their last four games. With a solid core of players returning, the upcoming 1966 season promised to be a bright one.

Like the Cougar football team, Warren McVea overcame a horrendous start to his college football career and redeemed himself over the Cougars's final four games, starting with the defeat of Mississippi.

Moved to flanker early in the season, due in part to the opening game debacle against Tulsa, McVea never got untracked as a running back in 1965. For the season, he ran the ball just 38 times for 135 yards—just 3 yards per carry. As a flanker, McVea fared better. He ended up with 17 catches for 341 yards and four touchdowns, at 20.1 yards per catch. He also returned 17 kicks for 428 yards, a 25.2-yard average, and one touchdown.

However, Warren McVea certainly proved himself an able pioneer for the integration of college football in the South. A year later, he would continue to integrate football fields that had never had black players set foot on them. But even more significant, his junior year would see one major difference—he would not be the only black man clad in red and white.

12 "WE WANT A FIELD HOUSE!"

When I got there [the restaurant], the players said there was a problem—they refused to serve Elvin and Don, and they said they could pick up their meals in the kitchen in the back ... We all said, "We're outta here"—even though we had already placed our orders.
    —UH STUDENT TRAINER BOB
    SMITH (AT SHREVEPORT)

Elvin Hayes and Don Chaney embarked on their sophomore basketball season without hype and expectations comparable to the Warren McVea gridiron story. There was no South Texas exhibition tour, no *Sports Illustrated* article, nor regularly mentioned comparisons to basketball legends in the news media. They completed most of their integration pioneering as freshmen playing in East Texas junior college gymnasiums.

It seemed like everywhere McVea played, he was the first African American to do so. Hayes and Chaney were the first to ever play against Auburn University when they met in the

Sugar Bowl Tournament in New Orleans in December 1965 and the first to play in Shreveport when they took the court against Centenary University.

Otherwise, the basketball duo ranked as impressive "seconds," becoming the second African Americans to ever play at Texas A&M University. This happened on December 9, 1965—one week after Larry Jeffries of Trinity University. These three occasions were the only times in their three-year varsity careers that they integrated a venue or became the first blacks to take the court against an opposing team.

Although not achieving the same high level of publicity—some would call it *hype*—as McVea, the two black UH sophomore basketball players in fact generated an impressive amount of optimism and anticipation going into the 1965–66 basketball season. Ten days before the Cougars opened their season on the West Coast on December 1 against a tough University of San Francisco team that had gone 24–5 and went to the Elite Eight the previous year, Guy V. Lewis sized up his team and his individual players. "I think we'll have a good team," Lewis said. "We should be stronger. But we could still be a better team and wind up with a worse record because of the schedule we play."

Three nights later, the Cougars would face Brigham Young, another 1965 NCAA Tournament team with high expectations for the new season, causing Lewis to remark, "A fellow told me today that the turning point in our season might be our first two games." The UH coach went on to evaluate his team and players, saying, "We'll have three sophomores playing a good deal of the time—Elvin Hayes, Don Chaney, and Paul Ozug. This is also the tallest team we've ever had and quite a contrast to our previous teams. I'd say, for the first time, we'll be able to compete with teams physically."

Another exciting newcomer was 6-foot-8 center/forward Don Kruse, the junior college All-American from Kilgore Junior College, where he averaged more than 28 points per game. "Don is an outstanding player," Lewis said, "but it takes a while for a transfer sometimes. However, Kruse is the most fantastic passer I've ever coached. Against a zone, he really whips that ball around. He's a really good shooter, too. Actually, he's passing up more shots in practice than he should."

Lewis also touted several returning players, such as senior cocaptains reserve forward Rich Apolskis and starting point guard Joe Hamood. Lewis said Apolskis "has improved his shooting quite a bit. From being a poor outside shooter, Apolskis has turned into a very good one. And he's the best on the team in taking that step to the bucket. Rich is also very tough and gives us experience off the bench."

The leader of the 1965–66 Cougar basketball team, however, was Hamood. Originally recruited out of Dearborn, Michigan, to play quarterback for the Cougar football team, Hamood explained how he ended up on the basketball court instead: "When I first came down here, I was homesick. I really wanted to go back home, but I talked to coaches Yeoman and Lewis, and they agreed that I could try basketball."

Assistant football coach Tom Boisture, who was from the same area of Michigan Hamood hailed from, said, "We recruited Joe out of Fortson High School, where he was all-state, to play quarterback here at Houston. He was the first athlete from his area to play in college. He was a Muslim.

"For whatever reason, there was a large Muslim population in Dearborn. Joe ended up playing just basketball after he got here, which turned out pretty well for Guy Lewis. After college, he played a little pro ball [with the ABA Houston Mavericks]. Unfortunately, when he was back home in Michigan, he died in an auto accident."

Hamood died in 1970, just days short of his 23rd birthday. He was generally regarded as the heart and soul of the Cougar basketball team. Bob Smith, the student trainer, said, "When Elvin and Don came to the varsity team that first year, it could have been a problem. Some of the older guys had been there a while, and now these two sophomores come along who are better than pretty much any of them were. All of a sudden the white guys aren't playing as much. I never really heard any griping or moaning. I think having a strong senior leader in Joe Hamood really helped. By Elvin and Don's second year, there was a changing of the guard, and it was *their* team. Not that first year, though. It was Joe's team."

Junior forward Leary Lentz said, "Joe was our leader. Everyone looked up to him. Elvin and Don even deferred to him. We started out a little slow Joe's senior year, but eventually we jelled, and we had a good chemistry by the end of the season, better than any of the three teams I played on at the University of Houston."

"Joe is our quarterback and team leader and certainly one of the better scoring guards we've had here," Guy V. Lewis said. "For us to have a real good club, he has to be not only a good scorer but our leader, playmaker, and feeder."

Lewis mentioned the other returning starting guard, Wayne Ballard. "You know how well Ballard can shoot the ball. He's a dandy." And the coach didn't leave out some of the other reserves. "Gary Grider, the guard, has the speed to help our press, and David Starks can help. We got a good boy out of Tyler Junior College in Bob Hayward. He's 6-foot-6 and a good shooter, particularly with the hook.

"Leary Lentz has improved the most since last year. He has combined better shooting with a more aggressive step toward the basket. He's also matured. He should be a much better player." Lentz eventually made the starting lineup and averaged 8.1 rebounds a game, second on the team behind Elvin Hayes.

Of his two newest Cougars from Louisiana, Lewis said, "Chaney will play a lot. He's very quick and a good shooter and ball-handler. He's also a 6-foot-5 guard who can rebound."

Lewis then said, "I think Hayes will hold up his end of the scoring, even though he's going to be in there with the big boys. He's strong and he's not timid. His biggest problem is fouling out. Hayes gives us something we've never had before—a good big man on the boards who can block shots.

"Overall, I'd say potentially we're better," Lewis said of his 1965–66 Cougar basketball squad. "We'll score more. I really believe this, even though we averaged 83 points a game last year. Even though we're taller, we're still going to fast break, and we're still going to use the pressing defenses.

"The press may look a little different, but I believe it can work for us. If they break through, Hayes might just knock the ball back down court. A boy like that is something new to me. We'll probably have more points scored on us this year than ever before. But we'll probably also score more."

* * * * * * *

While the 1965–66 UH basketball Cougars didn't lose their first game on national television like McVea and the football team, they also got off to a rather rocky start. First, at the last practice before the San Francisco game to start the season, Chaney suffered a knee injury, and he had to sit out the game. Thus the Cougars's firepower coming off the bench was limited at best.

San Francisco then proceeded to hand the Cougars a 75–67 defeat. The Dons were led by senior Don Ellis, who had 21 points and 16 rebounds. Hayes was held to just 2 first-half points because he was charged with three quick personal fouls and spent an extended amount of time on the bench. He did wind up with 20 points and 10 rebounds. The Cougars climbed back into the game, but a late 7–2 run by San Francisco in the last two minutes sealed the win for the Dons.

After the opening defeat, Lewis remained optimistic. He said, "We'll be good, better than San Francisco, and I don't mind saying so. If we get the chance to play them in March, well, we'd just like the chance to play them again, that's all."

Lewis also would have liked to have seen Chaney have the chance to guard Ellis with the opportunity to shut him down. "He hurt his knee in our last workout at home," the coach said. "Nobody knew about it. He didn't say anything. Not having him out there hurt our pressing defenses. It looks like he'll be out for our next game, too."

The Cougars's second game was played on Saturday, December 4, against the Brigham Young Cougars in Provo, Utah. It proved to be the only bad loss UH would suffer that season. BYU had a fine 21–5 record the previous season, averaging 94.3 points per game. Lewis said, "Brigham Young is a different kind of team than San Francisco. They're taller and more of a fast breaking team. They'll be a lot tougher." The BYU team also got to play a 22-game exhibition schedule in the summer of 1965, touring South America for the US State Department.

Although Hayes and Hamood each scored 24 points and Hayes had numerous blocked shots (but was called for goaltending six times), the BYU team blew out UH 111–82 behind Dick Nemelka's 39 points and numerous fast break layups by other BYU players.

The 0–2 Cougars then returned home to begin preparations to go to College Station to take on the Texas Aggies on Thursday, December 9. "We need to get together and become a team," Lewis said. "In both games, we took shots we shouldn't have. We were beat on the boards."

Hamood called a players-only meeting after the two games. "There was no closeness on this team—not like last year," the cocaptain said. "We just weren't playing together. The locker room was as silent as a tomb. No spark. We talked about it. Since we've come back, we've had two good workouts in a row. We played like a team."

Lewis also made some changes in his lineup. He installed Leary Lentz into the starting lineup—where he remained for most of the season—in place of Paul Ozug, and Gary Grider would start in place of Wayne Ballard. Rich Apolskis got the starting nod over Don Kruse for the Aggie game. And Chaney's knee was healed enough to enable him to make his varsity debut against the Aggies.

While the Cougars played a strong first 30 minutes of the game and led 70–57 with 10 minutes to go, the Aggies, led by All-American John Beasley's 29 points and Dick Rector's 18, came back to outscore the Cougars 36–18 in the last 10 minutes to take a 93–88 victory. Hayes again led the Cougars with 24 points, but only 5 of them came in the last 10 minutes, as the Aggies used a sagging defense on him to help them mount their comeback. Hamood added 20 points, and Chaney, in his first varsity action, chipped in 7 points.

Neither Hayes nor Chaney could recall any racial incidents at the game, nor was there any mention of the integration of college basketball in College Station by the local media. That integration had happened a week before the Cougars took the court against the Aggies.

However, Cougar-fan Sam Swearengin did recall years later, "We played two games against the Aggies that year. We heard on campus that Elvin and Don had caught some flak from their fans up there. The

Aggies also had Randy Matson, the Olympic shot putter, on their team. He was only 6-foot-6 but was playing center against Elvin. Apparently the Aggies made a big deal about how Matson supposedly outplayed Elvin and how an all-white team beat up on a team with black players. When we played them at Delmar in January, we demolished them, and Elvin was terrific against Matson."

After starting the season 0–3, the Cougars finally returned home. Before the university completed Hofheinz Pavilion in 1969, the Cougars played at three venues in Houston. Their actual home court, Jeppesen Field House on the UH campus, only seated 2,500 fans. The 1965–66 season would be the last time the Cougars would play there, because the building's seating capacity was just too small to accommodate the crowds that came to watch Hayes, Chaney, and the rest of the Cougars compete like never before.

Another place the Cougars played, beginning in the early 1960s, was Delmar Field House, a Houston Independent School District facility on the northwest side just off Highway 290, about 15 miles from the UH campus. Completed in the late 1950s, the arena first hosted Cougar games in March 1961, when UH defeated Marquette University, 77–61, in the first NCAA Tournament game ever played in Texas. The Cougars started playing some of their regular season games there in 1962, the first against eventual national champion Cincinnati on February 1. The seating capacity for Delmar was 5,200. After the 1965–66 season, the Cougars played their home games there exclusively until Hofheinz Pavilion opened in December 1969.

The third "home floor" the Cougars used through the years was the old Sam Houston Coliseum in downtown. A multipurpose venue, the Coliseum was built in 1937 and torn down in 1998. At the time it was finished, the facility had been advertised as having the world's largest arena air-conditioning system. The Coliseum was also home to the Shrine Circus, the Houston Livestock Show and Rodeo (before it moved to the Astrodome in the 1960s), ice hockey (when Gordie Howe played for the WHA Houston Aeros from 1974 to 1977), and the city's most historic concerts. Elvis Presley played there on

*Don Chaney drives the
lane at Delmar Field
House, circa 1966
(Courtesy of UH Athletic
Department)*

October 13, 1956, and the Beatles on August 19, 1965. The arena also hosted professional wrestling, World Team tennis, and high school, college, and pro basketball. The Houston Mavericks of the old ABA played their games there in 1967–68 when Joe Hamood and Leary Lentz were team members.

The last game the Houston Cougar basketball team ever played at Sam Houston Coliseum happened on Saturday, December 11. It also was their first victory of the 1965–66 campaign, when 5,100 curious fans showed up to see the home debut of Elvin Hayes and Don Chaney. The Cougars did not disappoint the home faithful as they rolled over the Wisconsin Badgers, 82–57.

The Cougars raced out to a 25–9 lead and never looked back. Hamood led the way with 23 points, while Hayes added 22 and 16 rebounds and Lentz, making the most of his starting opportunity, had 15 points and 15 rebounds.

After this initial victory, the Cougars were off to Autry Court on the Rice University campus to participate in the sixth annual Bluebonnet Classic Tournament on December 15 and 16. Their opening game was against the LSU Tigers, and they set a single-game tournament scoring record with a 110–87 thrashing. Hayes led with 31 points, with Hamood adding 18. Chaney had his first double-digit-scoring game with 12 points.

The next night, the Cougars faced undefeated Texas A&M just a week after losing to the Aggies on their home court. UH got a measure of revenge, scoring a 90–85 victory that won the Bluebonnet Tournament title. Hamood and Don Kruse led a balanced scoring attack with 20 points each, while Hayes and Wayne Ballard chipped in 17 and 13, respectively.

Now squared with three wins and three losses, the Cougars traveled on Saturday, December 18, to Fort Worth to play the TCU Horned Frogs, which had a dismal 6–18 season in 1964–65 and started out this new season 1–3. The Cougars proceeded to set a Daniel Meyer Coliseum scoring record in a 132–102 rout. Hayes led the way with 33 points, 16 rebounds, and six blocked shots to go along with four goaltending calls. Hamood chipped in 22 points along with Wayne Ballard's 20. Chaney had a solid all-around game with 8 points, 8 rebounds, and six assists.

Two nights later, the Cougars faced their biggest test of the young season against the seventh-ranked Providence Friars, with their All-America guard Jimmy Walker and future NBA star Mike Riordan on their roster. The Friars were rated, along with St. Joseph's team, as one of the top two teams in the East, and Providence was coming off a 24–2 record the previous season. A crowd of 5,200—with several hundred more turned away at the gate—packed Delmar to witness the Cougars's best performance of the season—a 102–89 win.

The Friars, thanks to their hot first-half shooting and a sagging defense that at times triple-teamed Hayes, held a 55–50 lead at the break. For the second half, however, Hayes said, "I quit trying to fake before I shot and just went straight up to shoot. That prevented them from sagging on me." The strategy worked. Hayes scored 21 of his 33 total points in the second half to go with 18 rebounds as the Cougars started the second half on a 24–8 run and never looked back. Jimmy Walker led the Friars with 30 points, but Lentz had 17 points and Hamood had 14 points and seven assists.

The Cougars enjoyed the Providence win and a short Christmas break before heading to New Orleans on December 29 and 30 to play in the annual Sugar Bowl Tournament, the prelude to the Sugar Bowl football game every New Year's Day.

Although New Orleans was in the Deep South, racially mixed athletics at the college level were not new to the Crescent City. Loyola University regularly competed against opposing black athletes in basketball, and the Sugar Bowl basketball tournament had integrated in December 1955 when sophomore Al Avant of Marquette University took the court.

What was also significant about the 1955 Sugar Bowl Basketball Tournament and football bowl game on January 1, 1956, was the controversy created by the football matchup of Georgia Tech against Pittsburgh. The Panthers had an African American fullback and defensive back named Bobby Grier. Georgia governor Marvin Griffin focused on Georgia Tech, all white, playing a football game against a team with an African American on its roster. In a telegram to the Georgia Board of Regents, Griffin said, "It is my request that athletic teams of units of the university system of the State of Georgia not be permitted to engage in contests with other teams where the races are mixed on such teams or where segregation is not required at such games. The South stands at Armageddon."

The Georgia Board of Regents eventually voted 10–1 to allow Georgia Tech to play in the game, which the Yellow Jackets won, 6–0, thanks in part to a controversial pass interference penalty against Bobby Grier. However, the regents, in a rider attached to their decision, outlawed future games in the State of Georgia between Georgia colleges and integrated teams.

The ban in Georgia lasted until 1968. Ironically, the first team to play Georgia in Athens with African American players on its roster was the University of Houston, the year after Warren McVea left the Cougars for the NFL. The Cougar roster included African American players Elmo Wright, who scored the Cougars's only touchdown in a 10–10 tie with an 80-yard first quarter pass reception; Paul Gipson, who ran 37 times for 230 yards; running back Carlos Bell; defensive end Jerry Drones; and linebacker Charlie Hall.

The Sugar Bowl Tournament did hold some significance for Hayes and Chaney, since both were Louisiana natives. Hayes said, "I used to think about playing in that tourney, but I never thought I'd get the chance. Now that I have, I'm just hoping we can win it."

Chaney added, "I never really thought much about it before, but I'm looking forward to it. My family will be there, and a lot of my friends, too. I have friends who go to Loyola."

While the Cougars did not integrate New Orleans or the Sugar Bowl Tournament, both games they played did carry some cultural significance. The first matchup for UH was on December 29 against the Maryland Terrapins out of the Atlantic Coast Conference (ACC). Referring to the scouting report on this opponent, Guy V. Lewis said, "It said that Maryland probably has the best six-man team in America. They don't have much of a bench except for 6-foot-8 backup center Rick Wise, but they play ball control, play tough defense, and rebound well. I guess it figures, since Bud Millikan was coached by Hank Iba. In fact, I think Harvey Pate and Bud were college teammates."

Maryland's bench was depleted because one of their key reserves, sophomore Billy Jones, had suffered a foot injury and did not make the trip. Jones, like Hayes and Chaney, was an integration pioneer. During the 1965–66 season, Jones became the first African American basketball player in the ACC. He suffered his foot injury a few days before the Terrapins traveled to New Orleans, ultimately missing a total of nine games in December and January.

As much as Maryland could have used Jones coming off the bench, the Terrapins still had enough firepower to edge the Cougars out, 69–68. The Cougars had a 7-point lead with less than three minutes left to play, but they let the game slip through their fingers. Neil Brayton of Maryland came off the bench despite four fouls to lead an 8–0 run for the Terrapins to take a 67–66 lead with a minute to play. Chaney scored from 20 feet out to give the Cougars a 68–67 lead, but Brayton sank a 15-foot jumper with 25 seconds left on the clock.

After the game, a frustrated Guy V. Lewis said, "I have nothing to say except that we blew it. The game never should have gone to the last shot."

The Maryland game would be the last the Cougars would lose for almost two months. The next day, December 30, they defeated Auburn, 89–76, in the consolation game, starting a then-school-record 14-game winning streak. The Auburn game also was significant because it was the first time the Tiger basketball team had played against African Americans, either at home, away, or on a neutral court like in New Orleans.

Hayes became the highest-scoring Cougar to ever play in the Sugar Bowl Tournament. The team had previously played there in 1956 and 1962. As a result, he was named to the all-tournament team. It was after the tournament that the praise started coming in for the Cougar star. For one, Maryland coach Bud Millikan said, "We tried to chop the big man down, but we couldn't. He's strong and once he gets the ball, he knows what to do with it. We put a man in front of him and in back of him and he still scored 28 points."

Auburn assistant coach Rudy Davalos added, "He's the best big man I've seen this year. He's better than anything in our area." Davalos's area included the Southeastern Conference and All-American Clyde Lee of Vanderbilt. It also featured the University of Louisville, which had future Hall of Famer Wes Unseld on its roster.

Davalos himself was somewhat of an integration pioneer. A San Antonio native, he played basketball for one season at Wharton County Junior College in 1956–57, the year before that college integrated the junior college ranks with Hank Allen. From Wharton, Davalos went on to Southwest Texas State University in San Marcos, Texas, and in 1960 helped the Bobcats win the NAIA championship.

Davalos was the only Hispanic player in the all-white Lone Star Conference. "I was called a few names—Spic, Wop, Dago, a Greaser, you name it," Davalos said. "It just made me play harder, because I wanted to beat their butts."

Later, in 1968, while he was still an assistant coach at Auburn, Davalos recruited Henry Harris to be the first African American athlete at the school and the second in the history of the Southeastern Conference, after Perry Wallace of Vanderbilt in 1965.

Nineteen years later, in 1987, with a bit of irony, Rudy Davalos became the athletic director at the University of Houston. The first Hispanic athletic director at a major university, Davalos went to the University of New Mexico in 1992 and remained there as athletic director until he retired in 2006. In 2003, he was named by *Sports Illustrated* as one of the 101 "Most Influential Minorities in Sports."

* * * * * * *

The trip to New Orleans was the first time Hayes and Chaney had played games in the Deep South. The Cougars only played four times in the South during Hayes and Chaney's three years at UH, with all the games played in their home state of Louisiana. Besides the Sugar Bowl Tournament to end 1965, the Cougars returned to New Orleans on March 1, 1966, to play Loyola University. They also played twice in Shreveport against Centenary, once when Hayes and Chaney were sophomores and again when they were seniors.

Despite some taunts from a few of the fans at the Sugar Bowl Tournament, it appeared to go fairly well for Hayes and Chaney. Hayes said, "I heard some racial comments from the stands, nothing on the court. You just tried to ignore it. If you're looking for stuff like that, you can usually find it."

The second win in the Cougars's 14-game streak was a 113–75 rout of the Mexican National Team at Delmar Field House on January 5. Hayes led with 36 points and 18 rebounds.

Three days later, UH finally played its first home game of the season at Jeppesen Field House. The opponent was Trinity, with Larry Jeffries, Trinity's first African American player. The Cougars blasted the Tigers, 95–52, before a sellout crowd of 2,500. Hayes dominated the game, scoring 30 points on 13 of 16 field goal attempts, taking down 21 rebounds and blocking six shots. He left the game with 5:44 to play to a standing ovation. Larry Jeffries, who came into the game averaging 19 points and 12 rebounds, scored only 12 points and fouled out of the game. Hamood added 18 points. Chaney missed the game due to a slight ankle sprain. The highlights came when Hamood twice stole the ball and then lofted alley-oop passes to Hayes, who slammed both passes through the basket with thunderous dunks.

As for the integration issue, the next game was the most significant game of Hayes's and Chaney's careers. The matchup was against Centenary University in Shreveport on Thursday, January 13, 1966.

In early 1966, there were still laws in the books in Shreveport that forbade whites and blacks from competing against each other. Orvis Sigler, the Centenary coach, undertook extraordinary measures to make sure the game was played. Sigler recalled the event: "We had a city ordinance back then—no mixing of the races. We broke that. We were the first ones. I had to go to the City of Shreveport and meet with the mayor and city council, and they rescinded the law. It was the beginning of open basketball in Shreveport. Heck, it was the beginning of open everything there. After that, we played several teams with blacks on them."

Once the game was on, a crowd of 1,900 packed Centenary's gym to watch the UH blast the Gents, 108–84. Tom Kerwin, Centenary's top player, had 34 points, but the Cougars put five players in double figures, led by Hamood's 26 points and 11 assists. Hayes contributed 20 points and 12 rebounds before fouling out with 11:45 to play. Chaney chipped in 16 points off the bench.

"The game with Houston was a groundbreaking event," Sigler said years later. "They beat the hell out of us, though. Guy Lewis and I were good friends. We would always schedule each other. Elvin was great that night. I don't remember any problems at the game—everything went smooth. People came out just to see them play—two Louisiana boys—one from the north just down the road in Rayville and the other from the south down in Baton Rouge."

The fact that Hayes and Chaney were the first African Americans to play in Shreveport did draw the attention of the local and national media. John Hollis of the *Houston Post* mentioned briefly in his article on the game, "Hayes, the first Negro to appear on Centenary's home court (Don Chaney came in later to make it a twosome), came back for 13 second-half points, but his total of 20 is five points under his nationally ranked season average. He finished with 12 rebounds."

Hayes and Chaney integrating Shreveport and Centenary made the Associated Press wire service story on the game. Part of the article, which was a roundup of scores from around the country, said, "At Shreveport, Louisiana, sophomores Elvin Hayes and Don Chaney became the first Negroes to play on Centenary's court as Houston beat Centenary 108–84. Both fouled out, with Hayes getting 20 points before leaving."

Although events at the game went well that historic night, afterward when the Cougars went out to get a postgame meal, Hayes and Chaney were denied service at a local restaurant. Several players and student trainer Bob Smith remembered the event.

Teammate Paul Ozug recalled, "I do remember when we traveled to Centenary in Shreveport, the restaurant wouldn't serve Elvin and Don. I had never seen that before, growing up in Gary, Indiana. I had black teammates in high school, and it was not a big deal."

Lentz remembered the event, as did student trainer Bob Smith, who said, "The kicker was that I usually took care of the travel arrangements—hotels, restaurants, etc. After the Centenary game, the players got into cabs to go eat. I gave out the money to them, so I was the last one to arrive at the restaurant. When I got there, the players said there was a problem—they refused to serve Elvin and Don, and they said they could pick up their meals in the kitchen in the back. The waitress said, 'Sorry, that's just the way it is.' We all said, 'We're outta here'—even though we had already placed our orders.

"I heard Elvin talk about this incident one time years later when we had a 30-year anniversary reunion for the first Final Four team. Elvin talked about the team and how they took up for him and Don. Elvin said that Guy Lewis had created a family-type atmosphere and that everything was for the team."

Hayes said, "I remember after the Centenary game across from the hotel. When we went to eat, the restaurant owner said, 'All y'all can come in here, but those niggers can't come in.' People made stupid

statements like that back then—those were the times we lived in. I have
to admire guys like Guy and Harvey, though. Everybody left with us.
That showed me they were my friends and they cared about me. Some
people wouldn't do that for you. I hold my teammates and what they
did for me and Don close to me."

Two nights after the win at Centenary, the Cougars faced another
tough road contest against the 13–3 Tulsa Hurricane. The Cougars
squeaked out a 1-point win over the 15th-ranked Tulsa squad, 72–71,
on a 15-foot basket by Joe Hamood with 20 seconds left. Coach Lewis
said, "It's our biggest win since beating Notre Dame in the NCAA
playoffs last year. I'd say bigger than the win over Providence. This one
was on the road, it was against a nationally ranked team, and we had
to come from behind to win in the last 36 seconds."

Two nights later, the Cougars enjoyed their biggest blowout of the
season, whipping St. Mary's University of San Antonio, 109–53, at
Jeppesen Field House. As was becoming the norm, Hayes led the Cougars with 29 points and 19 rebounds.

After a nine-day layoff, the Cougars tested their mettle against three
different Southwest Conference opponents on Wednesday, Thursday,
and Friday in cramped Delmar. The Cougars began this tiresome task
with a 1-point victory over Baylor in overtime after blowing a 4-point
lead. Hamood sank the game-winning free throw with nine seconds
left to give the Cougars a hard-fought 92–91 victory.

The next night, UH scored its second rout of the season on the
TCU Horned Frogs with a 100–79 win, with Hayes having his best
night of the season up to that point, scoring 33 points, 27 rebounds,
and six blocked shots in only 33 minutes of play. After two games in
two nights, Lewis said, "They were tired, but they played well. What
are we going to do tomorrow? We're going to sit around and think
about the Aggies and growl."

The Cougars then completed their sweep of SWC opponents by
defeating the Aggies, 97–85, before a packed house of 5,600 fans. It
was estimated that another 3,000 fans were turned away at the door.
Hayes broke a 56–56 tie with a basket with 16 minutes left. Over the

next 8 minutes, he scored 14 points to give the Cougars some breathing room in overcrowded conditions.

Toward the end of the Aggie game, the red-clad Cougar faithful started chanting, "We want a field house! We want a field house!" With the winning streak and the exciting level of play, the Cougars were showing that they were starting to attract large crowds, prompting Coach Lewis to say after the game, "The need for a field house could become real serious."

Indeed, UH began to hatch a plan for an on-campus basketball arena. On the Monday after the Aggie game, Athletic Director Harry Fouke met with UH President Philip G. Hoffman to discuss the possibilities. "We're working," Fouke said, "and that's about all I can say. It was under discussion today. Our biggest problem remains financing."

Eight days later, Rich Burk of the *Cougar* wrote an editorial: "The students are unhappy with each passing game about the seating situation. After paying $24 for an activity book, students are finding it useless for basketball because there is no place to sit . . . But for now students merely want a seat for basketball games. Other universities are concerned about the situation as well. How can UH continue to schedule national powers such as Michigan, Providence, Brigham Young and others when all that is available is far from adequate for the crowds the team now draws?"

Burk finished his editorial by saying, "The need for a field house is acute. It is a situation that will no doubt get worse before it gets better. But something must be done. WE WANT A FIELD HOUSE!"

Eventually, after the A&M game at Delmar, UH put into motion the plans to build what ultimately became known as Hofheinz Pavilion, which opened on December 1, 1969.

* * * * * * *

After the three-game sweep against SWC foes, the Cougars extended their winning streak to 14 with five relatively easy home wins against less-than-stellar competition. The closest margin of victory for the Cougars over this stretch was 15 points.

Elvin Hayes blocks a shot at
Delmar while Leary Lentz (#30)
looks on, December 1965
(Courtesy of UH Athletic
Department)

The streak included a 112–84 victory over Lamar Tech, a 97–77 rematch win over Tulsa, a 125–96 rout of Centenary, and a 140–87 pounding of Southwestern University. The 140 points were a new single-game high for UH. In addition, Hayes set a new individual single-game scoring record at Houston with 55 points. He also set single-game records for most field goals with 24 and most rebounds with 30.

This unprecedented momentum carried the Cougars to a 111–96 victory over the Miami Hurricanes on February 17 and a whopping 152–108 rout of Texas Wesleyan College in a packed (as usual) Jeppesen Field House. In the TWC contest, the Cougars broke the first-half and single-game scoring records they had set just days earlier. They raced out with an 85-point first half and coasted to the win. Nine Houston players were in double figures, led by Hayes's 28 points. Don Chaney scored a season-high 20 points to go with his nine steals on defense.

At the time, the 152 points were just 2 points shy of the NCAA record for points scored in a game. Furman had scored 154 points in

1955. UH had numerous chances to tie the record in the last minute of the game but missed several easy opportunities.

"If I'd only made my layup," said Gary Grider. "We had several chances at the record. Lou Perry took a couple of shots. And Snuffy Starks. And John Tracy, too." Seldom-used John Tracy, who had been Don Chaney's white roommate when Chaney was a freshman, missed a layup at the final buzzer that would have enabled the Cougars to tie the record.

What now awaited UH was its game against the University of Dayton Flyers at Madison Square Garden in New York City on Thursday, February 24. The Flyers, like Houston, carried a 19–4 record into the contest. Madison Square Garden officials estimated the game would draw the largest crowd of their college basketball season, about 12,000.

The Flyers were led by 6-foot-11 senior center Hank Finkel, averaging 21 points a game, and by sophomore forward Don May, averaging the same number of points along with 12 rebounds per game. Guy V. Lewis said before the game, "For all it means to the team and school, it is our biggest game of the year. Dayton is a fine ball club, and it will take an all-out effort to beat them."

To add to the interest and importance of the game, it was announced one day before tipoff that both Dayton and Houston had been selected to play in the upcoming NCAA Tournament.

Unfortunately for the Cougars, they played their worst first half of the season, hitting only 23 percent of their shots, as Dayton raced out to a 37–21 lead at the break. Coach Lewis said, "I thought we were ready to play. That first half of basketball was the worst I've seen since I've been here coaching basketball. I thought we were going to have to burn the place down to get a basket."

The Flyers's lead extended to 45–26 with 15:45 to go. The Cougars got back into the game by using a full-court press, but May scored Dayton's last 4 points to seal the 71–69 win. Hank Finkel scored only 7 points, but he pulled down 17 rebounds. Hayes had 22 points and 17 rebounds, and Joe Hamood had 14 points and Don Chaney 13. Lewis was philosophical about the loss, saying, "Maybe this will help us in the long run. We did come back strong against a good club in the second half. We had a chance to win it."

The Cougars returned to the South to face two easy opponents: Portland at home and Loyola of New Orleans away. They beat Portland, 109–84, and wrapped up a 21–5 regular season three nights later with a 103–77 win over Loyola. In the latter game, the team received a scare in the second half when Hayes came down with a rebound with 14:04 left and sprained his left ankle, thus missing the rest of the game. During the time he did play, the Cougars put on a dunking clinic. Hayes managed 22 points, 15 rebounds, and five blocks. Joe Hamood matched Hayes's 22 points, and for the second straight game, Don Chaney scored 16.

Also of significance was that with the 103 points the Cougars scored against Loyola, UH became the highest-scoring regular season team in college basketball history, up to that point. They also became the first team to average 100 points a game for the regular season, scoring 2,601 points in 26 games.

* * * * * * *

Going into the NCAA Tournament, the Cougars got some good news. Two days after his ankle sprain in New Orleans, it was determined that Hayes's injury was not serious. Trainer Bob Smith said, "There was little or no swelling. He's ready to start working out."

The Cougars's first-round NCAA Tournament game was to be on Monday, March 7, in Wichita, Kansas, against Colorado State University. Excitement on the UH campus was building. Fans were offered two ways to travel to Wichita to see the game. Either they could travel on now-defunct Braniff Airlines for $39.50 round trip, or they could spend $44.50 and ride the Santa Fe Super Chief to Wichita.

Before the matchup with Colorado State, however, the accolades started pouring in for Elvin Hayes and the Cougars. Hayes was designated second-team All-America by the *Sporting News*. He ended the regular season ranked seventh nationally in scoring (27.2 points per game), ninth in field goal percentage (.565), and fifth in rebounding (16.9 rebounds per game).

Miami coach Bruce Hale said, "He's the best big man we've seen, sophomore, junior, or senior."

"He's the best I've seen," agreed Don Butcher of the Detroit Pistons. "He's so strong that if someone blocks his shot, he can still get it in the basket."

"He's the strongest I've played against," added Loyola's Barry Geraghty. "When he goes up for a shot, he takes you with him."

"He impressed me most," concluded Portland coach Al Negratti, "when he moved to the corner and hit a couple of jump shots. We didn't know he could do this."

Bob Feerick, general manager and scout for the San Francisco Warriors, was impressed with both Elvin Hayes and the entire Cougar basketball team: "I'll go on record and say Elvin Hayes is the best big man I've seen. I told Guy Lewis that Hayes could probably play for the Chicago Bulls, the new NBA team. They'll probably have the first draft rights the year Elvin graduates, and he'll probably be their first pick.

"He's small for a pro center, but he could play there. He has such tremendous physical ability. The thing about Hayes is he's already an outstanding ballplayer and there's still room for improvement. Like his driving. He drives well, but he needs to be smoother. It'll come. Boy, is he strong. Like Russell of the Celtics. That's who he reminds me of. There's no telling what that big guy will accomplish if he keeps improving. He and Alcindor of UCLA may dominate the game."

Feerick also said, "Guy Lewis's team at Houston is a really fine outfit. It could go all the way this year and win the national championship. I've seen a lot of the top teams this season, and it strikes me there is not a lot of difference in any of them. Houston has a strong outfit. It has Hayes for a big man, and that little guard, Joe Hamood, is a fine one. It has Wayne Ballard, who can hurt you outside, and this Lentz, listen, he's a fine player. Lentz is a lot better ballplayer than people think.

"I like Houston's chances. Guy can go to his bench and get help. Like this Chaney. He's a good ballplayer. And Kruse and Grider . . . Houston is a lot like Texas Western for that. Good starters and three or more guys on the bench who can go in and get the job done."

Coach Abe Lemons was always honest. He coached Oklahoma City University in the first round of the NCAA Tournament against eventual national champion Texas Western University. Lemons honestly

assessed his team's chances against the favorite. "We can't beat 'em,"
Lemons said. "Play them any way you want and they're tough." He
was speaking to Guy V. Lewis as the Cougars were working out at the
Wichita Field House in preparation for their game against Colorado
State the next night. "You guys are going all the way."

"All I'm concerned about right now is Colorado State," Lewis
responded.

"Ha," Lemons said. "You're going to be national champions. You'll
beat Colorado State. And we saw Oregon State play UCLA. They pass
the ball around so much it puts you to sleep. A two-footer is their idea
of a long shot."

Then on the day of the Cougars's game against Colorado State,
someone brought Lewis a copy of a Wichita newspaper with a banner
headline that said, "Houston to Win NCAA—Lemons." Guy Lewis
grabbed the paper and said, "Oh no! Doggone that Abe!"

Leary Lentz was also high on Houston's chances in the NCAA
Tournament. He recalled, "I thought we had the best team in the coun-
try that year. We started out slow, but because of the leadership of Joe
Hamood, we jelled as the season went on. We were just as good as
Texas Western or any of the other teams by the end of the season."

Colorado State presented a tough opening game. The Rams featured three top players: 6-foot-2 guard Lonnie Wright, who went on
to play for the Denver Broncos in the American Football League and
the Denver Rockets in the American Basketball Association; 6-foot-9
center Dale Schlueter, who played ten NBA seasons; and 6-foot-8 forward Bob Rule—the same Bob Rule that Guy Lewis had tried hard
to recruit from Jerry Tarkanian's Riverside Community College in the
spring of 1964. "We thought he was one of the best junior college
boys in the nation," Lewis said. "He can do everything, but he's only
the third-leading scorer for Colorado State, so you can tell what kind
of team they have."

The Rams gave the Cougars all they could handle in their opening round, UH eventually escaping with a hard-fought 82–76 victory.
The Cougars built an 11-point second half lead, but Hayes picked up
his fourth foul with 16:52 left in the second half and had to go to the

bench. Within two minutes, the Rams cut the Houston lead to two, 53–51. Hayes then reentered the game with 14:41 to go and his team built back its lead to 8 points and eased to the victory when Rule fouled out with 7:02 to go in regulation.

Hayes ended up with 18 points and 12 rebounds in limited playing time. As usual, Hamood helped pick up the slack with 23 points and five assists. Wayne Ballard chipped in 13 points and Chaney a season-high 11 rebounds. Rule led Colorado State with 18 points, including several baskets on dunks that rivaled those of Hayes, who might not have wound up playing for UH had Rule committed to Lewis in the spring of 1964. Hayes said of Rule, "He was tough. Man, he went up for a rebound one time so high I didn't even know where he was."

After the game, Abe Lemons—whose team lost, 89–74, to Texas Western in the late game in Wichita—spoke again on Houston's chances of winning the NCAA championship. "I wasn't trying to needle Guy with my earlier prediction," he said. "I'm a right good prognosticator. As a matter of fact, I was getting kind of mad there when Guy's team almost let Colorado State catch 'em. It'd made me look bad if Houston had lost."

The next matchup, in Los Angeles on March 11 at Pauley Pavilion, UCLA's brand-new arena, pitted the 22–5 Houston Cougars against the 20–6 Oregon State Beavers. The game would feature two teams with completely contrasting styles of play. As Lemons earlier alluded to, the Beavers played the game at a much slower pace than did Houston. They led the nation in defense, while the Cougars led in scoring. During the season, UH had taken almost a thousand more shots than Oregon State.

UCLA Coach John Wooden, whose 1965–66 team split their games with Oregon State, gave his assessment of the Beavers: "It's a very deliberate club, a sound club. It is also a very good club. It works for the shot it wants, and it will pass the ball around until it gets it."

The Beavers also were a very short team, their tallest player being 6-foot-6 center Ed Fredenburg. Forward Loy Peterson was their leading scorer at just 13.1 points per game. Interestingly, the other Oregon State forward and team captain, Charley White, was the team's first African American.

A couple days before the Houston–Oregon State game, Guy V. Lewis said, "The way we will play, that's what bothers me most. If we play well, and play our game, we'll be all right."

At the Cougars's last practice at Jeppesen two days before, they did not look sharp. "We're going to have to pick up our feet or we might as well forfeit to Oregon State," Lewis fumed. "We might as well stay home because we aren't going to win playing like we have today."

Then, as if the lethargic practice wasn't enough, late in practice the aforementioned fight between Elvin Hayes and Paul Ozug took place. Punches were landed, but the scuffle was brief. Rich Burk, reporter for the *Cougar*, said, "Even after the fight, the air in Jeppesen Field House was thick."

"I don't think the fight did a thing," Lewis said. "I don't know what's the matter with us."

Once the game finally unfolded, Oregon State won the battle of playing styles, holding the Cougars to almost 40 points under their season per-game average. The Beavers held on for a tight 63–60 win. The defense-oriented team worked and worked and worked some more for open shots, one time passing the ball 21 times before shooting. Rick Whelan led Oregon State with 24 points, with Loy Peterson adding 13 and ten rebounds, while Charley White chipped in 10 points and ten rebounds.

Houston held a slim 30–28 halftime lead, but Oregon State held Hayes to just 3 second-half points. For the game, Oregon State shot 62 percent from the field, while the Cougars shot just 31 percent. Hamood led the Cougars with 18 points, and Hayes ended up with 14 points and ten rebounds.

All that now remained in the 1965–66 season for the Houston Cougars was the consolation game the next night against the University of the Pacific. The Cougars bounced back from the Oregon State loss to defeat Pacific, 102–91, the 14th time UH went over 100 points in a game.

UH started slow, getting down 21–6 with 13:38 to go in the first half. Guy Lewis then benched all his starters except Hayes and inserted Paul Ozug, Gary Grider, Rich Apolskis, and Don Kruse into the lineup. The strategy worked. By halftime, the Cougars were up 47–43. The starters came back to start the second half and gradually extended the lead to 76–59 before coasting home with the victory. Hayes put up 31 points and 28 rebounds, while Hamood and Wayne Ballard scored 18 and 13 points, respectively—both in their last game in Cougar spangles.

After an inauspicious start to their varsity careers, Elvin Hayes and Don Chaney's sophomore season turned out well. After starting 0–3, the Cougars went 23–3 the rest of the way, with the losses being by 1, 2, and 3 points. Although the Cougars would lose the senior services of forward Wayne Ballard and the play and leadership of point guard Joe Hamood, plus the steady play of Rich Apolskis off the bench, the future looked bright for the 1966–67 season.

The season of UH's varsity basketball integration proved to be a huge success. One apparent comparison loomed in the near future and begged a key question: If given the opportunity to play in the Astrodome, would Hayes and Chaney fare better than Warren McVea had in his first indoor football game, when the Cougars lost to Tulsa?

13 THE *REAL* WONDROUS WARREN

Houston is the most explosive team I've seen.

—MEMPHIS STATE COACH BILLY "SPOOK" MURPHY

Interest and excitement about the 1966 Houston Cougar football season began almost as soon as the 1965 season ended with its 3–0–1 finish. Warren McVea, like the rest of the Cougars, redeemed himself in those last four games, and it looked like he and the team could have a breakout season.

Just two days after the 16–16 tie with Florida State, Bill Yeoman and others were already talking about the potential of 1966. Yeoman thought the Cougars would improve but also face a much tougher schedule. The just-concluded season had been challenging, with the opposing teams rolling up a 55–43–6 record, and 34 players from the Cougars's ten opponents were picked in the 1965 NFL draft, whereas no Cougars were.

"We'll be more experienced next year," Yeoman said, "and as a result, we should be better. We'll have more competition at the positions with the youngsters we have coming up, and I feel that will help."

Yeoman was encouraged by the way the Cougars performed in the last four games. "It's got to mean something to the kids," Yeoman said, smiling. "They now know they can go out there and play with anybody—that they're capable of beating the top teams. We won't have to worry about that part of it again."

Off campus, the positive end to the 1965 season appeared to be leading to more public interest in the program. In December 1965 and January 1966, just a couple miles from the University of Houston campus, the King Center Drive-In Theater, on the corner of Holmes Road and South Park Drive, showed highlights of the Cougars's 1965 season before the main feature.

However, the National Collegiate Athletic Association dealt a mighty blow to this great momentum in January. NCAA officials asked the UH to present findings of a university-conducted investigation of its own football program following "a complaint registered by a disgruntled former coach." After the facts were revealed, the NCAA placed the school on three years's probation, with no television or bowl appearances allowed for the 1966, 1967, and 1968 seasons.

The probation, which only covered football, was the fourth most severe penalty the NCAA had handed down up until this point in its history. Only Auburn, Indiana, and North Carolina State had ever suffered stiffer penalties, each of them affecting all sports.

The violations included providing free transportation to student athletes during holiday and semester breaks in 1963 and 1964, providing transportation for parents to freshman games in 1964, providing parents and friends of prospects plane tickets to Houston and excessive entertainment, and conducting winter and spring out-of-season football practice in 1964 and 1965.

Many people assumed that the violations were the result of the recruitment of Warren McVea. Some were, but the majority weren't, records showed. On October 1, 1967, some 20 months after the probation went into effect, Dan Cook of the *San Antonio Express-News* explained the violations in his column and talked about who was responsible for exposing them:

"J. D. Roberts was an assistant Houston coach and Bill Yeoman was head coach. That was fine with Yeoman but Roberts did not care for the arrangement. He wanted the positions reversed and he made this clear to Houston officials. They balked. In fact, they said no.

"Roberts then told of some wrong-doings that his fellow members on the Houston coaching staff were guilty of and he threatened to expose these things . . . he might have been using this information to chop down Yeoman.

"But whatever the case, Roberts wasn't bluffing. He went to the NCAA and blew the whistle. He blew it loud and clear. It was a matter of simple fact that shortly after he sang the sour song he was among Houston's unemployed."

According to Cook, part of the problem related to McVea involved his mother receiving transportation to Houston in the fall of 1964 to watch her son play in a Kittens game: "McVea became involved through the strong ties with his mother. She wanted to see him play a college game. Somebody on the Houston staff sent her a round trip plane ticket so she could go to Houston and see Warren play as a freshman."

Cook concluded by writing, "McVea makes a wonderful fall guy. But actually there were about four cases—besides the plane tickets for Mrs. McVea—that caught Houston in the homespun web."

Phil Woodring, a Cougar defensive end during the three years of probation and a time period when the Cougars fashioned a 21–7–2 record, said, "J. D. Roberts. He was something else. Not too many of the players were fond of him. What he did you don't do to your own people. All I know is he cost me three bowl rings."

Although the news of the three-year probation dealt the UH football program a large setback, they still had to prepare for the upcoming season. For the first time since Yeoman took over the program in 1962, the Cougars had a lot of experience on both sides of the football—eight offensive starters were returning, including five on the line. The skill positions looked solid, too, with Bo Burris back at quarterback, Dick

Post at running back, Ken Hebert at receiver, and Warren McVea at either running back or receiver. Three of the four defensive linemen were returning, along with three of the four spots in the secondary. Greg Brezina was the only holdover at linebacker, however.

Spring practice began on March 21 with a schedule that included four scrimmage games. The first would be in the East Texas town of Lufkin on March 25, the second in the Golden Triangle town of Nederland on April 2, the third against the varsity exes on April 15 at Jeppesen Stadium, and the fourth the annual red-and-white game at Grob Stadium in Spring Branch (on Houston's west side) on April 23.

Spring training did not bring forth the same excitement and anticipation as the arrival of Warren McVea on the varsity team had the previous year. The spring training 1966 scrimmage crowds were, in fact, disappointing. For example, in the spring of 1965, the Cougars scrimmage in San Antonio had brought an overflow crowd of 10,000, who had shown up hoping to catch a glimpse of their hometown star. Another at Jeppesen Stadium had drawn 4,500. When Yeoman's team played its first scrimmage of 1966 in Lufkin, only 500 fans appeared. The final scrimmage in Spring Branch—about 15 miles from the UH campus—drew just 1,500.

Although the crowds and the fanfare seemed lighter, Warren McVea had a good spring. He was not hampered by injuries and played well at the flanker position. At Lufkin, he caught four passes from Bo Burris for 71 yards and two touchdowns. In the first half of the exes game, he scored on an 88-yard pass from Burris and a 14-yarder from Dick Woodall before sitting out the second half.

Going into the summer, McVea got two other boosts. Yeoman felt his star player needed to have a healthier, more durable season. A weight-lifting regimen would do the trick. Even more significant, Yeoman decided to have running back Dickie Post work with McVea in the weight room. When McVea had first arrived on campus, the incumbent star running back had not immediately accepted him. "Being from Pauls Valley, Oklahoma, Dickie had some of that inbred Southern racism in him," tight end Tom Beers said. "He was very standoffish. It wasn't just with Warren, though. He was that way with players from up North, too. You know, Yankees. Me, being from Michigan, it took him a while to warm up to me. The same thing with Warren—it took a while."

McVea had his own views: "Assistant Coach J. D. Roberts did not like blacks, period. He never spoke to me. Being from Oklahoma, he got in Dick Post's head. He was telling him I might take his job. We didn't get along at first. Coach Yeoman made us work out together over the summer. Dickie was a big-time weightlifter. We ended up being friends. I ended up having a good season in 1966. I was in shape and more durable."

The other factor that helped relieve the stress for McVea was the arrival of additional African American players on the team. Now with McVea would be fullback Paul Gipson, flanker and return specialist Don Bean, and backup fullback J. B. Keys.

Paul Gipson, out of Washington High School in Conroe, Texas, 30 miles north of Houston, eventually became the workhorse running back in 1967 and 1968. At Washington High, it was rumored that in his senior season, Gipson averaged almost 30 yards per carry running the football.

Once he settled in as the starting fullback, Gipson ran for 1,100 yards in 1967 and 1,550 yards his senior season in 1968, earning second-team All-America honors. He ended up being a second-round draft pick of the Atlanta Falcons in 1969. Unfortunately, his pro career was cut short by injury.

Dick Woodall, the starting quarterback in 1967, said, "Gipson ended up being our best offensive player, and we had some good ones—Warren, Ken Hebert, etc. Paul could block, too. He was a physical specimen."

"Paul was a magnificent player," Yeoman said, "and a great person, too. I think it was Paul who helped speed up integration of Southeastern Conference football teams.

"Let me tell you why. In 1968, the year after Warren left, we were playing Ole Miss in Jackson. One of our alumni and boosters, Charlie Jones, was sitting by this Ole Miss fan who, early in the game, kept hollering, 'Give the ball to Leroy!' over and over, obviously meaning give the ball to Paul.

Paul Gipson, circa 1967
(Courtesy of Myron McReynolds)

"I could hear this guy down on the sidelines. He was being that loud. Well, Paul ran over Ole Miss that day. He had over 200 yards and two touchdowns, and we won 29–7. By the end of the game, that Ole Miss fan was saying, 'We've got to get ourselves some Leroys!'

"The next week, we go to Athens, Georgia, to play Georgia. They were undefeated and we tied them 10–10, even though we ran all over them. Well, Paul ran for like 230 yards against them. The Ole Miss game and the Georgia game changed a lot of attitudes in the SEC. People are very serious about their football down there, and they would not accept their losing, and they would especially not accept losing to a football team whose workhorse is a black running back. That was something the people down there would not accept nor tolerate.

"What that Ole Miss fan meant when he hollered, 'We gotta get us some Leroys!' was, if we have to go get our own black players to win football games, let's do it. I think their fans also picked up on how wonderfully the black players conducted themselves on and off the field when we went to play in the South. Our guys conducted themselves with class and dignity. It was not long after those games that the SEC started to integrate."

In an interview years later, former Miami Dolphins All-Pro safety Jake Scott recalled his days at Georgia and confirmed what Yeoman had said about running over the Bulldogs. When asked what his most profound on-field memory at Georgia was, Scott replied, "I guess when we got lucky and tied Houston in 1968, 10–10. We went 8–0–2 and Houston just kicked the hell out of us.

"We got lucky and tied it up. Afterward, Coach [Vince] Dooley said, 'I hope we can meet them again in a bowl somewhere.' And teammate Brad Johnson and I looked at each other and said, 'I guess he wasn't at the same game we were at; I don't want to see those guys again.' That's a true story."

"If you looked it up, they killed us," Scott continued, "Erk Russell, our defensive coordinator, said we were going to have to hold them to 200 yards rushing. I think they had 220 yards rushing in the first half, and they fumbled like five times inside our two-yard line.

"But that was an embarrassing game, and we got lucky to tie. They were running the Veer option and we couldn't stop them. We got lucky at the end of the game, and Jim McCullough kicked a field goal to tie the game for us. We had a great football team, we really did. We could play with anyone at the time, except maybe Houston."

Another African American player on the UH roster for the first time in 1966 was Don Bean, a Beaumont native who came out of Hebert High School in 1964. While at Hebert, Bean played in the same football backfield as future All-Americans Jerry LeVias, who went to SMU, and Mel Farr, who attended UCLA, as well as Jerry Ball Sr., father of future NFL All-Pro nose guard Jerry Ball Jr. Those four also ran track on the same 4×100 relay team that set a national record.

Bubba Smith, who went to neighboring Charlton-Pollard High School, said of Jerry Ball, "He was a 9.4 sprinter who went off to college for a little while, but he got a girl pregnant and he didn't want to leave her, so he ended up coming home. Believe me, he was just as good as those other three guys in that backfield and relay team."

"I was the biggest and slowest on that relay team," Mel Farr said. "That shows you how much talent we had. LeVias was the fastest at 9.5. Jerry Ball ran a 9.6, Bean ran a 9.7, and I ran a 9.8. We were state champs in the 4×100, and we set a national record. We never lost a race while I was in high school."

Don Bean went to Drake University as a freshman but ended up at Southern Missouri Junior College. It was there that Cougar assistant coach Bum Phillips heard of Bean because of his coaching connections in the Beaumont area. As Bean was heading back to Drake after a year at Southern Missouri, he was informed that the University of Houston wanted him.

Don Bean turned out to be a valuable return man for the 1966 and 1967 Cougars. In the spring of 1967, Bean also became the first African American baseball player at the University of Houston.

The third new black to play on the 1966 football team was backup fullback J. B. Keys. A native of Hamtramck, Michigan, the same hometown as Cougar teammate Tom Paciorek, Keys described how he became a Cougar. "Coming out of high school, I was set to play at Michigan State, but it turned out I didn't have the grades. I ended up going to Eastern Arizona Junior College. After a couple of years there, I ended up at Houston because Bill Yeoman knew my high school coach from his days back at Michigan State.

"Unfortunately, in my second year at Eastern Arizona, I messed up my ankle. It never really fully healed, and I lost a lot of speed. In fact, Coach Yeoman said after I got to UH, 'You're not as fast as I thought you were.'

"I had a great time at the University of Houston, though. Although I didn't get to play much, I got to play with some great players and teams, and I got my education.

"There was also no animosity over race at UH on our team. I had no problems. When I first came to UH in the summer of 1966, I rode down from Michigan with Tom Beer. He was a really good guy. Tom Paciorek and Bo Burris were two of the best guys I've met. There were a couple of times during games some of the black guys were called names, and Tom and Bo were the first guys to come to our defense."

Another change for the 1966 Cougar football team was the new playing surface in the Houston Astrodome. After the disastrous attempt to play on grass in 1965, Harris County Domed Stadium officials replaced the dead grass with a new synthetic playing surface called Astroturf.

Astroturf, manufactured by Monsanto Corporation, eventually became the standard playing surface for most college and professional teams for the next 30 to 35 years until it was gradually replaced by field turf. So the UH Cougars, who in their 1965 season opener against Tulsa became the first football team to play indoors, would also become—in their September 23, 1966, opening game against the Washington State Cougars—the first team to play a game on Astroturf.

*   *   *   *   *   *   *

As the summer passed and football season got closer, optimism abounded. Coach Yeoman gathered the Cougars together for a team meeting a couple days before fall practice started on September 1. The team would be preparing for its first game of the season, against Florida State in Tallahassee—the same venue where UH ended the 1965 season with a 16–16 tie. Yeoman was very optimistic. He said, "It's gonna be fun to go out and practice with this squad."

The coach soon got some disappointing news. Another African American slated to be on the 1966 roster was sophomore wide receiver James Harris, who was expected to battle for a starting role. Right as fall practice began, Harris was removed from the team.

Quarterback Bo Burris described what happened. Harris was a wide receiver capable of earning a starting position. "He was a great athlete," Burris said. "He was 6-foot-1 and could easily dunk a basketball like it was nothing. Well, apparently he robbed a drug store in the Richmond/Rosenberg area, and that was the last we heard from him."

Yeoman was counting on numerous players who were returning to the offensive and defensive lines and the skill positions. The Cougars arguably had the best skill position players in the country in 1966 and 1967. Sometimes it was questioned why McVea wasn't utilized more in the offense during his career. Injuries played a factor, but, as Yeoman said, "We had the best backfield in the country, bar none."

McVea agreed: "We did have the best skill players out there. Also, when Coach Yeoman went to the Veer, neither Dick Post nor I were much in the way of blockers. I was only 182 pounds, so I moved to flanker, and Paul Gipson went to fullback until he got hurt and then suspended. I then went back to running back. But we spread the ball around in 1966 and '67 because we had so many good skill players."

All the starting skill-position players from the team went on to play professional football: tight end Tom Beer, fullback Paul Gipson, running back Dick Post, quarterback Bo Burris, wide receiver Kenny Hebert, and flanker/running back Warren McVea.

At fall practice, Yeoman also found some younger players to fill positions of need. Stepping in at right offensive tackle was sophomore Bill Cloud. On defense, three sophomores became starters. In the secondary, Johnny Peacock became the new starter at left cornerback. In the linebacking corps, highly touted high school All-American Skippy Spruill from Odessa would man the middle linebacker spot, while defensive coordinator Bum Phillips's son, Wade, would play right side linebacker.

The Cougars had not won a road game since the 1962 Tangerine Bowl. The week before they opened the new season at Florida State on September 17, the team held its final preseason scrimmage. Burris threw for three touchdowns, and Don Bean showed his potential as a return man with a 75-yard punt return touchdown.

UH being on probation for the season did not appear to dampen its enthusiasm for the upcoming season. Tom Beer said, "The probation won't prevent us from winning ten games and the national championship."

As for the opening game, Florida State's weakness appeared to be on defense, as they had returned only four starters, while the Houston offense had returned eight. The host team had received bad news when it found out its best defensive lineman, Mike Bugar, would be lost for the season with a knee injury. But being the home team seemed to play to Florida State's favor, for the Seminoles had not lost a home opener since 1959. Even so, the Cougars were installed as a slight favorite to win.

UH used turnovers and big plays to defeat their hosts, 21–13, at Doak Campbell Stadium. Florida State ran a school-record 91 plays, compared to the Cougars's 45. The Seminoles also outgained UH, 368 yards to 237, and held the ball for 38 of the 60 minutes. One of the keys to Houston's victory was seven Florida State turnovers, including three interceptions by defensive back Tom Paciorek.

The other key for Houston was the big play. Florida State broke out to a 7–0 lead after a game-opening 92-yard drive, but a short time later, they missed a 20-yard field goal attempt. McVea and the Cougars struck back. Starting at their own 20-yard line after the missed field goal, Burris hit McVea about 15 yards downfield, and McVea easily outraced the defenders 80 yards for a touchdown, tying the game at 7–7 early in the second quarter.

Then after a Paciorek interception that gave the Cougars the ball on the Florida State 33-yard line, Burris hit wide receiver Ken Hebert two plays later with a 28-yard scoring strike to make the score 14–7 Cougars.

Early in the third quarter, the Cougars used another big play on special teams to extend their lead. Dick Spratt returned a punt 81 yards for a touchdown to increase the margin to 21–7.

The Seminoles added a fourth quarter touchdown, but that was as close as they got. Sophomore defensive back Johnny Peacock, making his first start, picked off a Florida State pass at the Cougar 3-yard line with 31 seconds to play to seal the victory.

* * * * * * *

The next Cougar game was a Friday night affair on September 23 in the Astrodome against Washington State, in history's first football game on Astroturf. Fortunately for UH and McVea, this season's home opener turned out much better than the one against Tulsa the year before. The Cougars prevailed, 21–7, before 36,108 fans.

McVea had another solid game. He caught three passes for 128 yards, rushed four times for 45 yards, and returned two kicks for 51 yards. Dick Post added 108 yards rushing and caught an 11-yard touchdown pass from Burris in the second quarter, and later the same two combined on a 29-yard scoring pass.

Washington State struck quickly in the first quarter on their opening drive as wide receiver Doug Flansburg scored the first-ever touchdown on artificial surface when he grabbed an eight-yard scoring pass from quarterback Jerry Henderson for an early 7–0 lead.

The highlight of the game, however, happened just before Post's third-quarter touchdown. Houston was backed up to its own six-inch line after a Washington State punt, when lightning struck. Burris described the next play: "The 99-yard touchdown pass to Warren in the Dome. It was 7–7 in the third quarter. Joe Arenas, the receivers coach, of course wanted to pass. He always wanted to pass on every down—he claimed there was someone open on every play.

"So Coach Yeoman shoves me in the game from the sidelines, and we were going to run a quarterback sneak. However, Bill Pickens, our right guard, was offsides on the play, and we were backed up even further, if that was possible. I called the next play—I had never done that before. I just threw the ball to a spot. Warren reached out for it—he had little hands, but the ball stuck. He caught it at about our own 44, and by the time he was at the 50-yard line, he was all alone."

The record-setting 99-yard touchdown pass gave the Cougars a 14–7 lead that they never relinquished. The final score was 21–7. Tight end Tom Beer summed up the feelings of many Houston players and coaches when he said, "I think we can keep up with anyone in the country."

In the days following the victory, the team found itself ranked No. 16 in the weekly United Press International coaches's poll. Its next opponent, the Oklahoma State Cowboys, would challenge that honor on October 1 under the Dome. Previously, the Cowboys had taken perennial Southwest Conference powerhouse Arkansas to the wire before losing, 14–10, on a last-minute Razorbacks touchdown. The Cowboys knew well the fleetness of the Houston team based on their scouting reports. James Dickey, former UH assistant, then on the OSU staff, said, "Houston is one of the fastest teams in the country. If they're having a hot night, it's something to see."

And quarterback Bo Burris did have a hot night. UH won, 35–9, before 43,743 Astrodome fans—the largest football crowd yet to be seated indoors. They saw Burris throw five touchdown passes to put the entire home team's score on the board. Beer caught three of them from 15, 5, and 17 yards out. Post reeled in a 5-yard score, and Ken Hebert caught a 48-yard bomb. Also, Don Bean flashed his big-play potential by returning the second-half kickoff 59 yards, and he later caught a 73-yard scoring pass from backup quarterback Dick Woodall, though the play was called back for holding.

McVea served mostly as a decoy, frequently double-teamed at his wide receiver position. He was shut out from receiving, but he said, "I don't know how many men they had on me. When they double-teamed me, though, it leaves someone else open."

Later in the game, when Paul Gipson suffered a thigh bruise, McVea switched to running back and contributed 58 yards on just six carries.

While the offense obviously performed well, it was the defense under the direction of Bum Phillips that impressed Coach Yeoman, who said, "This was the first time our defense has been able to contain a team in a long time. I don't know what happened. If I did, I'd sell it."

The Cougars now had an extra week to prepare for an Astrodome matchup against Mississippi State on October 15. The Bulldogs had embarrassed the Cougars in the Astrodome, 36–0, the previous season. Houston defensive tackle Paul Otis stated the week before the game, "We haven't forgotten the way they walked over us last year. They humiliated us, and since then maybe we've learned about revenge, too."

Another record-setting crowd of 47,870 showed up for the game. They saw their favorites whitewash the Bulldogs, 28–0, after getting off to a fast start with 14 points in the first quarter and never letting up after leading 21–0 at the half. Gipson scored the opening touchdown on a 1-yard run, the first touchdown on the ground for Houston in the 1966 season. Dick Post scored the second touchdown on a 9-yard scamper and ended up with 83 yards on 19 carries. George Nordgren, who had been a substitute player the first three games, ran for 80 yards on 9 carries and scored from the 5-yard line in the third quarter.

The one negative that came out of the Mississippi State game was the injury situation at skilled positions. Beer broke his right hand, and Paul Gipson injured his shoulder, forcing him to sit out the second half, thus providing Nordgren a timely opportunity. McVea, who had zero yards in the game rushing or receiving, was the victim of a cheap shot on the sidelines by a Mississippi State defender in the second quarter, putting McVea out the rest of the game with a bad ankle.

In the postgame, Bulldog coach Paul Davis offered numerous superlatives to describe UH: "Houston has a great football team. They have as much team speed as anyone I've ever seen. Tonight, Houston was better. Houston has so much quickness: in the line, in the backfield, in the secondary.

"Bo Burris did a great job of picking us apart. We felt we had to stop him, and we couldn't. We wanted to put pressure on him. There were several times back there we should have had him, but he got away. He's awfully quick. Burris and Spurrier are pretty close in abilities."

The coach was referring to Florida quarterback Steve Spurrier, who would eventually win the 1966 Heisman Trophy.

Yeoman also had praise for his Cougars, who now stood at 4–0, the best start in school history. "I'm pleased with the progress," Yeoman noted, "but we have a long way to go. I thought Burris had an outstanding evening, and the defense performed very well. The kids are more attuned mentally. They have a great deal of pride in what they are doing."

Despite the undefeated start to their season, the Cougars still lacked respect in the national polls. They were still ranked 16th in the UPI poll, the same spot they occupied after the Washington State game. In the Associated Press poll, which in the 1960s only ranked the top ten teams, the Cougars were among several teams in the "Also Receiving Votes" category.

The next challenge would be the annual matchup with Ole Miss on October 22. The revenge-minded Rebels, who had lost their first-ever game to Houston the year before, carried an uncustomary 3–2 record into the game. It was evident that the Rebels were now taking the Cougars seriously. The week started with Ole Miss coach John Vaught refusing to exchange game films with Houston. In response, Yeoman said, "I got quite an inkling they are viewing us differently than in past years when they wouldn't exchange game films with us.

"I have great respect for Coach Vaught and his team. They may do the same thing, but they do it well. He'll test you every conceivable way you can be tested. They're definitely the finest defensive team we've ever been exposed to." Yeoman was not exaggerating with his assessment of the defense. Led by All-America defensive tackle Jim Urbanek, the Rebels ranked second in the nation in total defense.

In the first four games of the 1966 University of Houston football season, no mention was made by the media, UH coaches, or Houston players about any type of racial incidents, either on the field or off. That, however, changed when the Cougars played Ole Miss in Memphis, Tennessee. First of all, there was some disagreement as to why the game was played in Memphis instead of the two usual home fields the Rebels used—in Oxford and Jackson, Mississippi. Some felt it was because UH had African American players and no such players had yet to play college football in Mississippi against white players.

Cougar offensive tackle Rich Stotter recalled, "The Ole Miss game in Memphis? I think the game was supposed to be in Jackson. I heard there were some veiled threats. We really didn't know what was going on with moving the game. Were there threats directed at Warren? I don't know for sure."

Dick Woodall added, "We played in Memphis in 1966 because they wouldn't let us into Oxford because of Warren, Don, and Paul."

However, Sports Information Director Ted Nance said, "Ole Miss had played a lot of prior 'home' games in Memphis, usually about one a year. They had a large fan base in Memphis, and when they played there, fewer students showed up, and that meant more alumni could buy tickets.

"Also, there was a group from Memphis promoting their new stadium, the Liberty Bowl, and they worked to get the game there. Hey, we were happy to play in Memphis. Whenever we would play in Oxford or Jackson, we would have to fly into Memphis and then take a bus there."

Once the team arrived in Memphis, the racial incidents and abuse quickly followed. The first incident happened at the airport. Fullback J. B. Keys, the fourth African American on the UH team, made his first road game when Paul Gipson's injured shoulder required him to remain in Houston. Keys recalled, "When we arrived in Memphis on the Friday before the game, airport officials met us at the plane. Usually your plane taxis up to the terminal and you enter the terminal to get where you need to go.

"In Memphis, we got off the plane on the tarmac, and there was a bus waiting for us to take us to the hotel. They did that so we wouldn't have to go through the terminal. I think they did it for security purposes, because maybe they thought there might be a problem if Warren, Don, and myself walked through the terminal."

When the team left the hotel the next morning to go to the stadium, they encountered abuse from fans. "The fans started in on us as soon as we came out of the hotel to get on the bus to go to the stadium," Woodall said. "Then the fans got on us again with more racial remarks when we got to the stadium, and the same thing happened getting back on the bus and going to the hotel."

Keys described another event that occurred with his white teammates before the game. "As players, we always got two tickets to each game, home and away," he said, "and they were always excellent seats. Well, before the game, since none of us knew anyone in Memphis, some of my white teammates gave their tickets to some little black kids.

"During the game, I remember looking up in the stands around the 50-yard line, about where the seats were, to see if the kids were up there. They weren't; they were made to go sit in the end zone where nobody was."

Then just before the game, one more incident took place. "I very likely wasn't going to play in the Ole Miss game," Keys said, "so Coach Yeoman told me before the game to stay right beside him at all times. As we were coming out of the tunnel to go into the stadium, Ole Miss was there, too. I remember one of the referees who was standing there said to Coach Vaught, 'Coach, how bad are we gonna beat 'em today?' Coach Yeoman couldn't believe his ears."

Before a disappointing crowd in Memphis of just 14,118, Ole Miss upset the error-prone Cougars, 27–6. UH turned the ball over nine times, including Burris's seven interceptions.

The Rebels only had to go a total of 76 yards to score 20 of their 27 points, thanks to these gifts. In addition, McVea dropped a certain

8-yard touchdown pass late in the second quarter that would have cut into the Rebels's 17–0 lead. On the very next play, Ole Miss intercepted a Burris pass at the 3-yard line. Although McVea would go on to catch three passes for 90 yards, he sat out the fourth quarter when his bad ankle stiffened up. "There's no way I should have broken loose those three times and not scored," he later said. "I just couldn't go on the ankle."

Tight end Tom Beer may have been able to haul in a Burris pass in the end zone, but the ball grazed his fingers before falling incomplete. "I had broken my hand the week before against Mississippi State." Beer said. "I had a padded cast on it for the Ole Miss game. Their coaches complained before the game, and the referees made me take it off.

"On the pass in the end zone, I touched the ball with my hands. I could have caught it with a pair of good hands. We played poorly though—a bunch of turnovers. Warren dropped a touchdown pass, too."

One of the reasons for the Rebels's success was their ability to steal Houston's play signals from the sidelines. Two Ole Miss players confirmed this fact of life that Saturday. Quarterback Bruce Newell said, "We beat Houston in Memphis pretty good. We had a bunch of interceptions. One of our coaches was stealing their signals."

Urbanek added, "In Memphis against Houston in 1966, we got Bo Burris frustrated. We had stolen their signals. It's a lot easier to intercept a pass if you know where the ball is going ahead of time."

After the game, Yeoman learned of the stolen signals. For the rest of the 1966 season, the Cougars alternated left offensive tackles Bill Cloud and Larry Perez to deliver the plays to Burris in the huddle.

Although the Cougars outgained the Rebels and had more first downs, they lost the war because of the turnovers. Rich Stotter said after the game, "It's one thing to get blown off the field, but another when you lose it yourself."

One of the few highlights was the first touchdown in a Cougar uniform for Don Bean. Replacing the injured McVea at wide receiver in the fourth quarter, Bean hauled in a 29-yard scoring pass from Burris to account for the only UH points.

"The fans were terrible in Memphis, with the taunts and the name-calling," Keys said.

"The only time I really remember the racism and taunts being really bad was when we played Ole Miss in Memphis in 1966," Dick Woodall recalled. "We heard it all at the game. I was right there close to the stands and could hear it all because Bo [Burris] started and I didn't play."

"Ole Miss was rough," said Warren McVea. "Their fans called me everything in the book from the stands."

After the season was over, though, McVea had kudos for the Ole Miss players. "Mississippi was the cleanest team we played last season," he said, "but I can't say as much for their fans."

Then, as if the sting of losing their undefeated status to Mississippi wasn't bad enough, on the Wednesday following the game, Yeoman suspended seven players for a curfew violation for the rest of the season. They even had to move out of the athletic dorms. Included in the suspensions were starting defensive end Royce Berry and fullback Paul Gipson.

Burris recalled how Gipson's injury and then his suspension affected the Cougars. "It's too bad Paul got hurt early in '66 and then got suspended," Burris said. "If he would have been at full speed and been able to play all season, we could have been even better."

"It was my low point at UH," Berry said. "We had just lost a big game to Mississippi in Memphis, and the following Tuesday we had a curfew, but I went to La Marque to go on a date. I got caught. It was my fault and my fault only."

Yeoman said the players would be allowed to participate in spring practice but added, "We're here to win football games, and we have to do it as a team, not individuals."

The coach then spoke of the effect of the suspensions: "Practice went about 1,000 percent better out there today. If those boys think they are upset, they should have seen me Tuesday night."

The suspension of Berry and Gipson meant adjustments had to be made. Backup George Caraway stepped into Berry's defensive end spot, while McVea slid over from wide receiver to running back, with Don Bean taking McVea's wide receiver role. Obviously happy with the move, McVea said, "This is where I want to stay for the next year and a half."

This distraction behind them, the Cougars geared up to face the University of Tampa Spartans on October 29 in the Astrodome. Although the Spartans had compiled a respectable 3–2 record, UH was listed as a 32-point favorite.

The Cougars covered the point spread and then some with their 48–9 rout of Tampa before 41,182 fans. Burris attempted only 16 passes, completing 8 for 246 yards, but four of the completions went for touchdowns. Ken Hebert, in probably his finest game as a Cougar, caught all four, ending the night with five catches for 205 yards, including bombs of 46 and 86 yards. Since he also kicked the extra points, he wound up with a school-record 30 points on the night.

The Cougar offense churned out 484 total yards. Dick Post, in his first game at fullback, churned out 118 yards on 15 carries and scored two touchdowns, one on a 24-yard pass from Burris and the other on a 23-yard second-quarter run.

McVea, in his first game at running back, ran eight times for just 18 yards and caught two passes for 30 yards. Also, not to be totally outdone, the Cougar defense picked off a school-record six Spartan passes on the evening.

After the game, Tampa coach Sam Bailey lavished praise on the Cougars for their team speed and specifically on Ken Hebert: "I've been in the football racket for 30 years, and this Houston team is the fastest I've ever seen. If we had two backs, either on offense or defense, with the speed of McVea or Hebert, there could have been 20 points difference. We just couldn't cover them all. Houston just plain outran us. Ken Hebert is the best receiver I've ever seen."

Next up in the Astrodome on November 5 was the Tulsa Hurricane, who had won the last three games in the series, including the 14–0 opening game of 1965 in the Astrodome debut of the Cougars and McVea's awful start to his varsity career.

Coming into the Houston game, for the fifth year in a row, the Hurricane was leading the nation in passing, while UH ranked ninth. Neal Sweeny had replaced 1965 All-America wide receiver Howard Twilley as the No. 1 wide-out. Sweeny came into the game with 45 receptions for 603 yards. The Hurricane also featured probably the biggest player in college football at that time: 313-pound defensive tackle Joe Blake.

Besides their awesome offense, the Hurricane, at 4–2, had a defense that had given up only 77 points in six games. Included as one of their victories was a 57–11 triumph over Tampa, the team the Cougars had just defeated.

In one of the finest performances ever by a UH football team, the Cougars almost matched the 77 points the Hurricane gave up in its first six games. UH rolled up a 73–14 blowout before 42,061 fans at the Astrodome.

If McVea had gotten off to a slow start in his first game at running back the week before against Tampa, and a bad start to his college career the year before with his four-fumble performance against Tulsa, he got his shot at redemption in this Tulsa game. He did all his damage in the first half as he rang up 160 yards rushing on just 11 carries, including a 5-yard touchdown run. On his only carry of the second half, he lost 2 yards.

But McVea was far from the only Cougar with a big day. The Cougars set school records for most points in a game with 73, most points in a half with 45 in the first half, most total yards from scrimmage with 585, and most rushing yards in a game with 433. Individually, Don Bean set a school record with five punt returns for 199 yards, including touchdown returns of 66 and 63 yards. Post ran for 124 yards and a touchdown, and Bo Burris had three short touchdown runs of 2, 1, and 1 yard.

After the game, mammoth Hurricane defensive tackle Joe Blake said, "I never thought any team would beat us this bad. They're the quickest team we've seen. McVea impressed me, but so did Post. He keeps churning and doesn't give up."

Tulsa linebacker Bob Buoniconti added, "One of the finest teams we've played. We heard about Post and McVea and Burris. We didn't know much about Bean. And that Post? He just doesn't go down."

"As I told Coach Yeoman," Tulsa coach Glenn Dobbs said after the game, "I think, tonight, this was the finest football team I've ever seen. They gave a tremendous effort, had great execution on offense, and were thorough with their play. They were just outstanding."

"We're big and slow. You can't catch those bugs—the type Houston has—with our big and slow ones. We can't come anywhere close to boys like McVea and Bean and even some of the others."

* * * * * * *

After the dominating win over Tulsa, the next matchup for the Cougars was a November 12 road contest in Lexington to take on the Kentucky Wildcats in their Homecoming game. After the Tulsa game, the Cougars found themselves leading the nation in total offense. In contrast, the 3–4–1 Wildcats led the nation in pass defense.

During the week of the game, however, the Cougars received some disappointing news that would affect their passing and return game. Don Bean, who had his finest performance the week before against Tulsa, was held out of the Kentucky game when questions arose about his eligibility. Bean had supposedly signed a letter of intent to play football at Drake University before coming to UH. There was no violation of NCAA rules, but UH decided to hold Bean out of action until the matter could be cleared up.

Luckily, the Cougars didn't need him. The offense had its second record-setting week in a row with a 56–18 mauling of the Wildcats. The Cougars set another single-game team mark for yards in a game with 649, beating the total from the previous week against Tulsa. Post and McVea combined for 335 yards on the ground, as Post had his best day ever as a Cougar with 187 yards on 24 carries, while McVea added 148 more yards on just 14 attempts. McVea broke off a wild 63-yard first-quarter scamper, as he dodged five defenders, and added two touchdown runs of 32 and 13 yards. Post added a 40-yard score on the ground, and Hebert hauled in a 60-yard touchdown pass from Burris.

Hebert recalled the game years later: "Post was great. He scored on a long draw play. In the second half, things got a little rough on the sidelines. I guess because they were getting beat so bad, some of their fans had a little too much to drink. The fans started throwing their half pint and pint liquor bottles at us. Bum Phillips advised us to keep our helmets on so we wouldn't get nailed.

Warren McVea cuts
upfield, 1966
(Courtesy of UH
Athletic Department)

"Since we had Warren, some people may have thought the fans throwing bottles may have been a racial thing—it wasn't. They were frustrated because they were getting their hats handed to them."

"We were everybody's Homecoming game before the Kentucky game," Yeoman also recalled years later. "But after that, everything changed. We were nobody's Homecoming game anymore."

Since Gipson was suspended, and Don Bean was held out of the game, and J. B. Keys did not play against the Wildcats, McVea became the first African American to play against Kentucky in Lexington at Stoll Field, which, in 1880, had been home to the first college football game ever played in the South, between Kentucky and Vanderbilt.

After the game, compliments for the Cougar team, Post, and McVea poured in. Charlie Bradshaw, the Kentucky coach, remarked, "Our people wanted to play, and were ready to play, even though Houston made us look futile at times."

Former SMU player and Heisman Trophy–winner Doak Walker scouted the game for the Denver Broncos and had high praise for Post, saying, "His height is a definite question mark. But I think some pro team will take a chance on him. When you're that small, desire is the most important part of making it. Personally, I'd have to lean toward the little man making it."

Walker was correct. When Post left UH, he was picked in the fourth round of the 1967 NFL draft by the San Diego Chargers. He was the AFL Rookie of the Year in 1967 and in 1969 was the AFL's leading rusher in the league's last year of existence with 873 yards. A knee injury in 1970 curtailed Post's career, however.

Now 7–1, the Cougars had an extra week off to prepare for their last two games of the season. Meanwhile, they rose back up to 14th in the UPI poll. The Cougars were leading the nation in scoring and total offense, averaging 36 points per game and 434.1 total yards. They also had an extremely balanced offensive attack, with their Veer offense averaging 220.8 yards per game rushing—10th in the nation— and 213.3 yards per game passing—11th nationally. And the Cougar defense had allowed only 97 points in eight games.

McVea also had a chance to break two national records with two games remaining. He stood a chance to break the NCAA records for most yards per catch and most yards per rushing attempt. Pete Dawkins of Army held the record of 30.9 yards per reception. McVea was averaging 29.5 yards per catch on 13 receptions and only needed two more catches to meet the minimum qualifying standard. The rushing record was one McVea could surpass but probably not break. One hundred rushes minimum were needed to qualify, and through eight games, he had only 46 rushing attempts. However, on those attempts, he was averaging 9.4 yards per carry.

On Monday, November 21, five days before the Memphis State game in the Astrodome, UH awarded Yeoman a new five-year contract.

The school also renewed each of his assistant coaches and gave them raises. The Cougars, having lost only 1 game in their last 12, had compiled the best two-year record among all college teams in Texas.

UH president Philip G. Hoffman said, "Yeoman has demonstrated competence as a coach and in the large dimension of building a sound, long-range football program which produces not only well-trained athletes but good students and future leaders."

Athletic Director Harry Fouke added, "Bill Yeoman and his staff provide an outstanding combination of leadership and technical knowledge of the game. The new contract means continued strength and added impetus in building the well-rounded athletic program which is our goal at the University."

Hal Lundgren of the *Houston Post* mentioned additional factors involved: "Under Yeoman, Houston has surpassed its attendance record two successive years, moved into the Dome for indoor football, and broken the color line by recruiting Warren McVea in 1964."

The Cougars reached No. 11 in the UPI poll. The only setback during this otherwise glorious week was the decision to hold Don Bean out of play because of the eligibility question.

The Memphis State Tigers proved to be far from a pushover. They had already fashioned a fine 6–2 record, and the rumor was that a win over Houston would send the Tigers to the Liberty Bowl in their hometown of Memphis. They were considered to be a fine defensive team, having shut out Tulsa earlier in the season.

In what was becoming almost a weekly ritual among opposing coaches, Memphis State coach Billy "Spook" Murphy spoke glowingly about the Houston offense, calling it "the most explosive team in the country."

"We beat Tulsa 6–0," Murphy reminded everyone, "and we felt pretty good about it. A couple of weeks later Houston runs up 73 points against the same team."

Although the Tigers learned the afternoon of their game with UH that the hometown Liberty Bowl had ignored them, they proceeded to shock the high-flying Cougars, 14–13, before 41,313 in the Dome.

UH had more first downs, 21–16, more rushing yards, 291–136, and more passing yards, 129–103. But three interceptions and two fumbles helped send the Cougars to defeat.

Memphis State scored two touchdowns in the second quarter and used them to hold on to their lead. Their first score was set up after the Cougars stopped them on their own 7-yard line. Two plays later, though, McVea fumbled on the Houston 19-yard line, and Memphis State took over, put the ball in the end zone, and took a 7–0 lead.

After Bo Burris hit Ken Hebert with a 5-yard scoring pass for a tie score, the Tigers went ahead 14–7 on a 36-yard scoring strike from quarterback Don Deaton to Mickey Duncan.

The Cougars finally mounted a sustained drive when they went 80 yards in the fourth quarter, the final 15 on another Burris-to-Hebert hookup with about eight minutes left to play. Instead of kicking the extra point to tie, Yeoman elected to go for the two-point conversion and failed. Later, the coach said, "We weren't moving the ball that well, we were having trouble stopping them, and I don't play to tie."

UH got one more chance with the ball on its own 21-yard line with 4:58 left to play. The Cougars drove 65 yards in 15 plays before stalling at the Memphis State 14-yard line. Then Ken Hebert missed a 31-yard field goal attempt with 1:20 to play. Said Hebert in the locker room, "I knew it wasn't good when I hit it; I did something wrong. I don't know what."

Although Dick Post ran for 152 yards and Warren McVea 113, and the Cougars outgained Memphis State 420 yards to 269, Coach Billy Murphy credited his team with making key plays. He said, "That's how you win games—by making the third-down plays. Our boys stuck to the game plan very well. We tried to keep the ball away from them."

Murphy also repeated after the game what he had said earlier in the week. "Houston is the most explosive team I've seen. The equal of anyone we've played. I wouldn't want to play them again anytime soon."

A couple days after the loss, Yeoman said, "I'm not taking anything away from Memphis State. They played well enough to win. The only thing we'd do differently is get into the end zone. We gained 420 yards to their 269. That's more than has been run up on those people in a long time."

* * * * * * *

All that now remained in Houston's 1966 season was the final game against the Utah Utes in the Astrodome on December 3. The week got off on a good note when Don Bean was cleared to play for the first time in three weeks.

The Utes had started the season 5–1, including wins over Oregon, Arizona, and Arizona State, before losing three straight games. Before the game, Utah coach Mike Giddings said, "The only way Houston can redeem itself for losing to Memphis State last week is to score 80 on us. If they can, they will."

Luckily for Giddings and the Utes, and thanks in part to four Houston turnovers, the Cougars won, 34–14, before 35,357 fans. The Utes kept things interesting in the first half, using two touchdowns from future Cincinnati Bengals All-Pro tight end and future NBC broadcaster Bob Trumpy to keep the score 14–14 heading into the second half.

In the third quarter, however, McVea entered the game for the first time. He had sat out the first half with a bruised shoulder. In just one half, McVea ran ten times for 103 yards. Included in those rushes was a 20-yard third-quarter touchdown scamper that put Houston up to stay, 21–14.

Hal Lundgren of the *Post* described the touchdown run: "McVea broke off the right side through a gap provided by Charlie Fowler and Tom Beer. After passing the scrimmage line, he made the kind of left turn they flunk people for on driver's tests—sweeping and without a signal. The 180-degree maneuver freed him from the Ute secondary, and such a condition is always fatal for the defense."

Taking up the slack in the first half and throughout the whole game were the two most reliable offensive players all season, Dick Post and Ken Hebert. Post, in his last game as a Cougar, ran for 172 yards on

28 carries, finishing the season with 1,061 yards rushing and a career total of 2,219 for his three seasons at Houston.

Hebert scored the last two touchdowns on passes of 4 and 10 yards from Bo Burris, who set a single-season school record of 22 touchdown passes—a record that would last until 1989, when Heisman Trophy–winner Andre Ware broke it.

Hebert's 16 points against Utah gave him the national scoring title with 113 points. Overall, he scored 11 touchdowns, 41 extra points, and two field goals. From his wide receiver position, Hebert added 38 catches for 800 yards.

In addition, Don Bean, back after his two-game hiatus, scored his third punt return touchdown of the season when he brought one back 60 yards.

Ten Houston seniors could say they were part of a turnaround that began with the last four games of the 1965 season when the Cougars went 3–0–1. The 8–2 record the Cougars fashioned in 1966 matched the season record of Houston's 1952 team. The team led the nation in total offense with 437.2 yards per game and wound up second nationally behind Notre Dame in scoring, averaging 33.5 points per contest.

Defensively, the Cougars gave up only 125 points in 10 games. They allowed only 52 first downs rushing the whole season, a school record that still stands. The Cougars also picked off 20 enemy passes, also a school record at the time.

Three Houston seniors spoke of playing at the next level. Dick Post said of his Cougar career and pro football, "I'm sorry to see it come to an end, of course. I wish we had one more game to play. It's just too much fun. I hope the pros realize I'm ready to take a shot at their brand of ball."

Tight end Tom Beer said, "You have to think about playing pro football; that's where the money is, and I'd be foolish to kid myself into thinking I didn't want to give it a try. If I do get a chance to play in the pros, I think I'll be better prepared because of playing two years here in Houston.

"This is the greatest town anywhere, the coaches are first class, and the Dome is the best place to play football anywhere in the world, I suppose. Any high school kid who doesn't come here is foolish."

"I think I'll get a chance to play in the pros," quarterback Bo Burris said, "I sure hope it's here in Texas, but if it's not, it'll be OK, too, as long as I get to play. I really enjoy the game too much to give it all up at once.

"I'm glad we came on so well last year after the bad start and again this year. That makes it all worthwhile, and when I think back on it later, I guess I'll be able to enjoy it more because we won."

As for Warren McVea, his 1966 season was his best in statistics and durability—the two not being independent of each other. It proved to be his best season at UH. The summer workouts with Post led to McVea being somewhat injury-free, and it showed in his 1966 statistics. While he ended up not breaking the NCAA records for yards per reception or yards per rushing attempt, he still fashioned some impressive numbers. McVea caught the required 15 passes (three for touchdowns) to qualify for the yards per catch record, but he compiled 414 yards on those receptions, a 27.6 average—short of Pete Dawkins's record, but still very impressive.

As for carrying the football, McVea averaged 8.8 yards per attempt, logging 648 yards rushing on just 74 attempts, 26 short of the required number to qualify for the record. He added five touchdowns rushing.

Combined rushing and receiving, McVea amassed 1,062 yards and averaged 12 yards every time he touched the football. Yes, indeed, he truly showed that he was "Wondrous Warren."

Although he did not integrate as many venues or experience quite the racism he encountered as a sophomore, McVea was the first African American to play at Lexington, Kentucky. Playing against Ole Miss in Memphis was the only real trouble he and fellow African American teammates Don Bean and J. B. Keys had during the 1966 season.

The Houston Cougars ended the season as the 19th-ranked team in the UPI poll. Also that fall, the men's cross country team finished 10th nationally. In the spring of 1967, Dave Williams's Cougar golf team was favored to win another NCAA title, and Lovett Hill's baseball team looked to be bound for the NCAA Tournament.

And in December 1966, Guy V. Lewis's Cougar basketball team was ready to take to the hardwoods full of hope and high expectations.

14 FINAL FOUR

*I was concerned about this game at the tipoff, because I knew
Houston has a good, strong team or they wouldn't be here.*
—UCLA COACH JOHN WOODEN
IN THE 1967 FINAL FOUR

Because of their strong finish to the 1965–66 season and the
return of experienced juniors Elvin Hayes and Don Chaney,
optimism and expectations for the basketball Cougars ran
sky high.

Although UH lost four seniors, including able team captain Joe Hamood, it still had experienced players who would
be playing their senior season: center Don Kruse, forward
Leary Lentz, and guard Gary Grider.

Three players off the freshman team were also expected
to add the depth needed to compete at the top of the standings. The top sophomore was 6-foot-7 forward Melvin
Bell from Clinton, Oklahoma, a former *Parade Magazine*
All-American. Bell had broken Elvin Hayes's freshman
scoring record. Another *Parade* All-American, Ken Spain,
was a 6-foot-9 center from Houston's Austin High School,

where he had led the school to a state title in 1964. His freshman year, he led the Kittens in rebounding. And Theodis Lee, a 6-foot-7 guard/forward from Monroe, Louisiana, averaged 18 points a game for the Kittens.

Other new additions were 6-foot-7 forward Andrew Benson, a transfer from Prairie View A&M University; 6-foot sophomore guard Neimar Hamood, Joe Hamood's brother; junior 5-foot-11 guard Vern Lewis, Coach Guy V. Lewis's son, who had transferred after two seasons at Tyler Junior College; 5-foot-11 senior guard Elliot McVey; and 6-foot-6 forward Bob Hayward.

Bell, Lee, and Benson were the second wave of African American basketball players to compete for the University of Houston. Like Warren McVea in his junior season of football, Hayes and Chaney were not the only two black faces; they had greater strength in more numbers. Hayes and Chaney breaking down racial barriers made for a smoother transition for Bell, Lee, and Benson.

Bell said, "There was only one time at Houston where I encountered any type of racism, and that was my freshman year when we went to some East Texas town to play some junior college, and when we went to a restaurant, they told me and Theodis Lee to go around back to pick up our meals. I couldn't understand it at the time. I never had any problems in Clinton where I grew up.

"Clinton was a small town, a farm town. I guess I was a little sheltered because I didn't go places growing up. Harvey [Pate] knew we might face some of this in some of those East Texas towns, so we ate several times at Sam Houston State before we traveled to East Texas to play a game."

Of the three new African American players, Bell was the most accomplished and talented. Many former Cougar players, fans, and coaches thought that Bell could have talent possibly even greater than Hayes. Unfortunately, even though he lettered three years, because of a knee injury suffered during a high school all-star game before he got to UH, his productivity proved to be limited.

Bill Worrell, a Cougar cheerleader and baseball letterman, said of Bell, "If he hadn't gotten hurt, he would have been a great one."

Howie Lorch, team trainer and Hayes's freshman roommate, said, "Melvin could have been as good as Elvin. His first varsity game, he scored 30 points. He was a Gus Johnson type. Melvin never got the chance to show his stuff." (Johnson was an NBA All-Star forward with the Washington Bullets in the 1960s and a 2010 Naismith Hall of Fame inductee.)

Larry Cooper played with Bell on the Kittens but redshirted the following season. Cooper said, "Melvin Bell was a great player. I think he hurt his knee in an all-star game in high school in Oklahoma. His first couple of varsity games, he scored a bunch of points."

"Melvin was as good as or better than Elvin," Don Chaney said. "He was my roommate after John Tracy. He was quite an athlete—a Gus Johnson type. Melvin was a special player."

Upon later reflection, Bell said about his knee, "I think I hurt my knee in an all-star game in Tulsa. It started swelling up after that. I eventually had to redshirt my junior year, and I had surgery to have my right kneecap removed."

Don Schverak said, "Melvin Bell could have been the best player ever at UH. He scored something like 60 points his first two games on the varsity. He was tough, too. His nickname was 'The Savage.' We used to have these legendary Saturday practices at UH—rough, tough scrimmages.

"Ken Spain and Melvin used to square off every Saturday morning and beat the shit out of each other. Sometimes they would actually fight. After practice, though, they would be friends. One would say to the other, 'Man, you got me good in practice today,' and that would be the extent of it.

"In fact, Ken Spain was my first recruit for Houston. I had graduated, but I was helping out at UH, and Ken was a midterm graduate in 1964. Ken had always wanted to play for the University of Texas. So Vern Lewis, who played with Ken at Austin High, drove him up to Austin one Saturday to meet basketball coach Harold Bradley.

"After Ken met with Coach Bradley, coach said, 'Let's go meet Coach [Darrell] Royal, I think you'd enjoy meeting him.' When they got there, Coach Royal kind of blew off Ken and said, 'I have to finish signing some papers. I'll be with you in few minutes.'

"When Ken finally went in to meet Royal, Royal looked over his half glasses at Ken and said, 'Well, well, who do we have here?' It pissed Ken off. He called me back in Houston and said, 'I'm not going to UT.'"

Theodis Lee, the other African American sophomore, came off the bench in a somewhat limited role in 1966–67, but by the time he was a junior, he was a starting forward. After his Cougar career was over, he played ten seasons with the Harlem Globetrotters and died at the young age of 33 after a short bout with cancer.

Bell said of Lee, "I first met Theodis Lee at an Ike and Tina Turner concert at Central State University in Edmond, Oklahoma. I ran into him at the concert and he said, 'Hey, you're Melvin Bell—I'm thinking about signing with Houston.' Obviously, he did, and when I was getting ready to come to Houston as a freshman, Coach Pate came and picked me up in Clinton and then we drove over to Monroe, Louisiana, to pick up Theodis, and we came to Houston."

A couple days before fall practice began on October 15, Coach Lewis gave an overview of what he expected from the 1966–67 squad: "Depending upon the maturity of our younger players, we could be as strong as last year. I would like to know right now that we could duplicate last season. I'd be satisfied because that was our best record in school history.

"Our strong points will be strong inside scoring, rebounding, and defense, plus good depth in the front court. Our weakness will be the lack of a proven outside shooter."

As the opening game at Delmar Field House against Albuquerque on December 1 approached, the UPI coaches and AP preseason polls were released. As expected, UCLA—with sophomore sensation Lew Alcindor now eligible to play varsity ball—was the No. 1 choice in both polls. The Cougars reached their highest ranking ever in the polls—sixth by UPI and seventh by the AP. "It's a lot easier to stay there than it is to get there." Lewis said. "The best time to be up there is March."

Lewis turned his attention to the Cougars's first opponent, Albuquerque, saying, "We've got to be ready to play Thursday, though. Albuquerque will already have played four games by then." The coach also announced that Melvin Bell would be in the starting lineup, with senior cocaptain Leary Lentz coming off the bench. The other four starters would be senior Don Kruse at center, Elvin Hayes at the other forward, and Don Chaney and senior cocaptain Gary Grider at guards.

"I have every confidence Bell will do a good job," Lewis said. "Of course, this doesn't mean Lentz won't start the other 25 games. I have every confidence in the world in him, too."

The decision to start Bell was a wise one. He scored 30 points in his varsity debut as UH beat the Dons, 91–84. Hayes added the other part of the potent front-line attack with 33 points, and Chaney added 14. "Bell held up extremely well for a sophomore," Lewis said. "In fact, I thought he looked like a senior."

Two days later, UH athletic director Harry Fouke and J. D. Morgan, his UCLA counterpart, confirmed in a joint statement what had been in the rumor mill since the end of last season: Houston would host UCLA on January 20, 1968, in the Astrodome. The classic match-up would pit two of the top teams and the two top players in the college game—Lew Alcindor and Elvin Hayes. "We were delighted this game could be arranged," said Fouke.

"A great many coaches around the country have asked me about it," Lewis said. "They have told me they want to schedule around the date so they can be here for the game."

Officials at the Astrodome and the University of Houston anticipated a potential crowd of 40,000, which would break a February 23, 1946, record of 22,822 at Chicago Stadium for a doubleheader featuring Ohio State versus Northwestern and Notre Dame versus DePaul.

An article in the *Houston Post* on March 16, 1966, three days after the Cougars had lost their second-round NCAA playoff game against Oregon State, was headlined, "Cougars to Meet UCLA in Dome?" This mention marked the first time the possibility of the game surfaced from off-the-court discussions. The article spoke of the potential matchup of Hayes versus Alcindor and the potential of 30,000 or more fans being present. UCLA coach John Wooden was quoted as saying, "Our schedule is filled for next season, and I don't know if it can be rearranged. I'll say this, a crowd figure like that could get our athletic director very interested."

When Fouke was asked about the possibility, he said, "We're working on it."

As it turned out, the potential Houston–UCLA basketball contest was the brainchild of Guy V. Lewis. "The game with UCLA in the Astrodome is my favorite game of all time," Lewis said, "but I really had trouble talking our athletic director, Harry Fouke, into it. The first time I mentioned it to him was in his office, and he kept saying, 'No, no, no, no. Just get out of here with that talk.'

"About a couple of weeks later, I went back again, and it was the same thing, 'Get out of here, don't even talk about that.'

"When I came back a third time, I said, 'Harry, now listen, dammit, we could have a good crowd, and I'm telling you we can beat them.' This time he didn't throw me out of his office, and he said, 'Dammit, if you believe in the game that much, come in and let's talk about it.'

"I said we could sell 35,000 tickets, and Harry said, 'You're crazy.' But I could tell he was starting to think about the possibilities.

"Harry then said, 'Well then, if we're going to do this, we have to get Judge Hofheinz [the Astrodome chieftain] involved.' So we went and talked to the judge in his suite up in the Astrodome.

"Harry and I told him what we wanted to do, play UCLA and all, and then the judge asked us, 'Where's the court going to go?' 'In the middle of the Dome,' I said. The judge came back with, 'But the fans won't be able to see the ball from that far away.'

"I told the judge, 'Well, can't the baseball fans that come here see that little ball pretty well? Our ball is a lot bigger, and most of our players are bigger than baseball players.'

"The judge said, 'Well, you're right about that.' So we had talked him into it. The only problem was, we hadn't even talked to UCLA about the game yet. Luckily, I knew Harry Fouke and the UCLA athletic director, J. D. Morgan, were good friends. Morgan was intrigued by the game, and he eventually convinced John Wooden the game would be good for college basketball if it was televised all over the country. John agreed. So the game was on."

Sports Information Director Ted Nance recalled that Harry Fouke and J. D. Morgan became friends through an event that dealt with integration in Houston. "Harry first met J. D. when he was UCLA's tennis coach," Nance said. "They came to Houston to play us, and they wanted to know if there were any clay courts in the Houston area to play on, because that was the surface the NCAAs were to be played on.

"Harry arranged it so UCLA could play at River Oaks, which was *the* country club in Houston. Problem was, UCLA had Arthur Ashe, the great black player, on its roster. The city of Houston was still somewhat segregated at the time, but it turns out there were no problems there and not a word was said about it. After that, Harry and J. D. became good friends."

* * * * * * *

Guy V. Lewis and the Cougars used the next phase of their schedule to find the right team chemistry, encountering only one blemish—an 86–75 upset by Michigan in Ann Arbor. Hayes saw the triple-team defensive alignment, and he and Bell experienced many goaltending calls against them that many believed were legal blocks.

Despite success that saw Hayes and three or four others always managing to score in double figures, Lewis was concerned with his team's lack of spirit in an 89–81 win over the Southwestern Louisiana Ragin' Cajuns. "We're supposed to be a pressing team," the coach told the media. "I can't kick about scoring 89 points. But the defense isn't getting us the ball enough. I wish I were a Houdini and could figure it out. I thought we would be better with the press this year than last. We run a combination of nine different presses. We used eight of them tonight and still didn't get the ball enough."

Lewis was unhappy enough with this early season play to shake up the starting lineup in hopes of seeing improvements. For the game against the Hawaii Rainbows on December 9, sophomore Neimar Hamood started at guard in the place of Gary Grider, and Leary Lentz started at forward in Melvin Bell's place because Bell was late for the game. Hamood made the most of his first start as a varsity player, scoring 11 points as five Cougars scored in double figures in a 93–59 rout. The Rainbows froze the ball for much of the first half, but the Cougars scored 61 second-half points to secure the victory. Hayes had 20, Chaney 18, Bell 13, and Grider 10. Vern Lewis said after the game, "Tonight's game may be the turning point for us this year. We played like we could all year."

Two days later, the Cougars played the St. Mary's University Gaels from San Francisco, winning their fifth game of the season against one loss, 90–74. They limited the Gaels to just 29 points in the second half. St. Mary's was able to tie the game at 42-all with 1:57 to go in the half, thanks to two technical fouls called by referee Bo McAlister against the Houston student section. When Elvin Hayes was called for goaltending, the student section erupted in protest and showered the court with paper cups. McAlister signaled the two technical fouls and then asked Fouke to escort one fan from Delmar Field House. As it turned out, the ejected fan was not even a student at UH but a basketball player from nearby Rice University.

When tied at 42, the Cougars slowly pulled away from the Gaels. Hayes led the way with 29 points, while Bell and Don Chaney, who also had six steals, each scored 17. Leary Lentz had 9 points and 12 rebounds.

The victory set the cross-town stage at Rice's Autry Court for the annual Bluebonnet Basketball Classic, the last one held at this location before UH took over hosting responsibilities the following season.

The Cougars bested Centenary, 97–66, and set a Bluebonnet Classic scoring record with a 111–85 victory over Idaho State. Hayes gained individual recognition with his 43 points against Centenary, also a new record. The Cougars were hitting 50 percent of their shots and seeing at least four players score in double figures.

The Cougars won their fourth-straight Bluebonnet Classic and their fifth in the seven-year history of the tournament.

Coach Lewis grew concerned over his team's sluggish first-half performances, but fortunately they featured rallies in the second. The bottom-line results were a 90–74 win over the San Francisco Dons and an 87–65 victory over the Washington Huskies. A high point was the noticeable improvement of Don Chaney, who scored 23 points and five steals against San Francisco. Hayes's playing time was limited against Washington because he tore the index finger of his right hand on the backboard. Of the latter win, Lewis said, "I thought we looked sluggish. We weren't up for the game. But they have the type of club that won't let you look good."

The Cougars took an eight-day break for the Christmas holidays and picked up the season on December 28 when they traveled to Jonesboro, Arkansas, for the annual Arkansas Holiday Tournament, hosted by Arkansas State University. They beat Kent State University as their first opponent, 85–73, despite the continued tendency to appear sluggish, especially after so much time off. Hayes had only had 5 points in the first half but scored 17 in the second as Chaney turned in one of his best performances, scoring 22 points and adding seven steals.

The next night, the Cougars took on host Arkansas State and won, 68–58, with Hayes leading the way with 23 points. This win wrapped up the 1966 part of the UH basketball season with an 11–1 record. But despite the impressive won-lost record, the team had two major concerns. The first concern was free-throw shooting. Throughout their first 12 games, the Cougars made only 62 percent of their foul shots. Gary Grider was the only starter shooting free throws effectively, at 78 percent. Even though Hayes led the team in free-throw attempts, he was only hitting 55 percent of them.

Guy Lewis declared, "Elvin is too good a shooter to be that low. He's capable of hitting 75 percent. He doesn't work hard enough at it."

The biggest concern for the Cougars heading into 1967, though, was the condition of Melvin Bell's damaged right knee. Although he averaged 15.3 points per game in the first 12 games, the knee had bothered him since the first day of practice back in October.

The Cougars's first opponent of 1967 was Tennessee Tech on January 2 at Delmar. The Eagles came into the game with a 4–1 record but saw the host team deal them a 95–69 defeat. Hayes led the Cougars with 26 points and 12 rebounds despite playing only 31 minutes. Chaney added 13 points with numerous steals, but it was the play from two players off the bench that was worth noting. Sophomore center Ken Spain had his best game of the season with

11 points and 9 rebounds in 29 minutes of play. Andrew Benson, a senior transfer from nearby Prairie View A&M University, hit all five shots he tried from the field and ended up with 10 points to go with 7 rebounds in just 14 minutes of action.

On the same day as the Tennessee Tech game, the Cougar basketball team was featured for the first time in *Sports Illustrated*. In an article titled, "Elvin, Melvin, and the Duck," writer Curry Kirkpatrick was not totally complimentary to the Cougars. When referring to the UH zone presses, Kirkpatrick wrote, "Their combination defenses are wild, risky affairs that do not produce the traps they were designed for, and could not stop Mary Poppins from bombing away all night from the corners."

Of the game against San Francisco, Kirkpatrick wrote, "Houston demonstrated a definitely human characteristic—laziness." He wrote of Hayes, "Though he loafs much of the time, The Huge E's potential as a pro is obvious."

One glaring inaccuracy in the article was the story of how Hayes obtained his nickname: "The Big E." The article said that "Big E" was a direct copy of "Big O," the name given to Oscar Robertson. However, John Hollis, the Cougar beat writer for the *Houston Post* during the previous season, said of Kirkpatrick's claim, "Not so. I gave Elvin the name, and the idea came from the aircraft carrier *Enterprise*."

When asked after the Tennessee Tech game about the Cougars's chances in 1967, Hayes himself said, "I think we are the team to beat. Most teams with a lot of 6-foot-7, 6-foot-8 players have a lot of average players. But we have big men who are good. Everyone says it will take a team with height and speed to beat UCLA. They are the two things we have. If we play them, we won't have to put three or four men on Lew Alcindor, either. Their other players are too good for that. I don't even think we'd have to double-team him."

Then, on Alcindor, Hayes cracked, "Yes, I think I can guard him by myself. Size isn't as important as defensive ability."

Inconsistency continued to plague the Cougars. With their record at 12–1, the Cougars traveled 90 miles east on January 5 to Beaumont to play the Lamar Tech Cardinals, where Hayes proceeded to play the worst half of his career—he was held scoreless. Luckily, the strength of the rest of the team was apparent as they ran out to a 43–31 halftime lead en route to an 82–62 win.

Bell picked up the slack in the first half as he scored 12 of his 14 points before the intermission. Bell also led the Cougars with nine rebounds. Hayes recovered to score 16 in the second, which ended up matching the game totals of Chaney and Lentz. Grider was also in double figures with 11.

Guy V. Lewis said after the game, "I don't think we had such a bad game. When your leading scorer doesn't have a point by halftime and you still win by 20, things aren't so bad. Bell did a great job, and so did Lentz, Grider, and Chaney."

Next for the Cougars, who had now won 33 games in a row at home on three different courts, was the West Texas State Buffaloes on January 14. In their previous game, West Texas State had given defending national champion Texas Western all they could handle before going down in an 85–73 defeat. The Buffs, however, were no match for the Cougars as they were pounded, 103–72, before a packed house at Delmar. The entire Houston starting five reached double figures in scoring, led by Hayes with 24 points in only 30 minutes. Bell contributed 17, Chaney added 16, and Grider and Lentz each had 12.

"That's what I love," said Lewis, "Everybody in double figures. At times, we looked like a great club tonight."

The Cougars now had a two-week break because of semester exams before resuming their season in Seattle on January 28 in their rematch with the Washington Huskies.

During the break, former Cougar All-America defensive specialist Gary Phillips, now part of the Houston radio broadcast team, spoke about Don Chaney and his defensive prowess. "He has tremendous reach to go with those hands," Phillips said. "He can stay away from a man and not appear to be close enough to steal the ball. Then somebody tries to make a long pass and he snaps it up. I think he's the quickest guard the university has ever had. He's their rover and he never tires. Keeping up with Chaney is like following a four-year-old around the house. Thirty minutes later, you're dead and he's still not tired."

"Chaney has quick hands and the feet to go with them, just like Phillips," Coach Lewis said, "what a dream guard combination they would have made in the press. Somebody thinks he's a safe distance from Chaney before he passes. Then Don reaches out nine feet and takes the ball."

Unfortunately, Chaney's stellar hands and quickness did not help the Cougars shake off two weeks of rust as they fell to the Huskies in Seattle, 81–78. Trailing by 13 with 5:50 remaining in the game, the Cougars pulled within one point at 79–78 but couldn't quite pull the game out. Once again, the entire starting five scored in double figures, but it was not enough.

UH also encountered another problem. After the game, Guy V. Lewis and others voiced their displeasure with official Charles Moffett. Lewis said, "He's the sorriest official I've ever seen in my life. I've never seen one guy dominate the game the way he did tonight." Of the last 17 fouls called in the game, 12 were against Houston, with Moffett making most of them. The Cougars were third in the nation in fewest fouls called against them, but that night they had 24 fouls to Washington's 18.

The Cougars tried to rebound three nights later by traveling to Las Vegas to play Nevada Southern (now UNLV). At the time, Nevada Southern was not a Division I team, but they carried a 13–2 record into the contest with Houston. In fact, Idaho State coach Claude Retherford, whose team had lost to Houston in the Bluebonnet Classic in December, said, "Houston wouldn't have any trouble with Nevada Southern in Houston. But I don't think they can win here."

UH proved Retherford wrong. The Cougars ran away from the Rebels, 103–83. Hayes hit 19 of 31 shots from the floor and ended up with 42 points to go with 14 rebounds. It was estimated that 12 of Hayes's baskets were scored on dunks. Chaney added 22 points, making 11 of 19 shots, and had six steals.

The team then put together another balanced scoring attack against Hardin Simmons and won, 92–85. One negative that came out of the game, however, was the deteriorating condition of Melvin Bell's right knee. He missed practice the day before the game after suffering further damage to the knee. He played limited minutes against the Cowboys, scoring nine points with six rebounds.

Coach Lewis said of the situation, "Bell was limping, and he told me it hurt. When he complains about the knee hurting, I know it must be bad."

The Cougars had to regroup to go back out on the road for two tough games against the Notre Dame Fighting Irish on a Saturday afternoon in South Bend and the Creighton Blue Jays the following Monday in Omaha.

The Fighting Irish's record for 1966–67 was deceiving. They started the season by losing 9 of their first 11 games but had rebounded with 7 wins in their last 10 games to stand at 9–12 for the year. The Irish were led by forward Bob Arnzen, who averaged 21.3 points per game. In the game, Arnzen led the Irish with 37 points in an 87–78 upset over the Cougars after racing out to a 44–26 halftime lead. Hayes, hounded by a scrappy Irish defense, was held scoreless in the first 18 minutes. Although he would end up with 30 points and 16 rebounds to spark a Cougar rally, UH still fell short in the end.

When the game was over, the Notre Dame fans charged the court and carried Coach Johnny Dee and Arnzen off the floor. Dee exclaimed, "It was our biggest game of the season, and one of the biggest wins since I've been here. We played a complete game today and never lost our poise."

Guy V. Lewis said, "This has been our problem most of the season. We just haven't been consistent; we just haven't been able to put two good halves together."

Two nights later, the Cougars remained inconsistent. The Cougars scored 52 first-half points but then let Creighton creep back to within 2 points with 4:25 to play. This time, the Big E came through. From that point, Hayes scored 7 of the last 9 points to give him 38 on the night, and Houston held off the Blue Jays, 87–80.

"Elvin was great tonight," Lewis said, "and he wasn't alone. The entire team had the poise and enthusiasm it takes to win on the road." Bell had 17 points, Chaney had 16, and Don Kruse, starting in the place of Leary Lentz, had 12.

Then it was back home, where the Cougars beat St. Mary's University of San Antonio, 122–58, scoring 75 second-half points with five players in double figures, led by Hayes, of course, with 30 points.

Now in mid-February, the Guy V. Lewis crew flew for a Saturday night encounter with the 14–7 Miami Hurricanes. Coach Lewis said, "There is no question that Rick Jones and Junior Gee are the finest guard combination on any college team this year. Miami is a very fast team with big inside men to back up the fast game. It will be a complete, all-around test for us."

What was expected to be a huge test for the Cougars on the road was nothing of the sort. UH raced out to a 57–37 halftime lead en route to a 105–86 drubbing of the Hurricanes. Hayes extended his streak of consecutive games scoring 30 or more points to six as he again led the way with 38. Don Chaney contributed 23, as Houston shot 57 percent from the floor and a surprising 88 percent (23 of 26) from the free-throw line. Hayes's performance raised his season scoring average to 28.7 points per game, which Lewis attributed to "getting the ball inside more to score." The coach also praised the rest of the team, saying, "Miami is a tough place to win, but the kids really got after it. We wanted this game badly."

The next game—another laugher—had more significance than just marking the Cougars's 20th win of the season. They defeated West Texas State, 120–76, sending the Buffalos into the depths of a 1–16 season. With 29 points, Hayes moved to within 4 points of breaking Cougar broadcaster Gary Phillips's career school scoring record of 1,452 points. Lewis pulled Hayes from the game with seven minutes to go, in spite of the West Texas fans yelling, "We want E!" The coach wanted his star player to break the record at their next home game against Creighton.

The best news to come out of the game was the play of Melvin Bell. In spite of his still-troublesome knee, he skied for 25 points, including several thunderous dunks. His family made the trip over from his hometown of Clinton, Oklahoma, for the game.

The team also got another bit of news: the Cougars would be pitted against the New Mexico State Aggies in Fort Collins, Colorado, in the first round of the 1967 NCAA Tournament. The winner of the game would face the Big Eight champion Kansas Jayhawks on their home floor in Lawrence, Kansas. New Mexico State, like Houston, was an independent and somewhat of a surprise choice to be selected for the tournament. Although the Aggies had defeated defending champion Texas Western twice during the season, they sported just a 14–9 record at the time of their selection. They were led by Coach Lou Henson, who had the head coaching job at Illinois in his future. The only common opponent for the two teams was Hardin Simmons. The Cougars had won their game, 92–85, but the Aggies had lost theirs, 87–77, in overtime. "I don't know much about them," Lewis said, "except that Coach Henson likes ball control."

Before the start of the tournament, the Cougars still had three regular season games remaining: home games against Creighton and Loyola of New Orleans and a March 4 season finale on the road against the Air Force Academy.

Playing before a packed house of 5,300 at Delmar Field House, Hayes became not only the all-time leading scorer in Cougar history but also the all-time leading rebounder in an 87–73 win over Creighton. After Hayes scored his fourth point early in the first half to break Phillips's record, the game was stopped, and Phillips joined Hayes from his broadcasting table to congratulate him on his achievement. Hayes ended up with 29 points, 18 rebounds, and 11 blocks. The rebound number put him ahead of the previous all-time leader, Don Boldebuck, who had 863 in his UH career. By the end of the night, Hayes had 867. After the game, Hayes said, "I kept telling myself it was just another game. The thought of the record was still there, I guess. I just couldn't hit at first in the first half. Gary told me I deserved to break his record. He was really glad I broke it."

In what would be the last home game for cocaptains Gary Grider and Leary Lentz and other seniors Don Kruse, Andrew Benson, and Elliott McVey, the now seventh-ranked Cougars took down Loyola of New Orleans, 106–64. Hayes scored 41, Spain and Lentz 13 each, and Grider 10 points and 11 assists.

Two hours before the game, Hayes found out he made the AP All-America team, joining Lew Alcindor of UCLA, Jimmy Walker of

Providence, Wes Unseld of Louisville, and Clem Haskins of Western Kentucky.

After the game, Guy Lewis said, "This was our best game all year because we played at both ends of the court. We were good on offense and great on defense."

New Mexico State coach Lou Henson was at the game to scout his team's first-round opponent. "I just saw one of the finest teams in the country," Henson said. "When one of their big men gets tired or in foul trouble, all Guy has to do is look down the bench and put in somebody better."

In the Loyola game, the Cougars received a mild scare when second-leading scorer Don Chaney played just 15 minutes because of a calf injury, which was ultimately diagnosed as a spasm or a strain, not a tear.

All that remained for Lewis's team was a road game against Air Force. Once on the court, they ran out to a 26-point lead and held on for a 90–80 victory. Hayes scored 23 points and had 17 rebounds, and Don Chaney, not feeling the effects of his calf injury, pitched in 19.

With a school record won-lost mark of 23–3 for the regular season, the Cougars had a week to prepare for the game with New Mexico State. The Aggies entered the game with the fourth-toughest schedule in the nation, which explained their being invited to the tournament despite their 15–10 record. They were also a very short team over-all. Center Wes Morehead stood 6-foot-5, but starting forwards John Gambill and Earnest Turner were each only 6-foot-1. Henson stressed his team's strong points, saying, "Teamwork has been the secret to our success. I've never coached a team with this much pride, cooperation, and desire. To put it bluntly, Houston is the only team I've seen this year that has a chance to stop UCLA. They're big, they're tough, and we're going to have our hands full."

The Aggies's strategy was to play tough defense, try to slow down the Cougars's attack, and play a deliberately slow offense. Their defense was ranked 13th nationally, giving up just 62.2 points per game, while the Cougar offense was second at 92.9 points per game.

As it turned out, the Aggies gave the Cougars all they could handle. But Houston held on for a tense 59–58 win, never leading by more than five points. The game was in doubt right up until the final second. With less than a minute to play, a Melvin Bell dunk gave the Cougars a 59–56 lead. Then the Aggies's Richard Collins made a jump shot to pull to 59–58. Lentz was fouled with 12 seconds left in regulation but missed the front end of a one-and-one, giving New Mexico State the ball for the last shot and a possible win.

With only three seconds showing on the clock, guard Vern Lewis stepped in front of the Aggies's Bob Evans, and the referee blew his whistle, calling a charging foul that ended any hopes of defeating the Cougars. "That was the most stupid thing I've ever done," Vern Lewis said. "Charging fouls can go either way. I could have easily been the goat."

Hayes scored 19 of the Cougars's 23 first-half points to keep the game within reach and ended up with 30 points as well as 14 of the team's 27 rebounds.

With pesky New Mexico State out of the way, the Cougars now traveled to the Midwest Regional Tournament in Lawrence, Kansas, on March 17 to meet the third-ranked Kansas Jayhawks on their home floor. Other games featured the 19–5 Southwest Conference champion SMU Mustangs against the second-ranked Louisville Cardinals, led by junior All-America center Wes Unseld and sophomore guard Butch Beard. If the Cardinals could win the Midwest Regional, they would host the Final Four the following weekend in Louisville. They were a nine-point favorite.

Kansas was a four-point favorite to defeat Houston. *Sports Illustrated* said, "Kansas should have no difficulty with a Houston team that just managed to get past the little New Mexico State Aggies by one point." The Jayhawks started four sophomores and one junior. Their leading scorers were 6-foot-6 junior forward Rodger Bohnenstiehl, who averaged 16.4 points per game, and sophomore sensation guard Jo Jo White, who averaged 14.

March 17 proved to be a day of upsets. SMU knocked off Louisville, 83–81, and the Cougars turned in their finest performance of the season by whipping Kansas, 66–53. It would be the two Texas teams in the Midwest final that Sunday the 19th. "I knew when I walked into

that dressing room that they were up like they've never been up before,"
Guy V. Lewis said.

It was a total team effort. Although Hayes was held to 10 points
below his season average of 29 points per game, other Cougars picked up
the slack. Melvin Bell had 11 points and picked up two key steals down
the stretch. Chaney, however, played possibly his best game as a Houston Cougar, leading the team with 20 points, the last 8 of them in the
first half to stake UH to a 32–29 lead. He also dished out several assists,
played his usual stellar defense, and broke the Jayhawks's press with ease.

"Chaney's long arms forced our playmakers to loft passes higher
and softer to get the ball into the corners and on the inside," Kansas
coach Ted Owens pointed out. "This allowed Houston's zone men time
to adjust and help their defense."

Kansas guard Jo Jo White added, "Chaney is the best backcourt
man we've seen this year."

Two days later, the Cougars punched their first-ever ticket to the
Final Four with a tough 83–75 victory over SMU. UH built up a 14-
point lead with nine minutes to play but let the Mustangs come back
to tie at 71-all with four minutes to go. From that point on, however, the Cougars outscored the Ponies 12–4 to take the win. Hayes,
who was named the Midwest Regional MVP, led the Cougars with
31 points—including 20 in the second half—and 11 rebounds. Once
again, though, Hayes was not alone in his contributions. Bell scored
11, Chaney and Spain had 10 each, and Grider had 9 and Lentz 8.

The Cougars returned home to Hobby Airport that evening
greeted by an estimated three thousand fans. As they prepared to
travel to Louisville for their first Final Four in school history on
Friday, March 24, they faced a daunting task. The team standing in
the Cougars's way was the top-ranked and undefeated UCLA Bruins.
The 28–0 Bruins were led by four sophomores in their starting lineup,
all of whom were high school All-Americans—the best among them
the 7-foot-2 center Lew Alcindor, the National Player of the Year,
who averaged 29.7 points and 15.3 rebounds per game. The other
three sophomores were forwards Kenny Heitz and Lynn Shackelford

and guard Lucious Allen. The only upperclassman who started was junior guard Mike Warren.

Before the game, Guy V. Lewis told reporters, "I haven't seen UCLA all year, but I think they rely on Alcindor for rebounding. Contrasting them with us, Hayes is not our sole rebounder." The coach also was concerned about the UCLA zone press: "They're quicker than we are. I've seen some great teams devoured by it."

UCLA coach John Wooden spoke words of concern of his own: "Hayes is a problem in himself. They are one of the largest teams we've faced. After Alcindor, they have us in size."

Although Hayes was the individual star of the game with 25 points and 24 rebounds, the Bruins handily took care of the Cougars in Louisville, 73–58. UCLA used a balanced attack. Shackelford had 22 points, Alcindor had 19 points with 20 rebounds, Allen had 17 points, and Warrant had 14.

The Bruins led 39–28 at the half and allowed the Cougars to get within 6 points later on, but poor shooting at the free-throw line contributed to the loss when Coach Lewis's crew hit on only 6 of 16. "I thought we had a lot of effort, but I was disappointed with our shooting," Lewis said. "You can't miss as many free throws, as many shots from the field, and turn the ball over as much as we did and expect to win. I don't think there's a team in the country that can beat UCLA."

Hayes made comments that would fuel the fire for the January 20, 1968, rematch in the Astrodome when he said about Alcindor, "I can't really say he should be the number-one player in the country. He's good, and he's going to get better, but I think Jimmy Walker [of Providence] is the best in the country." Asked if he was looking forward to the January 20 rematch, Hayes replied, "You know it."

From the UCLA side of the postgame interviews, All-America guard Mike Warren said, "Don Chaney did a tremendous job on me. He's the toughest—always trying to steal the ball. I'd have to say Elvin Hayes is the best big man I've played against. He's real tough."

Elvin Hayes dunks over
Lew Alcindor at the 1967
Final Four in Louisville
(Courtesy of Myron
McReynolds)

"I was concerned about this game at the tipoff," Wooden said, "because I knew Houston has a good, strong team or they wouldn't be here."

There was one game left for the Cougars: the NCAA third-place consolation game. Their opponent was the University of North Carolina Tar Heels, who had lost the other semifinal game to the University of Dayton, 76–62. The Tar Heels were making the first of Coach Dean Smith's 11 Final Four appearances.

The third-place game was one Coach Smith would like to forget. UH blasted North Carolina, 84–62. Sophomore Ken Spain led the way coming off the bench for the Cougars with 24 points and 14 rebounds. Hays had 23 and Chaney 19. The Cougars ran out to a 42–23 halftime lead and never let up. The key of the game was UH's rebounding. The final box score showed the Cougars holding a 72–46 advantage. Leary Lentz led with 17, and Hayes had 16, Chaney 8, and Bell 7.

Asked if it was his best game of the season, Ken Spain replied, "Are you kidding? It's the best game I've ever played in my life!"

Don Chaney passes the ball past Lew Alcindor for an Elvin Hayes layup at the 1967 Final Four (Courtesy of Myron McReynolds)

Between the UCLA loss and the North Carolina win, there was a bit of controversy concerning Elvin Hayes. A Louisville paper said that after the UCLA game, Hayes accused his teammates of "choking" against the Bruins.

"I never said that," said Hayes after the North Carolina game. "I've been with most of these men since they were freshmen, and they've never been the type to fold under pressure. I don't think you'll find too many guys capable of standing up to it like they can."

"He just never said it," Chaney insisted. Of the report, Lewis quipped, "Nobody on the team took it very seriously. We all got a laugh out of it."

The newspaper's accusation dismissed as malarkey, the 1966–67 basketball season ended as by far the most successful in school history, the Cougars finishing at 27–4. Hayes finished with averages of 28.4 points and 15.7 rebounds per contest. Don Chaney's per-game scoring average jumped from 8.8 as a sophomore to 15.3 as a junior, and his rebounds per game rose from 4.8 to 5.2.

Overall, the 1966–67 school year went down as the greatest in history for UH sports. The football Cougars finished 8–2, ranked 19th in the nation, and was the national leader in total offense. The men's cross country team finished 10th in the nation, while the golf team won its 10th NCAA title in 12 years. And the baseball Cougars, led in large part by football players Bo Burris, Ken Hebert, and All-American Tom Paciorek, finished second in the 1967 College World Series, losing to Arizona State in the championship game.

The excitement of these successes helped set the stage for the senior seasons of Warren McVea, Elvin Hayes, and Don Chaney—seasons that packed more thrills and excitement than ever before.

15 HALFBACK IN THE CROSSHAIRS

They were going to shoot him if he scored a touchdown.
One time Warren had beat their safety, but the guy caught
him and tackled him. On another run, he was wide open
on his way to a touchdown, and he just flat fell down.
—UH COACH BILL YEOMAN ON WARREN
MCVEA DEATH THREATS AT OLE MISS

After leading the nation in total offense, finishing in the top
ten in defense, and fashioning an 8–2 record in 1966, Bill
Yeoman and the Houston Cougars were enthusiastic about
the new season. Although he had to replace players such as
Dickie Post, Tom Beer, and Bo Burris on offense as well
as his entire defensive line due to graduation and injury, Yeoman was excited when he greeted 80 players for spring training. Manning the skill positions would be Warren McVea,
Ken Hebert, and Don Bean.

Replacing Bo Burris would be key for the new season.
The quarterback for the Cougars would be senior Dick

Woodall, a hometown product from Westbury High School. Wood-all was born and raised in Lufkin, 119 miles northeast of Houston. His family moved to the Bayou City in 1959, when he was in the ninth grade. Houston, as most Southern cities, was still segregated, so Woodall saw no African American fellow students at the brand-new Westbury High on the Southwest side.

"I didn't get to play football my senior year at Westbury—I was hurt. I didn't play a down," Woodall recalled. "TCU and some smaller schools offered me a scholarship in football, and UT offered me a base-ball scholarship. Houston was the only school that offered me a full ride. Coach Yeoman gave an opportunity when no one else would.

"When I got to UH, there were seven quarterbacks recruited, some with some pretty big reputations. I asked myself, 'What am I doing here?' I backed up Bo Burris for two years. I got to play as a sopho-more but not so much as a junior. Bo was one of the best athletes to ever go through the school. Did I want to play? Sure I did, but Bo was outstanding.

"I did have a good senior year, though. I was fortunate. I was sur-rounded by great athletes—Hebert, Gipson, McVea. We had a good all-around team. I'm also going to go on the record and say our defense was better than our offense. They were much more consistent than we were. On offense, we would stop ourselves sometimes with turnovers. On a good night, though? Our Veer offense was unstoppable."

This starting UH quarterback didn't think it was "a big deal" hand-ing off and throwing the ball to black players in the same backfield: "I was fortunate to have two parents who raised me right. Playing with Warren and the others didn't bother me one bit, not one iota. I truly believe most of the team felt this way. The most important thing was that we were an extremely close team. Going to UH and playing foot-ball were five of the greatest years of my life."

When spring training started, however, five Cougar starters were missing: Tom Paciorek, Ken Hebert, and Don Bean were playing var-sity baseball on the Cougar team that would finish second at the 1967 College World Series, while McVea and defensive back Mike Simpson were running track.

The Cougars played their first scrimmage of the 1967 spring on April 8 at Jeppesen Stadium, against the UH alumni team. Coach Yeoman said before the game, "It will be a very interesting game to watch. It should be close and exciting. The boys have done very well this spring. They have shown a lot of hustle and a willingness to learn."

Yeoman built up quarterback Woodall, who, he said, "exhibited a very fine arm during practice. I don't believe I have ever seen better passing."

The day before the scrimmage, Don Bean returned to the football team after spending 14 games on the UH baseball diamond. In the scrimmage, he returned the opening kickoff 102 yards and later scored on a 28-yard pass from Woodall in the third quarter, and the varsity won, 35–21. Freshman newcomer running back Jim Strong of San Antonio also contributed to the win with 138 yards rushing on 16 carries.

The next scrimmage was down the road in McVea's hometown of San Antonio on Saturday, April 15, for a night contest at Northeast ISD stadium. To accommodate the six thousand fans for the scrimmage between the Cougar Red and White squads, McVea took a break from his track schedule to suit up. He did not disappoint his fans, either. He returned the opening kickoff 97 yards for a score. He then ran for a 65-yard touchdown in the second quarter and had another 44-yard scoring run called back because of a penalty. The hometown hero ended up with 136 yards on only eight carries, as his Red team defeated the Whites, 41–7.

Another player who contributed to the win was freshman wide receiver Calvin Achey from Englewood, Colorado. Achey returned a punt 54 yards for a score. Over the next three seasons, he would be the other starting wide receiver opposite Cougar All-American Ken Hebert in 1967 and consensus All-American Elmo Wright in 1968 and 1969. Achey also witnessed the God-given talents of McVea. "I had never seen anyone as quick as Warren—he had this peripheral view where he could somehow see and sense guys coming at him," Achey said. "I didn't know how good Warren was until that Red–White scrimmage in San Antonio.

"I was a freshman, and we're getting ready to play before a good crowd. We warmed up, and as we were getting ready for the opening kickoff, Warren was nowhere to be seen. He finally shows up, pulling up his pants, and he hadn't warmed up at all. Warren proceeds to take back the opening kickoff for a touchdown. Before the half was over, he had a couple of other long touchdowns and three or four other runs I couldn't believe."

At the end of spring training, Yeoman and the Cougars got some good news and then some bad news. Royce Berry, the starting defensive end who had been suspended for the remainder of the 1966 season for missing curfew after the Ole Miss loss, came back to the team and had a solid spring. On the last day of spring practice, Yeoman told him he had been chosen captain for the 1967 season. However, in the final series in the final spring scrimmage, Berry injured his knee and had to miss the entire 1967 season.

Also that spring, Yeoman almost got to play the role of innovator again. Having integrated his team and invented the Veer offense, Yeoman almost combined the two when he set out to recruit who could have been the first black quarterback in the South and therefore the first to run the Veer offense. The innovative coach had set his sights on a star quarterback and baseball pitcher from Minden, Louisiana. His name was Vida Blue, and four years later he would become one of the biggest names in baseball when, at the young age of 22, he won both the Cy Young and Most Valuable Player awards in 1971 as the young pitching ace of the Oakland A's. Overall, in 17 major league seasons, Blue would compile a 209–161 record, pitching in three World Series.

At the time in 1967, Yeoman said, "This young fellow is going to become the first big-name black quarterback. He's going to be the best left-handed passer since Frankie Albert. That name alone will sell tickets."

Years later, Yeoman explained, "We went over to Louisiana to see Vida play. He was a phenomenal athlete. In the end, though, he had to help his family."

Blue may have been a better quarterback than he was a pitcher. He led Desoto High School in Minden to a 10–2 record as a senior. In 12 games, Blue amassed 5,084 yards of total offense: 3,484 yards passing with 35 touchdown passes and 1,600 yards on the ground.

Bill Yeoman, circa late 1960s
(Courtesy of UH Athletic
Department)

Longtime UH sports information director Ted Nance recalled Blue's recruiting trip to Houston. "Vida came and visited," Nance said. "Carroll Schultz, one of our assistant coaches, used to come back from watching Vida's games with these wild stories about how tough Vida was. Carroll said Blue caused about three opponents a game to be carried out on stretchers.

"When Vida first came to Houston, he came by my office, and I showed him some pictures. We then took him to the Astrodome before an Astros game, and he went out to the mound and wound up. He looked over his back shoulder like somebody hit the ball over the fence off him, and he said, 'One of these days.'

Nance continued, "When it came close to the time for Vida to decide on signing with the A's or playing football at U of H, the Shreveport paper had an eight-column headline that said, 'Decision Due for Vida Blue.'"

Blue even considered playing baseball for the Cougars, but basketball player Melvin Bell explained, "I remember Warren McVea showed Vida around campus when he came to visit. The baseball coach, Lovette Hill? The only racial tensions any of us black players ever felt was with him. He didn't want Vida Blue for the baseball team—can you picture that?"

McVea confirmed, "I talked to Vida when he came here and I showed him around. The coaches really wanted him to come here."

Blue spoke of his recruitment and how close he came to becoming a dream Veer quarterback at UH: "I went to an all–African American high school—Desoto High School in Minden, Louisiana. The faculty was all African American and most went to Grambling or Southern University, so they tried to talk me into going to one of those two schools. Eddie Robinson of Grambling came to see me play. Ralph Waldo Emerson Jones, the president of Grambling, was also the baseball coach. He said I couldn't play both sports. It was then I decided to check out U of H.

"I had offers from all over the country, but I decided to go see Houston because they ran the Veer offense. When I came to Houston, that was my first plane ride—Shreveport to Houston.

"Once I got there, Warren McVea was the one who took me to the campus. I was impressed with the campus and the college. Warren then took me over to the Astrodome to see an Astros game. I spent most of the game looking at the roof. I did get a bottle of dirt I scooped up from the Dome—I still have it all these years later. Later, when I was with the Giants, I got to actually pitch in the Astrodome."

Blue continued, "There was a very good chance I would have gone to U of H. Football was actually my best sport. Coach Yeoman used to call me up when I was trying to decide whether to go there or not, and he would sing me a song over the phone that went something like, 'Vida Blue, where were you?'

"When I think back, the University of Houston was the only college in the South that offered me a scholarship. I also didn't realize that I would have been the first black quarterback in the South.

"The reason I didn't go to U of H was that my father died and the money to sign with the Oakland A's was good. I think it was a $5,000 bonus. My mom wanted me to go get my education. I told her I could always go back and get my degree. It turns out it was probably a blessing in disguise. I have good knees today, and baseball was pretty good to me. Sometimes I think about how different my life would have been had I gone to Houston—could I have taken football to the next level?"

* * * * * * *

The summer before the 1967 football season, McVea hoped he would stay relatively healthy his senior season—like the summer before, when he worked out with fellow running back Dickie Post. Instead, McVea suffered an injury that would hamper him throughout what he expected to be his definitive year at UH. He was hanging out at Lloyd Wells's photography studio with several college and pro players from the area—Bubba and Tody Smith, Otis Taylor, and others—and throwing around a football. McVea described what happened: "Otis threw me a hitch pass, and I felt my groin muscle pull. I didn't think anything of it at the time. It was my fault, though. I didn't rehab it like I should have. Bubba Smith did show me an exercise to help the groin muscle, and that helped. But it still bothered me the whole season."

Before fall practice, Yeoman and the Cougars received two pieces of good news. Paul Gipson—like Royce Berry—had been suspended for the remainder of the 1966 season after missing curfew, but he would be able to play in 1967. Gipson had dropped out of school in the spring, returning to his hometown of Conroe and working at a country club. To be eligible for the 1967 season, Gipson attended both summer sessions at the University of Houston. He had to hitchhike from Conroe every day to get to campus. He did the work required and was declared eligible.

The other good news Yeoman received was that McVea was named to the *Playboy Magazine* preseason All-America team.

The Cougars were going to need the full talents of Gipson and McVea, because their 1967 schedule was one of the toughest in history. The ten teams the Cougars would play had a combined record of 60–39–1 in 1966. Two traditional football powers, Michigan State University and the University of Georgia, were new to the schedule.

The Cougars opened the season with always-tough Florida State and faced back-to-back Saturdays at Mississippi State and Ole Miss in October.

Probably the most intriguing game was the matchup between Houston and Michigan State in East Lansing on September 23. The Spartans were coming off a national championship season in 1965 and an undefeated 1966 campaign, the only blemish being a 10–10 tie with Notre Dame in an epic battle.

Even though the Spartans had lost 12 of 22 starters, including All-Americans Bubba Smith, George Webster, Gene Washington, and Clint Jones, they still featured such All-America candidates as quarterback Jimmy Raye and Beaumont products defensive lineman Tody Smith and defensive back Jess Phillips.

Then there was the relationship between Spartan coach Duffy Daugherty and Bill Yeoman—an assistant coach under Daugherty from 1954 to 1961. Daugherty actually scheduled the game out of his friendship with Yeoman. The game had been slated several years before when Michigan State was on its way to a national championship and UH was still struggling to become a football power.

For the new season, the Cougars added several more African American players to their roster: Carlos Bell (basketball player Melvin Bell's younger brother), Larry Gardner, Otis Stewart, tight end Harold Smith, and defensive end Jerry Drones (A. Z. Drones's younger brother). Smith and Drones had played for legendary high school coach Emory Bellard at San Angelo Central High School. Smith became the first black starter on defense for the Cougars. The younger Drones was nicknamed "Snake" by his UH teammates; Achey said it was because Drones "was like a snake on the defensive line. He would move around and slither past the blocker and then he'd strike you."

"First of all," Drones explained, "I had my nickname before I got to Houston. My JV basketball team in San Angelo called me that. I used to drive down the lane toward the basket like a snake. Harold Smith called me 'Snake' when we got here to Houston and it stuck. I moved to San Angelo in 1954, not long after *Brown v. the Board of Education*. I went to integrated schools. I got to play for Emory Bellard. Also on that coaching staff at San Angelo Central was future Texas Tech coach Spike Dykes.

"I wasn't highly recruited out of high school like my brother A. Z. was. I was only 165 pounds coming out of high school. Cougar coach Ben Hurt said my recruitment was like a 'cow and a calf' deal. Harold Smith, who was much more heavily recruited than me, was the 'cow,' and I was the 'calf.' Unfortunately, Harold was injured at UH and eventually went into the service. The only offers I had were from UTEP and Houston. I eventually chose Houston because it seemed like a school that was building something good.

"I had fun at Houston. It was a great group of guys and teammates. I never had any problems with anybody on the team. I was in the third group of blacks that came to campus, so I didn't run into many problems.

"I also got to play freshman basketball at UH. I had played at San Angelo, and the UH frosh team only had five players, so they talked me into playing. I really enjoyed it. I played for Harvey Pate. He was a really good person. He did a lot for the school. I remember going up into East Texas and playing against schools like Tyler, Kilgore, East Texas Baptist. I know a couple of years before I got there, the team wouldn't spend the night in hotels, but by the time I played there, we did. We really didn't run into any problems at those schools."

* * * * * * *

Before the Cougars took on Michigan State in their second game of the season, they had to be careful not to overlook their opening opponent of the season, the always-tough Florida State Seminoles, on Friday, September 15, in the Astrodome. As far back as spring training, Yeoman warned about the Seminoles: "If a lot of people around here don't start thinking about our first opponent, Florida State, there won't be much to be happy about on our way to Michigan State. Florida State thinks it has a really good team this year, and not too many people are going to disagree with them. They play Alabama in their second game, and I think they have a real good chance of beating them."

Luckily, the backfield tandem of Gipson and McVea never gave Florida State a chance. The Cougars trounced the visitors, 33–13, before 40,336 fans under the Dome. The home team ran up a 33–0 lead before the Seminoles notched 13 meaningless fourth-quarter points. Gipson and McVea each ran for 103 yards, Gipson on 19 carries and McVea on 15. Gipson scored on 2- and 10-yard runs, and McVea scored from 10 yards out. McVea sat out the entire second half to help rest his tender groin muscle for Michigan State.

After that slaughter, the Cougars prepared for the biggest game in school history: a September 23 trip to East Lansing, Michigan, to take on the No. 3–ranked Michigan State Spartans before 75,000 rabid fans. Yeoman said, "The guys were really looking forward to playing Michigan State."

McVea concurred: "I always got fired up to play the good teams. Tody Smith and Jess Phillips, who I knew well and hung around with in the summer, were always giving me a hard time, telling me about what they were going to do to us at Michigan State."

Duffy Daugherty said before the game, "We have a lot of respect for Bill Yeoman, and we don't have anyone who runs like Warren McVea, and we may regret this whole thing."

Quarterback Dick Woodall said, "Going into the game, we weren't intimidated or nervous. We had a good year in 1966, so we knew we were good. Beating Florida State in our opening game also gave us a lot of confidence."

Truth be told, many at Michigan State were not taking the Cougars or the game seriously. J. B. Keys was on the traveling squad to Michigan State. He said, "It seemed like Warren knew everyone. He was friends with Tody Smith. He met us at the airport. He had two or three other Michigan State players with him. They took one look at Warren and Don Bean and me, and they pointed at us and started laughing. Tody said, 'Don't laugh at them, I know how good they are.'"

Yeoman added, "We were much smaller, yet we had one distinct advantage—we were faster. The truth is, we weren't going to overpower anybody. We just had a bunch of little ol' guys. When we came out, the Michigan State students laughed at us. Heck, our right tackle, Larry Perez, was just 5-foot-8 and 216 pounds."

Keys said, "At the game there were more people than I'd ever seen in my life—75,000 or so. Coach Yeoman told us before the game what the Michigan State players would do. He said in the tunnel going into the stadium that the Spartan players would go right up to us instead of going around us and make a lot of noise to try and intimidate us."

Achey recalled, "The Michigan State game was my sophomore year. I was on the traveling squad for the first time. First of all, things didn't start well for me that day. Backup quarterback Ken Bailey and myself overslept, and the bus to the stadium had to wait for us—that didn't go well. When we got to the stadium, our locker room was a mess—straight out of the 1940s. There were a couple of ratty old double doors that led to the concourse and the tunnel that led to the stadium.

"Coach Yeoman said the Michigan State players would make a bunch of racket in the tunnel to try to intimidate us. Then, right before they would take the field, they would get silent. Coach Yeoman said when they did that for us to start laughing and cutting up. There were 76,000 fans there. There were a lot of folding chairs around the field. We had to go through them, and when we did, fans were yelling things like, 'Hey Yeoman, go home!' Or something like, 'Hey! Get your little guys and go home!' The thing is, we were so much quicker and faster than they were."

Yeoman described an incident in the tunnel: "Before the game, I told the players, and particularly defensive tackle Jerry Gardner, not to give an inch, not to change their path to the field, not their walk or anything. As Gardner came through the tunnel, one of the Michigan State kids got a little too close. Jerry forearmed him and dropped him. It was kind of indicative that we would not be intimidated."

September 23, 1967, in what is still considered the biggest day in University of Houston football history, was also Warren McVea's greatest day as a Houston Cougar. In front of what proved to be the official stadium count of 75,833 Michigan State faithful, Houston blasted the third-ranked Spartans, 37–7: the team's worst loss since 1947. McVea racked up 155 yards rushing on only 14 carries. In the first quarter, he had runs of 48 and 33 yards the first two times he touched the ball.

Then, just before halftime, McVea scampered for a 50-yard touchdown run to put the Cougars up for good, 10–7.

In the third quarter, on their first possession, Woodall hit Ken Hebert on a post pattern for a 77-yard touchdown for a 17–7 lead. In the fourth, Woodall hit flanker Don Bean on a 76-yard bomb. "Bean ran straight down the field, past a guy he'd been outrunning since grade school in Beaumont, Jess Phillips, and caught the pass for a 76-yard score," Yeoman remembered.

Mike Simpson added a 41-yard interception return, and Ken Bailey scored on a 2-yard run for the final 37–7 margin. When the game was over, many stood in disbelief. Woodall recalled, "I don't know if there was a bigger game in UH history or for Coach Yeoman. It was a huge win."

Warren McVea, 1967
(Courtesy of UH Athletic Department)

Harold Smith remembered that special day: "The Michigan State fans just kept watching Warren run by them all day. They were stunned at the end of the game." And Achey said, "Their fans were pretty quiet when we left."

In the press box toward the end of the game, *Daily Cougar* reporter Tim Fleck said positive comments ranged from "Fantastic team" to "Never seen anything like them" to "McVea is literally unbelievable."

Spartan defensive back Drake Garrett called McVea "the best back I've ever seen. His moves . . . you don't know what he's going to do next. He's there . . . and then he's not."

Daugherty said, "Their speed got us," and "McVea is the most talented runner I've seen in a long time."

Years after the historic game, Yeoman said, "It was so big because of all the media being there. We had an enormous press corps there because of all the big games MSU had played and was supposed to play later on in the year, like Southern California and Notre Dame. It was such a big win for our program because of all the exposure we got."

The sports news media was stunned and shocked, as was the rest of the country. The *New York Times* reported Alabama tying Florida State, the team Houston had blasted the week before, and the Cougars beating Michigan State on the same day: "The odds of Michigan State or Alabama giving up 37 points to any team in the country would have been 100 to 1 on Saturday morning. The odds of both of them doing so simultaneously would have been 1,000 to 1."

The *Times* continued, "It couldn't possibly happen—but it did Saturday. When in the history of intercollegiate football was there ever recorded on one such day twin fantasies as Alabama being tied by Florida State, 37–37, and Michigan St. losing, 37–7, to Houston? Florida State and Houston? How could such Johnnys-Come-Lately even belong on the same field with such longstanding Goliaths of Samsonian strength as Alabama and Michigan State?"

Cougar linebacker Wade Phillips said, "Against Michigan State, we were supposedly this big underdog, and we beat them. We had also beaten Florida State badly the week before. On the plane ride back to

Houston, we heard that Florida State had tied Alabama. When we heard that, everyone got excited."

Sports Illustrated dispatched legendary sportswriter Dan Jenkins to East Lansing to cover the game. In his article titled, "The Spartans Get Stabbed by Mac the Knife," Jenkins spoke of the Cougars's team speed: "Unfortunately for the good-natured Duffy Daugherty, what Houston showed up with last week were the speediest athletes this side of a bobsled run. Led by the 180-pound McVea, it looked as if everyone on Houston's team could run the 100 in 8.6."

Jenkins quoted Daugherty as saying, "We're not that bad. But even if we had played better, it would only have made the score closer. That team of theirs, you either catch 'em for a loss—or boom!"

Of McVea, Jenkins said, "Surely all of the epic open-field runners in college football's history were arthritic Step 'n Fetch-its compared to Wondrous Warren McVea, who runs like a blinking light . . . like a ZIP Code . . . cracking through the cavern of Spartan Stadium in East Lansing, darting and wriggling, streaking and spinning, doing this Z, then this V, then a long –, and finally a 6."

Jenkins also described McVea's three memorable first-half runs: "The first time McVea touched the ball, he cut this way and that for 48 yards, and the second time, he burst loose for 33 yards—both bobbing, weaving, beautiful runs that made it seem like he was in Flint one second, Ann Arbor the next, and Grand Rapids the next. You knew that the Spartans were in trouble.

"Later, on the same play, an off-tackle quickie called 23-G, he went 50 yards for a touchdown—well, 50 in the statistics, but more like 80 with all of his cuts and feints. A run by Wondrous Warren seems to last six or seven minutes."

When the team returned to Houston's Hobby Airport that evening, an enormous crowd was there to greet the Cougars. An airport official said, "I've never seen anything like it."

Cougar faithful on hand to greet their heroes at Hobby held up signs like, "Bring on Green Bay!"; "Big 10 Ain't So Big!"; and "MSU—Just a Workout!"

Achey said, "There were five to seven thousand people there waiting for us. It was crazy." And Harold Smith added, "When we got back to Houston, the plane couldn't even dock at the gate, there were so many people there."

"It was unbelievable because there were between ten and eleven thousand people there." Yeoman said years later. "We had to park 150 yards away from the terminal because they couldn't corral all the fans. It was a real nice trip home after a big win. It was very special."

The effects of the victory over Michigan State lingered for days, even weeks afterward. First, the Associated Press named Warren McVea Back of the Week and Bill Yeoman Coach of the Week.

Joel Williams said, "After the Michigan State game, it was announced that they were going to show the game on campus the next week at the Student Center—the place was packed!"

Houston Chronicle sports columnist Wells Twombly wrote, "What made it all so sweet was the way in which the school's alumni came out of hiding. On the Monday after the Michigan State Carcass was discovered on the turf, downtown Houston looked like the British Army at Saratoga. Red Coats were everywhere. People who used to let the impression get around that they'd really gone to Baylor or Texas A&M or Rice dropped their masks."

Woodall concurred years later: "Downtown Houston after the Michigan State game was crazy. After that game, people wore their UH stuff. The alumni were coming out of the woodwork."

Wade Phillips added, "The Monday after the game, I went to my math class. There were a lot of students in the class, and I didn't really know my professor at all. All of a sudden at the start of class, he says, 'Wade Phillips, stand up!' I didn't know what was going on. He then said, 'These guys just beat Michigan State!'"

Ted Nance said, "Warren was supposed to be on the cover of *Sports Illustrated* the next week. A photographer came out, and that guy must have snapped 500 pictures of Warren that week. At the last minute, Warren got knocked off the cover because Purdue upset Notre Dame."

After the biggest win in school history and the hoopla that sur-
rounded it for the next few days, there was of course the fear of a
letdown the next week when the Cougars took on the Wake Forest
Demon Deacons out of the ACC in a Friday night tilt at the Astrodome. Wake Forest came into the game 0–2 after losing to Duke and
Clemson. Before 41,769, the Cougars showed no signs of sagging
spirits as they scored three first-quarter touchdowns and routed Wake
Forest, 50–6.

McVea started the scoring with a 70-yard touchdown reception
from Woodall. Ken Hebert added touchdown catches of 50, 8, and
13 yards.

However, with the Cougars up 28–0 in the second quarter, a controversy erupted on the field between the fiery Hebert and McVea.
McVea did not get out of his stance to take a pitchback, allowing quarterback Woodall to be clobbered. Hebert proceeded to chastise McVea
and shoved him in the huddle. McVea shoved Hebert back and was
promptly removed from the game. Yeoman reportedly grabbed him
by the arm for a discussion, but McVea jerked his arm away roughly.
Some say McVea also shoved his coach. Brushed aside as a "boys will
be boys" incident—a heat of the moment confrontation between two
competitors—McVea did not return to action for the rest of the game.
Yeoman didn't pull him; McVea simply refused to go back in. Later,
McVea said, "I was really hot. I was shocked at Kenny. I guess I was a
little embarrassed. The whole thing was over right in the huddle, and
we apologized to each other. I could have gone back in, but it was 28–0
and they didn't need me. I had this sore groin. Why should I abuse it
against a team we're going to beat bad? If they had needed me, I'd have
been in there."

Defensive back Bill Hollon said, "Hebert was a winner. He didn't
think Mac was putting forth enough effort. It was not a racial thing,
just a disagreement between two players."

Hebert recalled years later, "The Wake Forest incident in the middle
of the field—it could have been handled differently. It was something
that happened in the heat of battle. We both had the same objective,
and that was to win."

* * * * * * *

After the Wake Forest rout, the Cougars stood at 3–0 and rose to
their highest ranking in school history, before or since. They were now
No. 2 in the AP poll and No. 3 in the UPI rankings. Next up was
an Astrodome contest with the tough, underrated North Carolina
State Wolf Pack. They, too, entered the game at 3–0. The week
before, the Wolf Pack had defeated Florida State, 20–10. This was
the same team the Cougars had beaten in week one. Those were the
only two games the Seminoles lost in 1967.

The three-touchdown underdog NC State pulled off at the time
what seemed to be an upset of gargantuan proportions, defeating the
Cougars, 16–6, before a record Astrodome crowd of 52,483. In hindsight, it was not as big of an upset as some would have thought. NC
State started off the year 8–0, rose as high as No. 10 in the AP rankings,
and beat Georgia, 14–7, in the Liberty Bowl.

The Cougars got off to a 6–0 lead as McVea ripped off 41 yards
on his first five carries. On the fifth carry, however, just ten minutes
into the game, McVea collided with 260-pound All-America defensive tackle Dennis Byrd and badly bruised his left shoulder. McVea
missed the rest of the game, and in his absence, the Houston offense
sputtered to its lowest output in two years. The Cougars only managed
222 total yards, with only 63 yards coming in the second half. UH also
fumbled seven times, losing three of them to NC State, and suffered
two interceptions.

"Our own mistakes killed us," Houston offensive guard Bill Pickens
said.

The loss dropped the Cougars to 10th in the AP and 12th in the
UPI polls.

UH now had two weeks to prepare for uncharted waters. On consecutive weekends, they would head to the state of Mississippi to play
Mississippi State in Starkville and then to Oxford to play Ole Miss a
week later. The Cougars would be the first teams with African Americans on their roster to play at both schools. In fact, these players would
be the first blacks to take the field against any all-white team on Mississippi soil.

The Cougars were heavy 19-point favorites against the Bulldogs, who were 1–3 that season, with their one win a 7–3 victory over 10th-ranked Texas Tech.

One of the biggest concerns heading into the Mississippi State game was the health of McVea. Even though there was an off week before the Cougars played the Bulldogs, McVea was still nursing shoulder and groin injuries. Yeoman spent the two weeks leading up to the game devising methods to compensate for McVea's potential absence. He switched flanker Don Bean to running back and promoted senior George Nordgren to starting running back. Yet, on the Thursday before the game, McVea said, "I plan to make the trip. I'm also pretty sure I'll be able to play, too. I know that in the past, most of the bruises and pains I have on Thursday suddenly disappear on Saturday. If that happens, I'll be ready for action."

Another concern was the fact that UH was bringing African American players to the State of Mississippi. "For whatever reason," Yeoman said upon reflection, "I was more worried about going to Mississippi State than Oxford the next week to play Ole Miss. My parents, though, were sure I'd be shot in Oxford. For whatever reason, I wasn't worried when I went there."

The experience brought back many memories years later.

Jerry Drones recalled his experience in Starkville: "We went for a walk down this little road close to the hotel. This guy comes out of his house with a hunting rifle and stood on the front porch—he most likely was just going hunting. The black players were in the front of the group that was walking down the road.

"We decided to turn around and go back. We weren't totally sure what the deal was. We knew things were still going on in the South, and we weren't sure what that guy was thinking. I really didn't run into too many problems in the South. We always stayed at national hotel chains like Holiday Inn, so I think that cut down on problems.

"At the stadium in Starkville, I didn't have a lot of apprehension. I was usually in the back when we would enter a stadium. At Mississippi State, I made sure I was in the middle or close to the front so I could get into the stadium. I just wanted to be on the safe side."

Cougar cheerleader Jimmy Disch recalled a humorous incident related to him by Cougar tight end Paul Daulong involving Paul Gipson and his roommate, Carlos Bell, in the hotel the night before the game: "Paul Daulong told me that to lighten the mood at Mississippi State in the hotel before the game, Paul Gipson got a white sheet and put it over his head and pretended he was in the KKK. He went to his room to scare his roommate, Carlos Bell."

Daulong remembered, "Gip was playing the KKK that night. He put a sheet over his head. He was just having fun. He was just a good ole country boy from Conroe."

At game time, Yeoman decided to hold McVea out of the game. Luckily, the Cougars did not need his services. Despite six fumbles, the Cougars blasted the Bulldogs, 43–6, before 17,000 fans at Scott Field.

Three of the Cougars's African American players made large contributions to that day's victory, with none bigger than Don Bean's. Bean, filling in for McVea, scored on a 9-yard touchdown run, but it was as a punt returner that he did the most damage. Bean returned six punts for 172 yards, including returns for 50, 65, and 76 yards, with the 65-yarder going for a touchdown.

The Associated Press game story mentioned Bean and integration: "Bean, a 170-pound senior, was one of several Negro players on Houston's team who became the first of their race to perform on the state gridiron."

Gipson contributed 87 yards rushing and a touchdown, and Jerry Drones was a catalyst for the defense. David Fink of the *Houston Post* said, "Greg Brezina dropped Mississippi State quarterback Tommy Pharr five or six times . . . while Jerry Drones accomplished the feat once. The rest of the time, the Cougars gang-tackled, but most of the time Brezina and Drones were the first ones there." The defense limited the Bulldogs to just 90 yards of offense and only four first downs. The Cougars rolled up 272 yards on the ground and 155 passing.

After the game, Yeoman said of Don Bean, "I'm glad he's on our team, not somebody else's. I'm very pleased that Bean broke for some long returns. He's been overdue . . . he's going to need to be even quicker next week when we play Ole Miss."

There were several incidents dealing with the integration of Scott Field. UH student Wally Lewis made the trip to Starkville and spoke about his experience in the *Daily Cougar*, saying, "When a UH Negro footballer was stopped for little or no gain, an extremely loud roar could be heard echoing from the partisan fans. Although half the sideline seats were vacant, the Negroes were placed in the end zone in a place someone in the press box described as 'the nigger section.'

"Other searing remarks could be heard from the stands, campus police, employees of the stadium, and the people working the down markers on the sidelines. When the Negro spectators, mostly teenage boys, began to yell for UH and boo State, Mississippi State troopers encircled the area . . . one UH fan encouraged the young fans to yell a little louder for the Cougars."

Lewis quoted an onlooker as telling the young men, "You might get hung for that." He said, "Within five minutes, a trooper threatened to eject the UH youth for encouraging the boys to enjoy themselves and yell for whom they pleased."

Lewis said, "The most humorous stunt pulled by some Mississippi State fans came late in the game when their cause was horribly lost. Obviously feeling persecuted by the fine play of Don Bean, Paul Gipson, Jerry Drones, and other Negro players, they tried to instill that 'old time' spirit in their ballplayers by playing 'Dixie.'

"After the game while eating dinner, one could hear State fans speaking favorably about a mutual admiration society known as the Ku Klux Klan."

It was also reported that Wally Lewis, right before halftime, took it upon himself to go down to the end zone and lead the segregated Negro fans in their cheering for Houston. Apparently, after the game, Lewis had to run and hide in his automobile to avoid the wrath of Mississippi State fans.

Tim Fleck, sports editor for the *Daily Cougar*, said, "Before the game in the press box, most of the comments were snide jabs at the ethnic composition of the UH squad. Afterwards, the comments very much sounded like, 'Just wait a few more years. Then we'll have our own Beans and McVeas.'"

One interesting incident happened after the game with the injured McVea, who had watched the game from the sidelines clad in street clothes. After the game, he was approached on the field by a group of Mississippi State fans, mostly young boys. Sports Information Director Ted Nance said, "All these little kids approached him after the game and surrounded him. They just wanted to get a look at Warren up close and maybe get his autograph."

Years later, McVea said, "I didn't play, and they were giving me the usual business from the stands—nothing racial—just the usual. I knew D. D. Lewis, the Mississippi State linebacker, and after the game I was on the field talking to him. Jack Littlefield, the UH equipment manager, would always wait for me, and we would go back to the dressing room together. I looked up, and all of these people from the stands were heading down to the field. I got so scared. I didn't know what was going on.

"They got right up next to Jack and me, and we were surrounded. I didn't know what was going to happen. Then everybody started asking me for my autograph. I've never been so scared in my life, but those ended up being the nicest people I ever met."

* * * * * * *

With the dismantling of Mississippi State, the Cougars turned their attention to the always-tough Ole Miss Rebels. Like Mississippi State, the game in Oxford on October 28 would be the first time African Americans would play against the Rebels at Hemingway Stadium. The Rebels carried an uncharacteristic 3–2 record into the game, but one of their victories was a 29–20 victory over third-ranked Georgia.

The Cougars, who had moved back up to ninth in the AP rankings, were installed as a five-point favorite. It was Homecoming for Ole Miss, and a sellout crowd was expected. "Ole Miss has a great collection of athletes and is one of the strongest teams we'll face this season," Coach Yeoman said. "If we play a level-headed game and give them our best, we can win."

As with the previous week at Mississippi State, there was a lot of apprehension with UH going into Oxford with African Americans on its roster. Some of this uneasiness dated back to the previous season, when the Cougars had played Ole Miss at Memphis. Before the game that week, a pregame pep rally on the Ole Miss campus resulted in McVea being hung in effigy while students gathered around and hollered, "Burn, nigger, burn!"

There also were group chants and brightly painted posters that spelled out the Ole Miss fans's feelings toward Houston's black players. One Cougar fan remarked, "It was unbelievable. Some of the slogans made the word 'nigger' seem like a compliment."

Yeoman recalled the few days leading up to the game in Oxford: "Once again, for some reason, I wasn't worried going into Oxford. My parents, though, were sure I was going to be shot. Once we got to Oxford, we had no trouble with the hotel accommodations. Because of the death threats and other potential for trouble, we had the players unplug their hotel-room phones at 10 p.m."

Jim Pat Berger, one of Warren McVea's closest friends, recalled, "I remember when we got to Ole Miss that Friday. Warren was usually upbeat, but on this day he was really quiet. I said, 'Mac, are you OK?' Warren said, 'Shit, Berger, we're in the territory where they don't like niggers!'"

Even fullback Paul Gipson, who had made light of Jim Crow the week before wearing the bed sheet to imitate the KKK, felt uneasy about Oxford. Jim Urbanek, All-America defensive tackle for the Rebels, said, "After the season, I went to play in the Hula Bowl in Hawaii. I remember Ken Hebert telling me that Paul Gipson brought a gun with him when they came to play us in Oxford."

Hebert said, "There was a bit of apprehension going into that place. I don't recall any incidents, though. We did all get to stay at the same hotel. Coach Yeoman wouldn't have allowed us to stay in separate hotels."

Dick Woodall recalled, "We were the first team with blacks to go into Oxford. We learned what racism is all about. I remember cars going by us at the hotel and the stadium shouting slurs at us."

Senior defensive back Tom Paciorek had a somewhat different perspective. "Integration was the furthest thing from my mind when we went to Ole Miss," he recalled. "To be honest, I didn't notice anything racial when we went there. I was 20 years old and my mind was some-where else. To tell you the truth, I was more impressed with the Ole Miss cheerleaders than anything—they were the epitome of a South-ern Belle."

Several of the African American players received death threats, including McVea. Yeoman remembered, "They said they were going to shoot him if he scored a touchdown."

An odd person to receive a death threat was white sophomore wide receiver Calvin Achey. "I'm guessing the reason I got it was that I was a wide receiver and my name is Calvin, which was a fairly common black first name back then," Achey said. "I kidded around with the other black players who got death threats. I said, 'You don't have anything on me!'

"I got a kick out of it, being from Colorado, where everything was integrated. I didn't take the whole thing seriously. I told the black players I had gotten a threat, and they seemed to get a kick out of it. I kidded them that during the game, I was going to keep my helmet off.

"I took the whole incident at the time as comical. I even thought some of our coaches may even have sent the death threats as a joke. I didn't think anyone would really do that. The black guys took it to heart, though. I remember some of them saying, 'It's just a bunch of crazy old crackers.' I guess in the end, I just didn't understand the whole thing, not having lived in their culture."

Yeoman remembered another incident on the Friday before the game: "We had a workout at the stadium, and I remember as we went onto the field, one Mississippi policeman said to another in a very loud voice, 'Have you ever seen so many fuckin' niggers in your life?'"

Jerry Drones recalled, "Just like at Mississippi State, when it was time to enter the stadium, the black players came out of the tunnel first so we could get the heck into the stadium. That reminds me of the next year when we played the Rebels in Jackson. We were up to eight to ten black players on the team, and we all came out into the stadium first, and I remember the Ole Miss fans saying things like, 'Do they have any white boys on the team?' I also noticed at Oxford the blacks had to sit together in stands that were basically outside the main part of the stadium."

It appeared that McVea was going to be able to play. He could have played the previous week against Mississippi State, but the Cougar rout of the Bulldogs had helped them save him for one more week. However, McVea would not start. That honor would go to George Nordgren, who rushed for 85 yards against Mississippi State.

Yeoman told the media, "I think our kids are in the right frame of mind now to play Ole Miss. We bounced back real well against Mississippi State last week, and if we don't make too many mistakes, I think we can make a whale of a game out of it on Saturday."

The coach was partially correct with his pregame assessment. The Cougars and Ole Miss did play a whale of a game, with the Rebels prevailing by a single point, 14–13, in front of 26,500 happy Homecoming fans. The Cougars made mistakes at key points that helped spell their defeat. The Rebels took advantage of two key fumbles and turned both into touchdowns on the ensuing first plays from scrimmage.

The first touchdown came early in the second quarter after a McVea fumble on his own 23-yard line. After a 5-yard illegal motion penalty, wide receiver Mac Haik hauled in a 28-yard touchdown reception from quarterback Bruce Newell. Usually reliable Cougar defensive back Gus Hollomon had fallen down on the play, leaving Haik wide open. The future Houston Oiler's touchdown and subsequent extra point tied the game at 7–7. The Cougars had jumped out to a 7–0 first quarter lead, thanks to punt returner Don Bean, who went all the way with a 75-yard touchdown return.

Then, with the score still knotted at seven with 44 seconds left in the third quarter, opportunity knocked again for the Rebels. A Paul Gipson fumble gave Ole Miss the ball at the Cougar 37-yard line. Once again, following Ole Miss head coach John Vaught's philosophy of going for a big play immediately after a turnover, Bruce Newell launched a pass to tight end Hank Shows at the goal line. Just as it appeared that Hollomon was going to intercept the ball, Shows turned back and ripped the ball out of Hollomon's hands and stepped across the goal line for a touchdown.

Yes, indeed, the quick-strike touchdowns were typical of Ole Miss. Bruce Newell said years later, "Coach Vaught usually tried to go for it all after a turnover, and we did that on both touchdowns in the Houston game. I remember Hank Shows taking the ball away from the Houston guy for our second touchdown in that game."

Although they were now down 14–7 heading into the fourth quarter, the Cougars were not quite finished. Early in the fourth quarter, Woodall connected on a 42-yard bomb to Achey to make the score 14–13. However, Ken Hebert missed the point-after attempt, his third missed kick of the day. He had missed a 20-yard field goal in the second quarter and a 42-yarder in the third.

"I'm proud of the effort," Yeoman said after the game. "But we're here to win, and we didn't. I knew we had to play without making any mistakes. They did it, we didn't, and we got beat. Those fumbles killed us, of course."

Adding to the narrow loss was the peculiar performance of McVea. He ran for 47 yards on ten carries in the first half, several times appearing to break in the clear for potential touchdowns. Twice the speedy running back was caught from behind by a defensive back. Then, on one play in the second quarter, McVea rode through a block by All-America guard Rich Stotter into a gaping hole on the right side of the line. As he sprinted into the open field, he fell down uncontested. What should have been a sure touchdown turned into a 14-yard gain. After his first-half performance, McVea did not play the rest of the game.

After the game, the Cougar star had no explanation as to why he was caught from behind or why he fell in the open field. Yeoman said, "I don't know why McVea tripped in the open field, and I can't say what made Hebert miss those three kicks, but it happened."

Years later, the coach shed some light on McVea's performance that October Saturday in Oxford. "As I had said, Warren did get a death threat at Ole Miss," Yeoman explained. "It said they were going to shoot him if he scored a touchdown. One time Warren had beat their safety, but the guy caught him and tackled him. On another run, he was wide open on his way to a touchdown, and he just flat fell down.

"I asked Warren about that a few weeks later, and he told me he was afraid to be out in the open and score like that—he thought he could be shot. Warren then told me that if it had been a one- or two-yard attempt to score a touchdown, he would have done it because there would have been a crowd of people around the goal line."

Another perspective came years later from Sam Swearengin, a UH student who made the trip to Oxford with a couple friends. Swearengin said, "We left Friday and drove all night. As luck would have it, I had a grandmother who lived in Oxford, so when we got there, we got ourselves a catnap and then went to the game.

"I felt at the stadium it was a very racially charged atmosphere. I felt very uncomfortable in the stands. Ole Miss fans were yelling all kinds of racial comments. They were saying things like we slept with niggers, we were nigger-lovers, all kinds of stuff. If we would have won that game, I honestly felt we would have been in trouble. I'm not sure what would have happened, but it wouldn't have been good.

"Warren was so fast. If he ever got in the open, no one could catch him. At the game, though, there were two or three times he broke into the open and should have scored. He was caught from behind a couple of times.

"We thought it was weird at the time. We were scratching our heads in the stands. How could anyone catch Warren? Then on another play, Warren was headed for a long touchdown, and he just flat fell down. No one was near him. Once again, we were talking amongst ourselves, saying, 'Why did he fall down?' We were wondering what the heck was going on.

"We didn't know about the death threats on Warren at the time. It wasn't until years later that those stories started to get out. In my honest opinion, it was those death threats that won the game for Ole Miss that day. Warren should have had two or three touchdowns."

* * * * * * *

After the heartbreaking loss to Ole Miss, the Cougars returned to the Astrodome on November 4 to face yet another foe affiliated with the Southeast Conference: the fifth-ranked Georgia Bulldogs. In spite of their lofty ranking, the Bulldogs entered the game as five-point underdogs. Yeoman said, "I guess the sportswriters who vote in the polls and the odds makers don't see eye-to-eye on our ball club. I was quite surprised to see us as the favorite. Georgia has a real strong football team, and we'll have to be at our best to beat them."

Georgia coach Vince Dooley had his take on the game, saying, "The thing that concerns me the most about Houston is their tremendous speed. Considering all factors, this is the finest football team we have seen this year, and it may be the finest we will see all year."

In spite of ongoing rumors that he was going to quit or be kicked off the team, McVea returned to practice during the week. For the first time in over a month, it appeared he would be playing. "I hope Warren will be able to go at full speed for Saturday," Yeoman told the writers. "He hasn't been able to go 100 percent since late September. We need him in there."

On the Monday before the game, McVea said, "I think I'll be close to full speed by the end of the week, and I felt close to that point in practice today." On a side note, the Saturday night game would be the first time in two years that McVea's mother, Mattie, would be able to see her son play, having missed so many games due to illness.

On Friday evening, another interesting racial incident unfurled. Ted Nance recounted, "We used to have press parties for visiting and local media and the athletic staffs of both colleges at the Astrodome club level on Friday nights before home games. Before we played Georgia in 1967, we were having a party while the two teams were having a light workout on the field. Harry Kalas, one of our broadcasters, was down on the field and decided to bring Ollie Matson, a scout for the Philadelphia Eagles at that time, up to the party. Within five minutes of Ollie's arrival, the Georgia people all excused themselves and left the party. I guess it goes to show you the South was still struggling with integration."

Charlie Miller, Nance's unofficial assistant sports information director, had the same experience: "When Harry Kalas brought Ollie Matson up to the Georgia party, the place cleared out. I remember saying to [UH athletic director] Harry Fouke, 'I don't believe what I'm seeing.'"

A record 53,356 Cougar faithful watched UH rally from a 14–0 deficit with 15 fourth-quarter points to edge out the Georgia Bulldogs,

15–14. The Cougars also overcame five lost fumbles to record the heart-stopping win.

The Bulldogs scored first on an 8-yard second-quarter run by Kirby Moore. In the third quarter, a 71-yard interception return by defensive back Terry Sellers set up a 12-yard touchdown run by Kent Lawrence to put the Bulldogs up 14–0.

The Cougars began their comeback with Gipson scoring on a 25-yard run. For the game, Gipson set a University of Houston single-game rushing record with 229 yards on 29 carries. Probably none of Gipson's carries was more important than the one that preceded the Cougars's last touchdown, a 57-yard pass from Woodall to Hebert with 4:29 to play. Before that spectacular scoring play, Gipson thundered 13 yards, and at the end of the play, he flattened Georgia safety Terry Sellers. Sellers, still feeling the effects of the collision with Gipson on the next play, let Hebert race by him to catch the Woodall bomb.

Years later, Woodall said, "Paul Gipson was a big reason we scored on that pass play to Kenny Hebert. Gipson was a specimen, an animal. The play before the touchdown, Paul ran over the Georgia defensive back, one of their best athletes. Before the next play, you could tell he was still dazed from the collision with Gipson, so I was screaming at Coach Yeoman to call the play to Hebert. Kenny was 10 yards behind the guy when he caught the ball."

After Hebert's touchdown made the score 14–13 Georgia, Yeoman decided to go for the win with a two-point conversion attempt. The obvious choice for the ball was Gipson. He took Woodall's pitchout and sprinted to the left corner of the end zone for two points and a 15–14 advantage.

The Cougar defense then proceeded to hold Georgia. After a Cougar punt, Carlos Bell recovered a Terry Sellers fumble at the Georgia 30-yard line to seal the win.

The Cougars dominated the statistical battle with 293 yards rushing and 112 yards passing versus just ten first downs and 168 total yards for Georgia.

McVea, healthy for the first time since September, ran for 79 yards on 16 carries. However, he also committed two costly fumbles. Houston

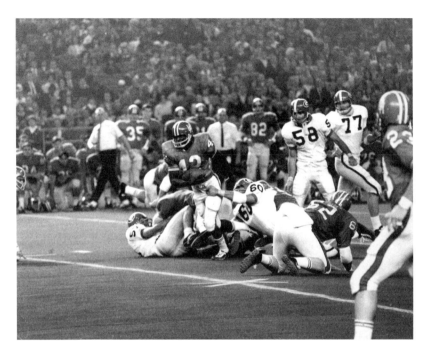

Warren McVea bursts up the middle against Georgia, November 1967
(Courtesy of Myron McReynolds)

fans—obviously suffering from short memories, considering McVea's early-season heroics at Michigan State—booed him when he entered the contest late in the game and cheered when he was later pulled.

Nevertheless, the mood in the Cougars's postgame locker room was jubilant. "There can't be many moments in life as big as this one," Yeoman exclaimed. "The kids were really up for this game. I'll tell you, our kids never let down, and it was a great win."

The victory enabled the Cougars to creep back into the AP rankings at No. 10, and for his efforts, Gipson was named the AP National Back of the Week.

*   *   *   *   *   *   *

Next up was Memphis State University at the Astrodome on November 11. The Cougars had revenge on their minds. The previous season, the Tigers had upset them, 14–13, ruining the hopes of finishing in the Top 10. Memphis State was having another fine season with a 5–2 record. The Tigers had lost to Florida State the previous week, 26–7, the same team the Cougars routed, 33–13, in their opening game. However, Memphis State also had defeated Ole Miss—the team that beat Houston, 14–13, two weeks before—in their opening game of the season by a 27–7 score.

The Cougars were not taking Memphis State lightly. Offensive guard Rich Stotter said, "They beat us last year when we kind of over-looked them. But none of us will overlook them this year. We want to make up for last year's loss."

"I don't think," Yeoman said, "that any of our players who faced them last year will forget what they did to us then."

Statistics had a story to tell. Going into the Memphis State game, the Cougars were fifth nationally in total offense, averaging 409.3 yards per game, while the defense was No. 10, giving up just 202.6 yards per game. The Cougars had notched 197 points through seven games, while giving up just 76.

Before 46,050 at the Dome, UH put together a 28-point second half to take down the Tigers, 35–18.

Gipson had another strong game, rolling up 154 rushing yards on 22 carries and scoring on touchdown runs of 5, 2, and 12 yards. McVea had his best game since Michigan State, rushing for 109 yards on 16 carries. Wide receiver Calvin Achey also caught a 52-yard third-quarter bomb from Woodall to give the Cougars a 21–6 lead.

The Cougars amassed 387 yards rushing and 502 total yards on the night. Thus, after eight games, Houston led the nation in rushing at 258.4 yards per game and in total offense at 426 yards per game.

Only one Astrodome game remained in Warren McVea's career, a night game against the outmanned Idaho Vandals on November 18. The Vandals came in with a 4–5 record and started 13 sophomores. The previous week, Idaho had lost to 0–8 Washington State, 52–14.

Before 40,464 fans, the Cougars rolled up 622 total yards, with a school record 511 of it coming on the ground, and set a single-game record for points in a game as they blasted their inexperienced oppo-nent, 77–6. Gipson once again led the rushing attack with 193 yards on 20 carries and first-half touchdown runs of 50 and 11 yards. McVea added 89 yards on nine carries, including a 58-yard second-quarter touchdown run that put the Cougars up 14–0. They never trailed. Fullback Carlos Bell had a breakout performance with 81 yards on just six carries. Through the air, Hebert caught touchdown passes of 30 and 25 yards from Woodall.

The 16 Cougar seniors were jubilant after their last home game. When asked about the outmanned Vandals, Tom Paciorek said, "Well, they did try hard. What can you say, really?"

"All you can say is that they were a young, inexperienced team, and we are a seasoned squad," Yeoman said after the game. "They gave it an all-out effort."

Two Cougar seniors were not sad about leaving behind the Astro-turf playing surface in the Astrodome. "Will I miss all the grass burns and bruises?" said Paciorek. "I don't think so."

When McVea was asked if he would miss the Astroturf playing sur-face he had played on the last two seasons, his response was, "Hell, no!"

All that now remained for the 7–2 Houston Cougars was a Novem-ber 25 road game against the Tulsa Hurricane, a team the Cougars had routed, 73–14, the year before. The Hurricane was 5–3, having lost two weeks earlier, 31–24, to the same Wake Forrest team the Cougars had demolished, 50–6, earlier in the season.

The Tulsa game brought the promise of offensive fireworks. The Hurricane was second nationally in passing at 267.1 yards per game, and they were eighth in total offense. In comparison, after nine games, the Cougars remained the top offensive team in the nation at 447.8 yards per game. They also moved up to fourth in scoring at 34.3 points per game. The difference in the game was potentially Houston's "Mad Dog" defense, which was giving up just 199.3 yards per game.

Yeoman, however, wasn't taking the Hurricane for granted, in spite of the Cougars's win the previous year and the fact that Tulsa lost to North Texas State University, 54–12, the week before. "I'm sure Tulsa will be ready to play us a darn good football game," Yeo-man said. "They've been getting ready for us since we beat them last year. We know that we're going to have to be at our best up there;

this is the only game of the season Tulsa cares about, if what I've heard is true."

Tulsa was indeed ready. The Cougars ran into a combination of a prepared Hurricane team and an old Houston nemesis—turnovers. The Cougars lost six fumbles and had two passes intercepted, as Tulsa scored 13 fourth-quarter points to upset UH, before 26,300 Tulsa faithful.

Those Cougar seniors ended their college football careers the same way they had begun as sophomores in 1965 at the Astrodome—with a loss to Tulsa.

The game saw the visiting team open the scoring to break up a see-saw defensive battle. Greg Brezina recovered a Tulsa fumble on their own 20-yard line. Six plays later, McVea scored the last touchdown of his college career on a 3-yard run, providing the Cougars with a 7–3 halftime lead.

On the first possession of the second half, Gipson scored on a 17-yard run to jack up the lead to 13–3. Hebert missed the extra point try. Tulsa scored on its next possession to narrow the gap to 13–9, heading into the fourth quarter.

Then came the Cougar turnovers and the Hurricane using them to its advantage—scoring two fourth-quarter touchdowns. Tulsa's Bob Murphy intercepted a Woodall pass, and Tulsa took over on the Houston 16-yard line. Five plays later, Tulsa quarterback Mike Stripling put the Hurricane ahead for good with a 1-yard plunge with 12:43 to play.

The next Houston possession also turned out to be costly, as McVea fumbled the ball back to Tulsa at the Houston 36-yard line. Two plays later, Stripling hit Harry Wood with a 33-yard scoring strike to up the Hurricane lead to 22–13.

And so it came to pass that the Cougars saved their worst performance of the season for their last game. Besides the eight turnovers, the offense had its second-lowest output of the season, gaining only 249 total yards, while the defense surrendered 287 yards.

Yeoman said, "I was afraid something like this might happen. I could see Tulsa getting higher and higher as the game went on, and anytime a team with so many good athletes gets its mind made up to win, it can do it.

"We fumbled too much, of course. But Tulsa's tackling didn't make matters any easier for us. We just lost the ball too many times to win, and they took advantage of most of our mistakes."

In retrospect, the 7–3 record and No. 16 AP ranking was somewhat disappointing. Although there were huge victories over Michigan State and Georgia, turnovers helped lead to the three losses to North Carolina State, Ole Miss, and Tulsa.

Linebacker Greg Brezina said years later, "We had enough talent to win the national championship. We had eight or nine guys on our team go pro." Actually, ten players off the 1967 team played in the NFL: Carlos Bell, Greg Brezina, Paul Gipson, Ken Hebert, Gus Hollomon, Warren McVea, Johnny Peacock, Mike Simpson, Rich Stotter, and Jim Strong.

In spite of the disappointing end to the 1967 season, there were many accomplishments and postseason honors, both individual and team. The Cougars led the nation for the second year in a row in total offense with 427.9 yards per game. The defense had allowed a school record 207.6 yards per game. Several Cougars achieved All-America status. Guard Rich Stotter was a consensus pick. Gipson, who rushed for 1,100 yards, was a second-team Associated Press pick. Hebert, who caught 28 passes for 626 yards and seven touchdowns, was a first-team wide receiver for *Look Magazine* and an AP honorable-mention pick.

McVea, thanks to his fast start, was named second-team United Press International and AP honorable-mention running back. In spite of being chosen for several All-America teams and being a fourth-round pick of the Cincinnati Bengals in the 1968 NFL draft, McVea's season was somewhat like the Houston Cougar team's season—somewhat disappointing. The year had started with much promise for McVea after the Florida State and Michigan State games. However, the star running back was beset by shoulder and groin injuries for most of the season.

These injuries resulted in McVea having a poorer season statistically in 1967 than he did the year before. He rushed 105 times for 699 yards in 1967, a clip of 6.7 yards per carry. In 1966, when McVea was somewhat injury free, he ran for 648 yards on just 74 attempts, an average of 8.8 yards per carry.

The Cougar star also fell off statistically as a pass catcher. McVea caught 15 passes for 414 yards and three touchdowns in 1966, while in his senior season, he caught just three passes for 86 yards and one touchdown.

McVea, however, had continued along with his other African American teammates to blaze the trail of integration on football fields in the South. The back-to-back weekends in October when the Cougars integrated the state of Mississippi were truly the defining moments of a successful season. Their efforts, which we now know included facing death threats, changed the course of history in American football. Integration would become the rule and not the exception—a fitting, long-overdue rule of conduct on football fields everywhere in the nation.

16 PRELUDE TO GLORY

If 55,000 Texans yelling for them can't rev them up, nothing will.
—COACH GUY V. LEWIS ABOUT MOTIVATING HIS
COUGARS FOR THE GAME OF THE CENTURY

As the 1967 football season wore down, anticipation for the Cougars's basketball season to get under way grew like rush-hour traffic on Houston's Gulf Freeway. The route ahead generated wild and exciting possibilities, beginning with the senior seasons of Elvin Hayes and Don Chaney and the return of other key players such as Ken Spain and Theodis Lee, along with the addition of junior college transfer George Reynolds. Few UH fans could avoid the thought of this season being the best in Cougar basketball history.

Adding to the preliminary angst that always precedes a new season of promise were several developments that posed a potential negative effect. The first happened just two weeks after the 1967 Final Four. The NCAA rules committee outlawed the dunk shot in college basketball, beginning in the 1967–68 season. Committee Secretary Cliff Fagan cited two

*Guy Lewis with Elvin
Hayes and Don Chaney
before the 1967–68
season
(Courtesy of Myron
McReynolds)*

reasons for the change: the dunk caused too many broken rims and backboards as well as an increase in player injuries.

Cougar coach Guy V. Lewis couldn't help but be outspoken: "In 20 years as a player and coach, I never saw one backboard cracked or broken. As for the steel rims, we might replace one a season. In my years as coach, I've not had one player injured because of dunking the ball."

He elaborated, "Elvin Hayes averaged maybe two dunks per game. In the just completed Final Four in Louisville, he had one dunk each against UCLA and North Carolina. But when Elvin had those dunks, everybody in Freedom Hall stood and cheered. Nobody got up from their seats, however, when Elvin hit a 15-footer from the head of the circle, proving what I've always said: The dunk is the most exciting shot in basketball."

While many basketball aficionados believed that the NCAA was aiming the rule at Lew Alcindor, Coach Lewis said, "I read somewhere once that John Wooden himself said that outlawing the dunk was directed at 'that crazy bunch from Houston.'"

Another big development involved UH basketball. Over the summer, the US State Department had chosen the Cougars to tour the Pacific for a series of exhibition games. However, after the Arab–Israeli war in June, the State Department decided that the Cougars would tour and play in South America instead. They departed Houston on August 17 and were scheduled to return home before the start of fall classes after playing a specially scheduled slate of 13 games against college and national teams from all over South America. Before the plane headed south, Lewis said, "We are really looking forward to the trip, especially the stops in Buenos Aires, Rio de Janeiro, and São Paulo. I expect the caliber of the opposition to be very high, perhaps surpassing many of next season's college opponents."

The Cougars won all but 1 of the 13 games, losing only to one of the top Brazilian teams, 73–69. Their victories included one over the best team in South America, the Corinthian team, which had never lost to an American team before meeting the Cougars. The final score was Cougars 67, Corinthians 63.

"They play a little different down there," Hayes said after the trip. "They don't call charging fouls. You could run right over a guy. There was a lot of contact. You might get a forearm in the mouth and no whistle."

Yet the reception for the northern neighbors was fun and exciting. "In Chile," Hayes said, "over five thousand people watched us work out for 15 minutes. The people were kind of small, and they would follow us for blocks. Everywhere you went, they'd be all around us. They'd run out of stores and block traffic. They loved to look at us. It was a great feeling."

Vern Lewis, Guy V.'s son, echoed the positive effects of the team's visits to Uruguay, Argentina, and Brazil. He said, "We lost only one game. We got in a lot of extra practice and games. It helped the camaraderie on the team. I felt it also gave us a running start heading into the season.

"When we went to Chile," Vern Lewis continued, "Elvin, Don, and Theodis Lee were with us. It was an oddity. The fans would crowd around those three. They had never been around blacks before. At first, it was a little scary. We didn't realize the fans just wanted a closer look."

Years later, Guy Lewis elaborated, "I've always felt like that trip brought us together as a team and had a lot to do with us winning 31 straight games that season. We rode a bus all over South America, and we had to cope with a lot of adversity."

As the tour ended and fall practice approached, the Cougars had to replace several key members of the 1967 Final Four squad. Gone were cocaptains Leary Lentz and Gary Grider, as was starting center Don Kruse. Just a few days before practice began, Guy V. Lewis received some bad news. Starting forward Melvin Bell, the team's second-leading scorer and rebounder, who was hampered by a bad knee throughout the past season, had surgery to remove his kneecap, putting him out for the new season. The coach was optimistic that he could use the team's unprecedented depth from the 1966–67 squad to take up the slack left by Bell's absence. Bell's forward spot would be manned by junior Theodis Lee, one of the key reserves on the previous year's squad. The center position now belonged to Ken Spain, the former *Parade* High School All-American from nearby Austin High School. Spain had also been a top reserve the previous season.

All that now remained was to identify the fifth starter. The most likely candidate looked to be junior transfer George Reynolds, who came to UH from Imperial Valley Junior College in California. "George is a valuable addition to our team," Coach Lewis said. "He's quick, passes very well, and is good at getting the ball to the open man. And he can play defense quite well." There was competition. Just two weeks before the season, the point guard position was still up for grabs—the other candidates were senior Vern Lewis and sophomore Tom Gribben.

Choosing the right personnel was crucial. Unlike the previous two seasons, when the Cougars had a strong bench, the strength of the 1967–68 squad would be their starting five. One day after a practice, Lewis said, "We won't be able to substitute players and have the substitutes several inches taller than the starters. The depth of the reserves will be thinner. This year is the first in my coaching career where the starting five completely dominate the rest of the squad. Last year, the first string and the second beat each other frequently in practice. This year the scores have been something like 34–4 in favor of the starters."

He added, "I think we'll be a better team than last year, and I think this could be the most exciting team we've ever had. If they hadn't ruled out the dunk shot, I know we could please the fans every game."

The season schedule included several tough opponents, such as Illinois, Brigham Young, Minnesota, Arizona, Michigan, Miami, and Marshall. At the end of December, the Cougars would travel to Honolulu to play in the annual Rainbow Classic. Some of the top teams competing in the tournament were Bradley, Marquette, and Ohio State. However, the game on the UH schedule that everybody had been eyeing for more than a year was the January 20 showdown with top-ranked UCLA in the Astrodome. The Cougars entered the season as the No. 2–ranked college basketball team in the land. More than 35,000 tickets would go on sale, and likely more than that number would be printed, many of the ticket-holders standing for the game. The game loomed as a mere warm-up for the final game of the Final Four as part of the March Madness in Los Angeles. But before the Cougars got to take the home court against Alcindor and the Bruins in January, they had to complete the first half of their schedule.

They opened in front of a packed house of 5,400 at Delmar Field House on December 2 against the Sacramento State Hornets, a team that had gone 15–11 the previous year. "I really can't say much about Sacramento," Lewis said. "I've never seen them play, and the people we play haven't, either. They are something of a mystery team." In a pregame interview, he added, "A week ago, we were so ready to play, it frightened me. But now I don't know. The past couple of days, we haven't accomplished anything in practice."

He proved to be overly cautious. The Cougars, led by Elvin Hayes's 35 points and 15 rebounds, trounced the Hornets, 100–79. The other four UH starters all reached double figures. Ken Spain had 20 points along with his game-high 23 rebounds. Don Chaney had 16 points, Theodis Lee 15, and George Reynolds 10. Reynolds, who had been named the fifth starter two days before the game, also dished out 11 assists in his Cougar debut, prompting his coach to say, "I thought Reynolds did a real fine job. The defensive play by both him and Chaney was really first-rate."

The Cougars's second game was against Abilene Christian College, also at Delmar, on December 4. For the first 20 minutes, Abilene Christian stayed with the Cougars, actually leading late in the first half, 36–34. In the second half, the Cougars broke out of their offensive doldrums and took a 90–75 win. Hayes led the way with 33 points and 21 rebounds. Spain had 18 points and 19 boards.

Even though the season was only two games old, student tickets for the UCLA game in the Dome went on sale the next day. UH students lined up as early as 1 a.m. for their chance at attending the game, which was still 46 days away.

Then it was back to Delmar on December 7 to play against the North Dakota State Bison (0–3). Opposing coach Harvey Schmidt said before the game, "Houston may well deserve the No. 1 ranking. They're that good. Not only are they big, but the Cougar guards are exceptionally fast."

Schmidt was right. Hayes poured in 38 points, 18 rebounds, and six assists as the Cougars blasted the Bison, 121–88. Hayes also made history. When he scored his 16th point of the night, he became the all-time leading scorer in Texas collegiate history, surpassing SMU player Jim Krebs's 1,753 points.

The game had extra significance despite the lopsided score. George Reynolds continued the solid start to his UH career with 17 points, 8 rebounds, and five assists. Theodis Lee had 16 points, while Spain had 13 points along with 11 rebounds. Chaney chipped in 12 points, and reserve guard Tom Gribben had 11.

Undoubtedly the highlight of the game came when, with seven minutes to play, Hayes leaped high in the air and slammed home an "illegal" two-handed dunk shot, prompting the Delmar Field House crowd to roar with delight. For whatever reason, Shorty Lawson, the closest referee to this dramatic action, had a clear view of the dunk but did not disallow the basket or call a technical foul. After the dunk, the crowd gave Lawson a standing ovation.

"We sure faked out the ref," Hayes later said. "I wasn't going to try it again. My luck was only good for one."

After three fairly easy victories, the Cougars now headed out on their first road trip of the year. They traveled to Champagne, Illinois, to take on Big Ten member Illinois on Saturday, December 9. The Illini were 1–0, having beaten Butler, 75–57. The Cougars towered over this opponent, with the Illini's tallest starter, Dave Schulz, standing at 6-foot-8 and their next tallest at just 6-foot-5. Before seven thousand fans at Assembly Hall, the Cougars overcame the slowdown tactics of the Fighting Illini with 19 first-half turnovers and only 20 shots from the field to come away with a 54–46 win.

What saved Houston was the fact that Illinois was ice cold from the field for the entire game, hitting on just 22 of 72 shots. The Cougars, meanwhile, wound up making 20 of 46 from the field. As expected, Houston out-rebounded the Illini 46–32. Elvin Hayes led the way with 20 boards to go with his game-high 25 points. The only other Cougar in double figures was Ken Spain with 10 points.

The bigger news was back in Houston, where tickets for the January 20 Astrodome game between the Cougars and UCLA went on sale to the public the first thing the following Monday morning (December 11). Tickets ranged from $2 to $5 apiece.

* * * * * * *

The Cougars wanted to maintain the momentum that had led them to a 4–0 record going into the Bluebonnet Classic Basketball Tournament on December 13 and 14 in Delmar Field House for the first time in tournament history. First-game pairings had UH playing George Washington University and Montana State playing Mississippi State. Facing a winless (0–3) George Washington, the Cougars expected this opponent to slow down the tempo, coming off a 108–68 shellacking at the hands of Syracuse.

Guy Lewis said, "I told the team after practice today that last year in the Bluebonnet Tourney, Centenary tried playing with the ball like Illinois did Saturday. We reacted pretty poorly to Centenary's slowdown—and had to fight for our lives to win."

This time the slowdown tactics didn't work. The Big E scored 40 points, Don Chaney 15, and Theodis Lee 13 as the Cougars triumphed mightily, 86–61. In the nightcap game, Montana State pulled ahead of Mississippi State for the first time at 72–71 with under four minutes to go and hung on for an 81–73 win.

The next night, the Cougars took on Montana State for the Bluebonnet Classic championship. Before the game, Wildcat coach Roger Craft praised Hayes and Chaney. "What can I say about Elvin?" Craft said. "He's fantastic. And that Chaney is one solid ballplayer. They really rate that No. 2 ranking."

UH lived up to that ranking, indeed. The Cougars routed the Wildcats 113–65 to win the championship. Hayes set a single-game tournament scoring record with his 45 points. He also set a tournament record with his 85 points in the two games, surpassing his own record of 70 set the previous year. His 23 rebounds gave him 38 for the tournament, another record.

In between the Bluebonnet Tournament on Thursday and the Brigham Young game on Saturday, Don Chaney took time out from his basketball schedule to marry Miss Jacqueline Dotson on Friday. Elvin Hayes served as the best man.

Brigham Young posted a 3–1 record, its only loss coming from a common opponent, Illinois, who beat them, 63–55, on their home court. Before another standing-room-only crowd of 5,400 fans at Delmar, the Houston Cougars ran their record to 7–0 with a 102–69 waxing of Brigham Young. The Cougars erupted for 9 points in the first 1:18 of play and never looked back. After the game, BYU head coach Stan Watts said, "They overpowered us. Our personnel just could not compete with Houston's size and agility. They are a fantastic team."

Just over a month now remained before the Game of the Century. Like Houston, UCLA started its season undefeated with wins over Purdue, Wichita State, and Iowa State, thus amassing a winning streak of 37 in a row. A sports writer asked Coach Lewis after the BYU game about the streaking Bruins. "Everybody asks about UCLA," Lewis replied. "I know we're all looking forward to it. But for now I'd like to enjoy this win."

But Elvin Hayes was ready to talk. "I think we're ready," he said. "We handled their big men tonight with no trouble. We'll take UCLA, too."

The Cougars now had to get their collective mind-set focused on the scheduled games before the UCLA classic. Next up was another Big Ten opponent, the Minnesota Golden Gophers (2–2) at Delmar. Before five thousand fans, UH scored more than 100 points for the fifth time in eight games, topping the Gophers 103–65. "If you had told me before this game that we would score 100 points against a ball-control team like Minnesota," Lewis said, "I would have said you were crazy. This team has really been tremendous these last three games."

There were two trains of thought at this juncture in the Cougars's great season—the next few games in the season and the Game of the Century scheduled for January 20. Before the Cougars embarked on a tough two-game road trip to face the Arizona Wildcats on December 22 and Nevada Southern the next day, school officials announced that December 20 would be the last day student tickets would be on sale for the UCLA game. Interest in *the game* was reaching a peak, since both teams stood a good chance of being undefeated by tipoff. While Dome officials had predicted a crowd of 35,000, estimates had now reached 45,000.

"A month or so before the game, things were crazy," Guy V. Lewis said upon reflection in later years. "The phone in my office kept ringing. I didn't have a secretary, so Harvey and I would answer the phones from people looking for tickets. Then I would go home, and there would be a bunch of messages from people either wanting to talk about the game or wanting tickets. It was nuts."

Sports Information Director Ted Nance said, "I started promoting the UCLA game during football season. There was a full-page ad in the football programs with Elvin and Lew Alcindor in it. I also started calling it the 'Game of the Century' to anyone who would listen.

"At first, sales were a little sluggish because people were interested in our good season the football team was having. We kept promoting it, though, and Guy kept talking about it. About a month before the game, sales really took off because of the promotion of the game and also the fact that people realized this could be a historic matchup of two unbeaten teams, each with a superstar player.

"To help promote the game even more, I put a life-size picture of Lew Alcindor's head right where it would be if he was really standing right there, which was about seven feet, four inches high in a room with an eight-foot ceiling [his office at UH]."

The first game of 8–0 Houston's two-game road trip was in Tucson against the 5–2 Arizona Wildcats. The Wildcats looked to be the Cougars's toughest opponent to date in a game played in the tiny on-campus Bear Down Gym, which seated just 3,600, somewhat comparable to Jeppesen Field House, the Cougars's current practice court. "They think we're gonna be scared, playing in such a small, old place," said forward Theodis Lee. "Well, we're not going to be because we're so used to good ole Jeppesen. In fact, we like the smallness of Jeppesen a lot, so I think we'll like playing in this gym."

Lee's words proved prophetic when he played the best all-around game of his college career. The Cougars held off the Wildcats, 81–76. Lee put together 20 points, 12 rebounds, and five assists. Hayes led Houston with 28 points, his second-lowest output of the young season, along with 15 rebounds.

The victory set the stage for a trip to Las Vegas to play the small college powerhouse Nevada Southern (University of Nevada–Las Vegas) two days before Christmas. In a fast-paced game, Hayes became just the 13th player in college basketball history to score 2,000 points in a career as the Cougars held off the pesky Rebels, 94–85. The Cougars led by just 46–45 at the half but stretched their lead to as much as 11 a couple times in the second half before hanging on for the win.

After the quick road trip, Coach Lewis downplayed the close scores. "I'm not concerned with how we win on the road," he said, "as long as we win. We've won three now this year away from home, and although we haven't played as well as we can in any of those games, we've gotten a bit better each game."

The Cougars's win streak would be seriously tested in Honolulu at the Rainbow Classic on December 28–30. The eight-team tournament featured such basketball stalwarts as Ohio State, which would end up in the 1968 Final Four; always-tough Marquette University; and UH's first-round opponent, 10th-ranked Bradley, which came to Hawaii after suffering its first loss of the season to none other than the UCLA Bruins, 109–73.

The International Center in Honolulu was packed on the first day of the tournament for the game between the Cougars and the Bradley Braves, thanks to heavy promotion by the local newspapers and the chance to see Elvin Hayes in action. Possibly not wanting to suffer another humiliating defeat for the second game in a row to a top-ranked opponent, Bradley stalled at the start of the game. With ten minutes left in the first half, the score was just 6–6. At halftime, the score was just 21–19 in favor of the Braves.

In the first half, the Cougars decided not to press and stay back on defense. In the second half, Guy Lewis decided to force the issue by coming out in a full-court press. Bradley finally collapsed about ten minutes into the second half. The Cougars went from a 46–45 advantage to make it 62–47, eventually surging to a 20-point lead before settling for a 69–52 win. All five UH starters scored in double figures, led by George Reynolds's 16 points.

The nationally ranked No. 2 Cougars were now 11–0 and set to face Marquette, who had beaten Ohio State, 64–60, in the other game of the opening round. The small and scrappy Warriors broke out to a quick 7–0 lead before the Cougars rallied to lead 38–35 at halftime. In the second half, Houston steadily pulled away for a 77–65 win. Elvin Hayes was the only Houston player in double figures, scoring a winner's-bracket record 45 points.

The championship game the next night came against the surprising North Texas State Eagles. North Texas had beat Northwestern, 83–66, in the semifinals the day before. Like Bradley, the Eagles went into a first-half stall against Houston. As a result, the game was close throughout. Reserve UH guard Tom Gribben came off the bench to score three of his four field goals late in the close game. With North Texas trailing just 42–41 with less than a minute remaining, the Eagles intentionally fouled the shaky foul-shooting Elvin Hayes. Hayes, however, drained both free throws, and Houston held on for a 45–43 win and the Rainbow Classic championship. Despite just 15 points against Bradley and only 12 against North Texas, Hayes nonetheless was named the tournament's Most Valuable Player. In spite of his relatively low-scoring total, Hayes had led the tournament in rebounding and blocked numerous shots.

* * * * * * * *

After ending the 1967 part of their season with a perfect 13–0, the Cougars started the New Year on January 2 at Delmar against another Big Ten opponent, the Michigan Wolverines, led by future Houston Rockets player and coach Rudy Tomjanovich. The 4–4 Wolverines were just one of four teams to beat Houston the previous season. Before another standing-room-only crowd of 5,400, the Cougars won their 47th consecutive home game, crushing Michigan, 91–65.

With just two weeks left before the Game of the Century, the Cougars had two games to play. First up was Centenary in Delmar on January 6. A win over the Gents would give Houston a school record 15 straight wins, breaking the record of 14 set by the 1965–66 Cougar squad when Hayes and Chaney were sophomores. The game was destined to be a mismatch—Centenary stood at 2–7.

Everything went as predicted. The Cougars rolled over the Gents 118–81 before another packed house at Delmar. Hayes had 40 points and 18 rebounds, but more significantly, he blocked 19 Centenary field-goal attempts. The Cougars showed scoring consistency. Lee had 17 points, Spain 13, and Reynolds 11. Chaney joined Hayes with a triple-double that included 11 boards and 15 steals.

The nation's top-two-ranked teams were both undefeated. Ten days before the Game of the Century, it officially became a sellout. Standing-room-only tickets were scheduled to go on sale a few days before the game. Astrodome officials were now expecting a record crowd of more than 50,000. Press interest was also becoming intense. *Sports Illustrated* assigned three reporters to cover the game.

Requests for press passes were staggering. Ted Nance said in the days leading up to the game, "I hate to guess how many may wind up here for the game and where we might put them all." As it turned out,

Nance issued a record 175 news media identifications. "I then have to find places for all of the radio and television broadcasters, as well as different scorers and statisticians. Things are moving along OK. The Astrodome people have been very cooperative . . . my phone hasn't stopped ringing."

Nance also had to handle numerous requests for interviews, the most frequent requests being Guy V. Lewis and Elvin Hayes. During that hectic time, Nance lamented, "Coach Lewis got stuck in Louisiana this week because of an ice storm over there. He finally got back here after a one-day layover. When he got here, there were calls from all over the country."

The Cougars had one more tune-up before the big game: a home game on January 13 against West Texas State. Because of the massive increase in interest in the team, KPRC/Channel 2 planned to televise the game. "We've never had a game televised from Delmar before, so this is all new," Nance told the news media. "But I'm glad they want us on television. That means a lot to the school."

In spite of the possibility of Houston looking ahead to the UCLA game, given West Texas State's record (1–4, and 1–18 the previous season), the Cougars won an easy 98–53 victory, their 50th consecutive home-game win. The Buffs kept the game close at first, being down just 15–12 with 11:17 to go in the first half. By halftime, however, UH's lead ballooned to 49–22. The second half was more of the same.

*   *   *   *   *   *   *

On Monday, January 15, five thousand standing-room-only tickets went on sale for $1.50 each to the general public.

The 12–0 Bruins, with the exception of a 73–71 nail-biter win over Purdue to open the season on the road, had not allowed any of their other foes to come within 12 points of them. They had one game to play before visiting the Dome, a January 18 home game against Portland. However, UCLA star center Lew Alcindor did not play in the game, having also sat out the Stanford game the week before. The day before the Stanford game, UCLA had faced the University of California. Late in the Cal game, Alcindor suffered a scratched left eyeball.

He then had to wear a patch over the eye and suffered from blurred vision. Throughout the week leading up to the Game of the Century, his playing status remained in doubt.

Guy V. Lewis, however, believed that Alcindor would play. Three days before the big game, Lewis said, "I have a sneaky hunch that Alcindor will play against us on Saturday despite his eye injury. Now I don't know exactly what makes me feel that, but let's say that it's intuition. I hope he can play, because that way the game will prove whether or not we're truly capable of beating UCLA."

Lewis then summed up his team's strategy and chances against the Bruins: "We'll probably play our normal fast-paced game on offense, and I'm sure they'll press as much as they did last March in Louisville, so we've been working against that in practice. We'll have to shoot as well as we can shoot. We're also going to have to reduce our turnovers and rebound like we're capable of doing.

"I don't think I'll have to fire up the players one bit. The importance of the game and the size of the crowd will do that for me. If 55,000 Texans yelling for them can't rev them up, nothing will."

Lewis knew his Cougars had a daunting task ahead of them. UCLA had stretched its winning streak to 47 games, and many called their 1967–68 squad the best in the history of college basketball. "I don't think that any team is really unbeatable," Lewis told reporters. "I feel that Johnny Wooden's bunch is the greatest college basketball team ever assembled, but I think they can be beaten. It will take a near-perfect game by some team to do it, but it can be done, and I think we have a chance to do it if we play up to our potential."

The Cougars's two top players also believed they had a chance to beat UCLA. Don Chaney said, "A million black cats can cross my path, and I still know we're going to win the game."

Elvin Hayes addressed his feelings: "I think we're going to be mentally ready for them . . . UCLA comes after you with that nasty press of theirs. We can beat the press, and we can beat them, if we play our game."

On the subject of Alcindor's eye injury, Hayes said, "I hope he can play and be at his best physically. That way, they can't alibi if we beat them. I think we're going to beat them even if he does play."

The Game of the Century was going to be the first-ever national broadcast of a regular-season college basketball game. TV Sports Incorporated, owned by future Chicago White Sox owner Eddie Einhorn, had sold the broadcast rights to the game to more than 120 television stations throughout the country. The game would also be broadcast by at least 30 major radio stations across the nation.

Throughout the week leading up to the game, writers and coaches made their predictions. The vast majority of writers and coaches picked UCLA. They cited many reasons, not the least of which was the Bruins's 47-game winning streak. The Bruins were also averaging 100.3 points per game and allowing just 68.9. UCLA was shooting 50.9 percent from the field as a team, while their foes hit just 39.3 percent.

UCLA didn't have to rely solely on Alcindor, either. Although he led the Bruins in scoring with 28.4 points per game and in rebounding with 15.4, he was far from being the only weapon they had. Guard Lucius Allen was the team's No. 2 scorer at 16.1 points per game, followed by Mike Lynn at 11.9, Edgar Lacey at 11.8, Lynn Shackelford at 11.5, and All-America guard Mike Warren at 10.9. They had a deep bench with players like Bill Sweek, Kenny Heitz, and Jim Nielsen. Guy V. Lewis said, "I think in a lot of cases their second group is as good as most teams's starters."

And then, of course, UCLA had legendary Coach John Wooden leading the charge, having coached the Bruins to three of the last four NCAA titles and seemingly poised to add a fourth title this season.

Lewis Cox of the *Dallas Times-Herald* predicted UCLA by 11 points. He wrote, "I never thought two tall boys like Lew Alcindor and Elvin Hayes could draw so many people. Houston has as good a chance as any team to defeat UCLA, but I favor the Bruins."

Dick Young of the *New York Daily News* also chose UCLA: "I believe UCLA to be a super team, above and beyond Lew Alcindor. If Houston should win, it would be because of the home-court advantage."

Jeff Prugh of the *Los Angeles Times* predicted UCLA would win with ease, writing, "UCLA has so many weapons that it can make a basketball game seem like a gangland slaying."

Sports Illustrated's Joe Jares said the Bruins would win by 20 points. He told his readers, "The Bruins are the best college basketball team I've ever seen."

About the only sportswriters whose chose Houston to win were local writers that worked for the *Houston Post*: John Hollis, David Fink, and renowned *Post* columnist Mickey Herskowitz. Herskowitz picked Houston to win by three, writing, "This is the right place, the right time, and the right team for an upset."

All the writers's predictions were made under the assumption that Alcindor would play. However, he had missed the Bruins game against Portland, a 93–69 UCLA victory, just two days before the Game of the Century. Nevertheless, Alcindor was finally given clearance to practice the day before the Dome game.

Of the college coaches asked to predict the game's outcome, almost none of them would go on the record. Several of them correctly predicted what a game of this magnitude would do for the game of college basketball. Notre Dame coach Johnny Dee said, "The setting, two great college teams, the record-smashing crowd, and the foresight to televise basketball's 'Game of the Century' will do more to publicize the sport than any other event."

University of North Carolina coach Dean Smith said, "The game will be a great step forward for basketball, what with 55,000 looking on in the Astrodome."

Two individuals coached teams who were common opponents of UH and UCLA: Bradley coach Joe Stowell and Minnesota coach John Kundla. Stowell said, "If anyone beats UCLA, it will be Houston. They have two things going for them that most teams don't have—tremendous size and a home court with 55,000 Texans in the stands."

Kundla, whose Golden Gopher squad had lost to UCLA by 40 points and to Houston by 38, said, "Both teams are better than last year. It will be a match of Houston's tremendous power against UCLA's amazing speed." Kundla also thought the home-court advantage would help: "Fifty thousand Texans making more noise than has ever been made before are bound to have an influence."

While stopping short of making a prediction on the outcome, the Minnesota coach did say, "I have some advice for Guy: Pray."

Those writers and coaches who gave the Cougars a chance to win because of their home-court advantage weren't entirely accurate. While there would be in excess of 50,000 fans rooting for the Cougars, the actual court and location of where the game would be played was not an advantage for Houston at all. The Cougars, like UCLA, had never played a game in the Astrodome.

An interesting quirk was the court that was to be used for the game. The floor from the Los Angeles Sports Arena was shipped to the Astrodome for use. UCLA had somewhat of an advantage over Houston, having actually played three games on the court earlier in the season, winning the LA Classic Tournament in December.

It was entirely possible that Houston and UCLA could meet again on the same floor in the Final Four, either in the semifinals or in the championship game.

17 THE GAME OF
THE CENTURY

As we were getting ready to enter the field to walk out to the basketball court, Guy V. turned and said to me, "Slow down, look around, and take all of this in. This is probably something you'll never see again."
—COUGAR ASSISTANT COACH DON
SCHVERAK ON ENTERING THE ASTRODOME
FOR THE UH–UCLA GAME

When January 20, 1968—the date of the Game of the Century—finally arrived, UCLA got some good news: after a Los Angeles eye specialist flew to Houston and examined Lew Alcindor, he cleared the Bruins's star to play in the game.

Many people associated with both teams as well as many fans who were at the game gave their recollections of the Game of the Century for this historic account. Several gave details about the atmosphere inside the Astrodome that night.

Joel Williams, son of famed UH golf coach Dave Williams, said, "There was a lot of anticipation leading up to it.

I sat up in the purple section of the Dome. The place was packed and it was rip-roaring. It was almost like a novelty."

Cougar football defensive end Jerry Drones said, "The crowd was crazy—it was something else. I was there with some recruits from Booker T. Washington High School in Houston."

Houston fan Jim Perdue described the scene: "I had prime seats. It was the most incredible crowd I've ever been around."

Charlie Miller, assistant to the UH sports information director, said, "I got to sit on the floor. I was two seats down from Wooden. I kept the stat sheets for shot attempts and blocked shots. It was quite a night, and wow, what a crowd."

Student trainer Howie Lorch said, "At the Game of the Century, when they opened up the centerfield doors at the Dome so we could go out to the court at around second base, we felt like the gladiators in Roman times. I still get goose bumps when I think about it."

Cougar football wide receiver Calvin Achey said, "People showed up in coat and tie. We sat in the theater-type seats in the Dome. I went in a red blazer. The electricity and the emotion in the Dome for that game was something."

Former Cougar quarterback Bo Burris had just finished his first season as a member of the New Orleans Saints when he attended the game. Burris said, "I sat by Jack Mildren. We were recruiting him to play quarterback at Houston, but he ended up being the wishbone quarterback on those great Oklahoma teams. I kept saying to myself, 'Boy, I hope we can keep the game close.' Right at the end of the game, Mildren got caught up in the excitement, and he said, 'Man, we just might win!'"

Another Cougar fan, Sam Swearengin, told his story years later: "I was in Alpha Phi Omega fraternity. We would sell programs at all the home games at Delmar, which only sat about 5,000 people. When we played at the Dome, we got there two hours before the game and we had 10,000 programs to sell. We were saying to ourselves, 'This is stupid—why so many programs?'

"Well, we sold every single one of them for a dollar each. The best thing about selling programs was we got to go to the games for free.

We sat in the yellow section of the Dome—it was hard to see, and the players were really small. It was an electric event, though. There were hardly any UCLA people there. The crowd was all Houston."

Cougar guard Vern Lewis gave his views on the Game of the Century: "Elvin got to showcase his talent that night. We all knew how great he was. To play the way he did on national television on that big of a stage was something else. Before that game, a lot of people didn't know much about Elvin. The Southwest Conference teams had quit playing us, and I felt the eastern press ignored us."

Most people forget that there was a game before the Game of the Century that night. Tyler Junior College played the UH freshmen. Poo Welch, who later came to play at Houston, was on that Tyler team.

Lewis continued, "Before the game, I ran into Coach Wagstaff, who had been my coach at Tyler. He said to me, 'Let me ask you a question: Do you honestly think you can beat UCLA?' I said, 'Coach, we're gonna beat them—we have Elvin, and I just know he's going to have a big game.'

"I also remember that before the game, we had to run to go out to the court, which was out in the middle of the Dome, somewhere around where second base was. By the time I got there, I was already winded. It was a long ways out there.

"The big thing I remember was the noise level. Usually when you're playing, you can hear some cheers. In this game, though, there was a roar pretty much the whole game—it was deafening."

Another player who remembered the long run to the court was UCLA guard Bill Sweek: "The Dome game was a surreal experience. The court was like a postage stamp in the Dome. It was a deluge of noise. We were so far away from the crowd, it was like there was a noise delay. The court was a long ways away, and it was a long run to get there. I was tired by the time I got out there to the court.

"The game was a huge event. The media, the TV, the venue. You could feel the tension. It was so different from any other game—no one had ever done this before. The lighting on the court was also weird. It was OK at the top of the key where Elvin was taking most of his shots, but it was not so good in the corners.

*The "Game of the Century" court in the middle of the Astrodome, January 20, 1968
(Courtesy of UH Athletic Department)*

"Elvin was gifted, but he was culturally different from Kareem [Lew Alcindor]. They were arch opposites—one city, one country. It seemed Kareem didn't like Elvin, and Elvin didn't like Kareem. It all played into the rivalry.

"In the days before the game, Kareem got poked in the eye, and we were concerned whether he would play. We also hadn't played real well leading up to the game. We were in a vulnerable state of mind. Coach Wooden was very uptight the two weeks leading up to the game.

"The Game of the Century was one of the only two games I missed in my college career. I dove off a diving board at the hotel pool when we played at Stanford, which I wasn't supposed to do. Coach Wooden suspended me for the Portland game a couple of days before we played Houston and also for the Game of the Century. To me the whole game was a fog, a dream. I felt so powerless to do anything."

UCLA assistant coach Jerry Norman spoke of the days leading up to the game and the atmosphere in the Astrodome. "First of all, while the game against Houston was important to us, it was more important to Houston," Norman said. "Houston was an independent, and the game was in the middle of our conference season. We were concerned about conference play. Back then only the conference champion went to the NCAA Tournament.

"Another factor in the game was that Jabbar couldn't see. However, if he hadn't been on the court, we would have lost by 10 or 15 points. As far as the atmosphere in the Astrodome, we were playing in the middle of the baseball field. We didn't play anywhere near the level we were capable of playing. We felt we were the better team. I didn't feel the crowd was a factor, though. We were concentrating on playing the game."

A former Houston player who was in his first year as an assistant to Guy Lewis was Don Schverak. Just before the Cougars came onto the baseball field from the door in centerfield to head out to the court by second base, Schverak recalled a moment that occurred between him and Guy V. Lewis.

"As we were getting ready to enter the field to go out to the basketball court," Schverak said, "Guy V. turned to me and said, 'Slow down, look around, and take all of this in. This is probably something you'll never see again.'"

Coach Lewis was correct. Before this game or since, there has not been a regular season college basketball game of this magnitude. The crowd in the Astrodome, the first national television audience for a regular season game, the nation's undefeated No. 1 and No. 2 teams, the two biggest stars in the college game facing off against each other, and the game going down to the wire were all factors.

* * * * * * *

On the night of January 20, 1968, before 52,693 screaming Houston fans, the University of Houston scored the biggest win in the basketball program's history as the Cougars won a heart-stopping 71–69 victory over the UCLA Bruins, breaking the Bruins's 47-game winning streak.

Elvin Hayes was spectacular, especially in the first half, when he rang up 29 points. For the night, the Big E hit 15 of his first 20 shots from the field and ended up with 39 points on 17 of 25 shots. He also pulled down 15 rebounds. His counterpart, Lew Alcindor, had but 15 points on 4 of 18 shots from the field and 12 rebounds.

After the Bruins got off to an early 10–7 lead, Hayes hit a pair of jumpers to give UH an 11–10 edge. After an UCLA basket, George Reynolds and Hayes each hit two baskets to give the Cougars a 19–12 lead, one they would never relinquish. With Hayes continuing his hot hand, Houston extended its lead to 37–28 before UCLA closed the gap to 46–43 at halftime.

The Bruins made a change at the start of the second half to try to slow down Hayes. Edgar Lacey, who had been guarding Hayes, was benched in favor of Jim Nielsen. That adjustment slowed Hayes to just ten second-half points and slowed him even more when he picked up his fourth foul with 12 minutes to go, thus limiting his aggressiveness. Sweek recalled years later, "Edgar Lacey tried to guard Elvin. He just didn't perform well."

Jerry Norman added, "Edgar didn't do anything against Elvin and wouldn't do anything, so we benched him. Nielsen did a good job of keeping the ball away from Hayes. We slowed down Houston's offense in the second half. They only scored 25 points. We had plenty of good shots in the second half. They just didn't fall for us."

Neither team was consistent in the second half offensively. UCLA slowly inched back into the game and finally tied it at 54-all with ten minutes to go on a Mike Warren jumper. However, the Cougars responded with the next 6 unanswered points to go up 60–54. UCLA soon pulled even again at 65 on an Alcindor free throw.

Hayes then hit a turnaround jump shot from the corner, and Don Chaney followed up with a basket to put Houston up 69–65 with 1:53 on the clock.

Lucius Allen of UCLA then hit a layup to close the gap to 69–67. Ken Spain missed a free throw and then proceeded to foul Allen at the other end of the floor. Allen drained both free throws, and the game was knotted at 69.

After Allen's foul shots, Houston worked the ball inside to Hayes, who was promptly fouled by Nielsen with 28 seconds to go. Hayes swished both free throws to make it 71–69 Houston.

UCLA never got another shot off, as an Allen pass intended for Lynn Shackelford in the corner was accidentally tipped out of bounds by Mike Warren with 12 seconds to go.

With the Bruins in a full-court press, Houston inbounded the ball to Hayes, who dribbled around in the backcourt before passing the ball to Reynolds with three seconds to go. When the buzzer went off to end the game, Reynolds flung the ball up into the air and the Astrodome was bedlam.

UH fans rushed the court, hoisted Elvin Hayes on their shoulders, and shouted, "We're number one! We're number one!"

Houston football player Calvin Achey said, "After the game, people were just euphoric!"

Cougar fan Jim Perdue said, "It was something else. UCLA was supposed to be unbeatable. Afterwards, the group of lawyers I worked with downtown at Fulbright & Jaworski, a bunch of Longhorns, were impressed."

Sam Swearengin, who had sold programs at the game, said, "Wow. Elvin scored 39 that night. We outplayed them. We were charged up. After the game, people stayed and lingered. Everyone knew it was a big event and it was historic. The celebrating lasted well into the next week. I hope I can always remember that night."

Cougar guard Vern Lewis, who played four minutes in the Game of the Century, said, "After the game, I ran into Coach Wagstaff, and he said, 'You weren't lying, were you!'"

Unfortunately, Cougar quarterback Dick Woodall didn't make the game. He explained the reason in a 2013 interview: "I had tickets to the UCLA game on the floor. However, my wife was pregnant and she was sick, so I stayed home with her. After the game, I went into the bedroom and said, 'This kid better be special, because I just missed the greatest game ever!' I never missed a basketball game, but I missed *that* one."

Cougar guard Tom Gribben, who got into the game late in the first half for four minutes, said, "I fed Elvin a bounce pass for a jump shot and I scored a basket. I had four shots in four minutes. One thing, though—Guy Lewis doesn't get enough credit for that game. He was the one who organized it."

UCLA shot just 33.6 percent on 26 of 77 shots, while the Cougars hit 30 of 66, a 45.5 percent rate. Houston also won the battle of the boards, 44–40. Houston had 20 turnovers in the game and UCLA 16.

Coach Lewis said, "When Elvin ended up dribbling the ball with time running out at the end of the game, it didn't bother me at all. I knew we'd be all right. He wasn't going to lose the game for us then."

Years later, however, Hayes said, "I got the ball and I started dribbling it. I was thinking, 'Why do you have the ball? Pass it. You shouldn't be dribbling the basketball.' That is the scariest moment for me in the game whenever I watch old films of it. I'm down there with one hand dribbling the ball.

"I'm boom, boom, boom, boom! And there's Jabbar and Lucius Allen there. They could have stolen the basketball—taken the ball from me and made a layup."

Don Chaney added about Hayes dribbling, "Elvin was a great shooter, but he wasn't the greatest ball handler. I was saying to myself, 'Somebody get to him and get the ball, get the ball from Elvin!'"

Guy V. Lewis went on to say, "Naturally this is the greatest moment of my coaching career. And this was the greatest basketball game I've ever witnessed. UCLA is a great ball club, and they never quit even when we got some good leads."

Hayes added after the game, "This was the greatest game we've played . . . I hit better this game than the last time I played against Alcindor."

"It was super all the way," Cougar forward Theodis Lee said. "They've got a helluva team, but we've proved we're better."

For UCLA, Lew Alcindor said, "I have nothing to say. About anything." When asked by a reporter if Elvin Hayes was the best player he had faced, Alcindor replied, "Oh, I guess so."

Bruin guard Lucius Allen commented, "Houston tonight was more disciplined, more methodical in what they were doing than when we played them in Louisville last year. I had never seen George Reynolds before. I thought he was very good. I was impressed."

Looking down the road, Allen said, "I just hope now that Houston wins all of its games and then we play them at the Nationals."

John Wooden said, "It was a fine game in a tremendous setting. It was anybody's game . . . no, I don't want revenge. Certainly I'd like to play Guy Lewis's team again—but not for revenge. When I start feeling that way, I'll quit. The biggest difference tonight was our ball handling. It was poor tonight."

As for Alcindor's eye injury, Wooden commented, "I wasn't concerned about the eye after Lew received clearance from the doctor. I was more concerned about his conditioning. But I played him for 40 minutes, and he seemed to hold up well. Houston is a fine team, an outstanding team."

Years later, players on both teams reflected on the Game of the Century.

Bill Sweek recalled, "Kareem had a minimal role in that game. He was tired and winded out there. You have to give Houston credit, though. They were so pumped, so ready. We really weren't at our best. Elvin and their whole team were ready.

"And oh, Don Chaney was something in that game. He was a great defender. He had those long arms. He was one of the only guys in the country that could guard either Lucius Allen or Mike Warren."

Lew Alcindor, now known as Kareem Abdul Jabbar, said, "We played the game at second base in the Astrodome. It was weird. It was like playing out on a prairie somewhere. I don't think either team felt very comfortable out there, but Elvin Hayes must have felt very comfortable—he had the game of his life."

Jabbar then reflected on what the Game of the Century meant to college basketball: "In seeing this game, people realized how popular this sport was, and if you made it available to its fans, people would watch it."

"During the game, we would score, there'd be dead silence," said Lucius Allen. "Houston would score, there would be dead silence, and then this roar would come down upon us. It took that long for the sound from the fans to get to us on the floor."

On losing for the first time in his college career, Allen said, "Coming off that floor, my legs were as heavy as they've ever been, because losing was not in my vocabulary at all."

Mike Warren echoed Allen's feelings. "It hurt," he said. "There was silence in the locker room. It was the first time we had lost. It was a terrible, terrible feeling. Elvin, though, had the kind of game that most basketball players dream about. He seemingly could not miss."

Don Chaney said years later, "People still remember that game. It was the 'Clash of the Titans' with two unbelievable egos, Elvin and Kareem, and neither one was going to step aside. Elvin was something. It didn't matter if Jabbar was in his face or not, the ball was going in.

"The Game of the Century brought about a lot more interest in basketball at U of H and in Texas. Before that, Houston was pretty much a football school. I remember for a whole week after the game, they showed it on a local television station every night."

The man whose star shined the brightest in the Game of the Century, Elvin Hayes, reflected on 1968 and the game: "It was one of the biggest moments in basketball history. Kareem had basically everything I wanted. He was the best player in college basketball; I wanted to be player of the year. His star to me was shining very brightly that year, and I wanted to replace his star with my star.

"I remember in the locker room before the game, we were all wondering, 'Will anybody be out there?' Then during the game the sound bounced around. The sound would go way up to the roof of the Dome and then come back down upon you.

"Even though we were way out there by second base and the lighting was different, it was still two baskets and a floor. To a basketball player, that's all you need.

"At the end of the game, there were 55,000 people in the place, and they were going wild. It was one of the most memorable moments in my basketball history.

"It just created euphoria and an atmosphere for college basketball that wasn't there previously. I think that game kicked the door down, opened the windows, and knocked the roof off the house. What we have today in March Madness is what I think the game in 1968 opened."

*Elvin Hayes shoots
over UCLA's Mike
Lynn during the
Game of the Century,
January 20, 1968
(Courtesy of UH Athletic
Department)*

When the polls came out the following Tuesday, January 23, the
Houston Cougars ascended to the top of the AP and UPI polls as
the nation's No. 1 college basketball team.

*   *   *   *   *   *   *

With the excitement of the Game of the Century behind them, the
Cougars now had to make their way through the rest of their regular
season. They had a week before their next game, against the Lamar
Tech Cardinals at Delmar Field House. The Cardinals were struggling
with a dismal 4–12 record. With a win over Lamar, the Cougars would
reach two milestones: their 50th consecutive home victory and Guy V.
Lewis's 200th win as the Cougars's head coach.

Both milestones were easily reached with a 112–79 win. The game was pretty much over not long after it started. The Cougars's full-court press enabled them to race to a 14–0 lead before Lamar could ever get the ball across half-court. The Cougars ended the first half leading 57–26 as Lamar hit just 7 of 41 shots.

The next Cougar game came just two nights later at Delmar against the Fairfield Stags out of Connecticut. Just three days before, the Stags had upset Niagara University and their All-America guard, Calvin Murphy. Coach Lewis expressed his pleasure with the attitude of his players and their approach taking the court against a lesser team after facing Alcindor and company. "I found it very gratifying that the players didn't let down one bit after the big win over UCLA," Guy V. told the media. "I wasn't sure what to expect from them against Lamar Tech, but they really got up for the game, and that's exactly what it will take from here on out."

Although Fairfield kept the game close for the first 13 minutes, when the score was tied at 32, the Houston Cougars pulled away from the Stags and recorded a 108–76 victory before another packed house at Delmar. With 48 points and 25 rebounds, Hayes recorded season highs in both categories. In addition, he blocked six Stag shots on the night. The Big E also passed basketball legends Jerry West and Rick Barry on the all-time college scoring list, moving into sixth place with 2,315 points.

Next up for the Cougars after more than a month at home was a trip on February 1 to New York City to play the Marshall Thundering Herd at Madison Square Garden, the team's last appearance in the old garden before the new one opened several weeks later. The old Madison Square Garden had not been kind during Houston's previous two trips. Both times the Cougars had lost to the Dayton Flyers, once in the 1962 NIT and then again at the end of the 1965–66 season, the sophomore year for Hayes and Chaney.

Marshall had placed third in the previous season's NIT and entered the UH game with a 10–5 record, with each of its five starters averaging in double figures in the points-per-game statistics. The Marshall game was somewhat of a homecoming for George Reynolds, who had played high school basketball across the Hudson River in Newark, New Jersey. Since the Cougars landed at Newark Airport, Reynolds served as the team's unofficial tour guide.

Also, for only the second time in the history of Madison Square Garden, a press conference was set up for a college coach and player. Guy Lewis and Elvin Hayes met the media to discuss the Marshall game and the Cougars's season to date. The precedent for such an event had been set just the week before when Wooden, Alcindor, and UCLA came to New York City to play Holy Cross and Boston College on back-to-back nights.

The Thundering Herd turned out to be a formidable opponent for UH, with the Cougars pulling off a sloppy 102–93 win before a surprisingly low turnout of 8,606. The Cougars had a difficult time handling the basketball, turning the ball over a season-high 25 times. Hayes started the game missing four of his first five shots but ultimately scored 39 points, while Reynolds continued his hot hand of late with 17 points and Theodis Lee contributed 15. However, it was reserve forward Carlos Bell who came up big toward the end of the game. After Ken Spain and Theodis Lee fouled out, Marshall closed the gap to 79–74 with 7:55 to play. Bell down the stretch had 4 points, five rebounds, four assists, and three steals.

Guy V. Lewis said, "We looked bad. We had far too many turnovers, and we just generally handled the ball poorly. Marshall has a pretty good team, and between that and our poor play, it was a tough, close game."

Now 20–0 on the season, the No. 1–ranked Houston Cougars had a nine-day break, their longest of the season. Their next game would be on the road in Shreveport on February 10 to once again play the Centenary Gents. Like George Reynolds returning to the New York area, the trip to Shreveport—which Elvin Hayes and Don Chaney had integrated two years earlier—would be a homecoming of sorts, since three of the Cougars's five starters hailed from Louisiana: Hayes, Chaney, and Theodis Lee, who had grown up in nearby Monroe.

To accommodate the anticipated large crowd in Shreveport, the game was shifted from the Gents's on-campus gym to the Hirsch

Memorial Center, which seated 9,500. Before 4,987 fans, the Cougars dismantled the Centenary Gents, 107–56, to raise their record to 21–0. Hayes, who earlier in the day had been chosen as Louisiana's Amateur Athlete of the Year, scored a season high 50 points and pulled down a school record 37 rebounds. Hayes raised his season averages to 35.0 points per game and 17.9 rebounds per game. Besides Hayes's individual rebounding record, the Cougars also set a team single-game rebounding mark with 85.

After the Centenary win, the Cougars returned for their first home game since January 29. The Cougars's February 15 opponent was the 14–7 Miami Hurricanes. They figured to be a tough test, especially their two leading scorers: sophomore guard Don Curnutt, with his 22.4 points per game average, and senior forward Rusty Parker, with his 22.3 average. Yet the potentially close contest against Miami never materialized. UH won easily, 106–64. During a 33–5 run, Chaney had six steals and fed the ball off for five Cougar layups before 5,600 screaming fans at Delmar.

The Cougars hit 51 percent of their shots (43 of 84) as they held Miami to just 35 percent from the field. The Cougars also won the battle of the boards, 68–40. A happy Guy V. Lewis said after the game, "This is the first time the team really let out since the UCLA game. The boys were ready to play. I could feel it all day."

The team was indeed on a roll. The 7–11 Air Force Falcons were scheduled to be UH's 24th straight victim at Delmar on Saturday, February 17. The Cougars marched to a 106–82 win. Unlike the previous game against Miami, where Houston saved its scoring outburst for the second half, the Cougars ripped Air Force for 65 first-half points and coasted to the win.

Now 23–0, and still ranked No. 1 in the land, the Cougars next faced Arlington State at home once again. Two days before this Thursday-night tilt, the Cougars found out their destination and opponent for the upcoming NCAA Tournament. They hoped to be placed in the potentially weak Mideast bracket, which would allow for a possible rematch with UCLA in the NCAA finals or semifinals. Since no independent team—as Houston was—had ever received a first-round bye in the NCAA Tournament, it was almost certain the Cougars would play a first-round game.

As it turned out, UH was in fact placed in the Midwest Regional and would play their first-round game in Salt Lake City on March 9. At the time of the tournament selection, the always-tough Loyola-Chicago Ramblers had a 13–6 record. If they won their first game, the Cougars would face the Missouri Valley Conference champion, which looked to be the powerful Wes Unseld–led Louisville Cardinals. The other half of the Midwest bracket would end up being Southwest Conference champion TCU against Big Eight champion Kansas State.

Before the NCAA Tournament, however, UH had to finish out the five remaining games on its regular season schedule. Here are brief accounts of what happened:

UH 130, ARLINGTON STATE 75. On February 22 at Delmar, Hayes became the third-highest scorer in college basketball history—behind Oscar Robertson's 2,973 points and Frank Selvy of Furman's 2,539 points. The Big E also became the all-time college leader in field goals made, surpassing Robertson. But the night against Arlington State, 3–18 coming in, belonged to Don Chaney, who received the game ball for becoming just the ninth player in Houston Cougar history to score 1,000 points in a career. Hayes now needed just 13 points to tie and 14 to move past Frank Selvy into second place on the all-time NCAA scoring list. It appeared that milestone would be achieved when Houston took on the 11–11 Valparaiso Crusaders at Delmar.

UH 158, VALAPARAISO 81. Hayes easily became college basketball's second-all-time-leading scorer as he scored a school record 62 points, breaking his own record of 55. As a team, the Cougars set NCAA records with 74 field goals and 158 points in a game. Houston's 158-point total beat the record of 154 set by Frank Selvy's Furman team against The Citadel. Selvy was the man Hayes had just passed on the scoring list.

UH 106, HARDIN-SIMMONS 82. In Abilene on February 26, the Cougars saw Theodis Lee play his finest game of the season, scoring 25 points, with most of his baskets coming from long distances. Hardin-Simmons made a game of it in the first half, tying the score at 50 with

1:31 to play, and they were down just 55–52 at halftime. In the second half, though, the Cowboys could only score one field goal during a 12-minute stretch as the Cougars ran their lead to 94–75 and coasted to the win. Hayes put up 40 points and 18 rebounds.

As the regular season wound down, individual accolades started coming in for the undefeated and No. 1–ranked Cougars. On February 28, Hayes and Guy V. Lewis were named by *Sporting News* as NCAA Player and Coach of the Year. Two days later, the Associated Press tabbed them for the same honors. In addition, Don Chaney and Ken Spain were chosen to the AP second team. Then Hayes and Spain received invitations to the Olympic Trials to be held in Albuquerque in the summer of 1968.

All that now remained for Elvin Hayes and Don Chaney in the regular season were two more games. The first would be their last home game on March 2 as they had their first-ever meeting with the Virginia Tech Gobblers. Tech, an NCAA Tournament team the previous season, stood at 14–9. At this point of the season, the Cougars had raised their season scoring average to 98.4 points per game. Since the UCLA game, UH had scored at least 100 points in nine straight games. The Cougars also led the nation in scoring margin and in rebounding at 61.7 per game.

UH 120, VIRGINIA TECH 79. The Cougars got off to a slow start as the Gobblers raced to a 7–0 lead. After that, however, Houston dominated and rolled to another lopsided win. Hayes reached yet another milestone as he hit the 44th out of his 51 points of the night. The Big E became only the fifth player in NCAA history to score 1,000 points in a season. He joined Frank Selvy of Furman in 1954, Oscar Robertson of Cincinnati in 1960, Billy McGill of Utah in 1962, and Pete Maravich of LSU during the same season.

UH 107, WEST TEXAS STATE 76. All that now stood between the Cougars and a perfect 28–0 regular season record and national title in the media polls was a March 4 road game in Canyon, Texas, to take on the West Texas State Buffaloes for the second time that season. "I'm very worried," Lewis said the day before the game. "They had a good team when we played them before, but they just hadn't put it all together yet. But they've done that now, and we'll have our hands full all night." But the drubbing took place before 3,008 fans in packed Buff Gym. For the evening, Hayes paced the Cougars with 39 points, 21 rebounds, and nine blocked shots.

With a perfect regular season in their back pockets, the Houston Cougars appeared to have all the momentum in the world as they looked to win their first national title. On March 6, three days before the Cougars were to face Loyola of Chicago in their first-round game in the NCAA Tournament, they received word that Hayes was named UPI Player of the Year and Don Chaney was named second-team All-America.

Later, however, they received some devastating news. UH found out that their season-long starter and point guard George Reynolds was ineligible for the tournament. It appeared Reynolds did not have the required 48 transfer hours needed to be eligible at the University of Houston. At Imperial Valley Junior College in California, Reynolds completed 56 hours of course work with a C average. However, UH did not accept several classes where he made less than a C, putting him below the required hours. The Cougars turned themselves in when they learned of the Reynolds situation. No other team ratted out Houston, nor did the NCAA discover the violation.

Guy V. Lewis learned of the ruling the Friday before the last two regular season games but didn't tell the team until they returned home from West Texas State. "I wasn't sure what effect it would have on the team, so I elected to wait until after our regular season ended," Lewis said. "I'll start Vern [Lewis] in George's spot. He's got experience playing in the tournament, and he's done a pretty good job for us all season coming off the bench."

18 THE DIAMOND AND ONE GAME

The game should be high scoring and fast. I don't think Wooden has the slightest intention of stalling. He is trying to psych us. I think we could handle it all right if they do try it.

—HEAD COACH GUY V. LEWIS BEFORE

THE FINAL FOUR GAME WITH UCLA

The Cougars now had to focus on their first-round opponent in the NCAA Tournament: the 16–8 Loyola-Chicago Ramblers. The Ramblers, whose tallest starter was just 6-foot-4, relied on the fast break and pressing defense to make up for their lack of height. "We're probably the smallest team in the country this season," Loyola coach George Ireland said. "We expect to be overpowered on the boards, but we're not going to change our tactics just because of that. We're going to press Houston from the moment they leave the dressing room."

The Cougars's Theodis Lee countered Ireland's statement with, "I can't see why Loyola's press should bother us too much. After all, nobody thought we could break UCLA's press, and we did, and that's what got us a win."

Lee was correct on his prediction. Houston broke the Ramblers's press at will and raced to a 94–76 win before 4,700 fans at Einar Nielsen Field House in Salt Lake City. Loyola also was the first team during the season to play man-to-man defense against the Cougars for the entire game. The Ramblers assigned 6-foot-3 sophomore forward Wade Fuller to Elvin Hayes.

Hayes responded to the mismatch with 49 points, 27 rebounds, and nine blocks. Almost unopposed, Hayes hit 20 of his 28 shots from the field. Houston won the fight on the boards, 63–52, and shot 50 percent from the field compared to just 37 percent for Loyola. Besides Hayes, Ken Spain tallied 15 points, Lee 13, and Chaney 10.

Vern Lewis, in his first game as a starter, fared well. He had five points and six assists, but more important, he handled the ball well against the Loyola press. "It was a thrill and a lot of fun," the younger Lewis said. "This was the longest I've ever had to play in a game, and it was the most pressure I think I've ever had on me."

"Vern did just fine," said his backcourt mate Don Chaney. "It felt a little strange out there without George, but Vern handled his job real well, and he directed the offense quite well, especially in the first half."

"Vern did a great job of getting the ball to the open man and beating their press," said the proud father, Coach Guy V. Lewis. "Our first half effort was tremendous in every phase of the game. I was glad to see us hustle so much. It's hard to get a team up for every game when people keep telling them they're going to win by 25 or 30 points."

With their first-round game behind them, the Cougars now traveled to Wichita, Kansas, for the Midwest Regional Tournament on March 15 and 16. The Cougars's Friday-night game would be the much-anticipated matchup with the eighth-ranked Louisville Cardinals. It would be the first time Elvin Hayes would face off with fellow All-American Wes Unseld. Unseld was so highly touted coming out of high school in 1964 that Adolph Rupp of Kentucky offered him the first scholarship to an African American athlete from the University of Kentucky.

The Cardinals had started slowly this season, playing 12 of their first 14 games on the road. However, they had proceeded to win their last 12 games, and their record now stood at 20–6. Guy V. Lewis said, "They lost several early season games but have come on strong and have won 11 or 12 in a row. Their strong points are similar to ours. They are very strong on the boards and have an impressive fast break."

The Cardinals featured a fine guard in Butch Beard, who figured to challenge Don Chaney for backcourt supremacy. Chaney said of Beard, "He does the same things I do, so it'll be very much of a challenge for me to outdo him. He's a better shooter than I am. I imagine I can play better defense than he can. I look forward to working against him."

Louisville also figured to get more play in the Houston matchup from 6-foot-9 center Mike Grosso, a transfer from South Carolina. When Grosso became eligible at the start of the second semester, the Cardinals had gone 9–0. Grosso had been nursing a knee injury most of the season but now appeared to be close to 100 percent. Cardinal coach John Dromo indicated Grosso would start at center against Houston and Unseld would be moved to forward to guard Hayes. Hayes and Unseld were already well acquainted—the previous summer, they had roomed together for two weeks at the Pan American Games.

The Cougars and Cardinals would play the early 7 p.m. game in Wichita, while surprise Southwest Conference champion TCU would play Big Eight champion Kansas State in the 9 p.m. nightcap.

The UH Cougars made a huge statement to back up their No. 1 ranking as they dismantled the Louisville Cardinals, 91–75. After Louisville jumped out to a 4–0 lead and was even with Houston at 13, the Cougars went on a 20–2 run to expand the lead to 33–15 and from there never looked back. That Cougar barrage was led by the stellar play of Chaney, who played the point on Houston's 1-3-1 zone defense. Chaney stole the ball six times during the 20–2 run and ended up with nine steals for the game.

The Cougars eventually stretched their first half-lead to 22 before Louisville scored the last 8 points to close the gap at halftime to 45–32.

In many eyes, however, the game was over. UCLA assistant coach Jerry Norman said, "We were very interested in seeing how Elvin

Hayes would fare against Wes Unseld. We figured we'd be playing the winner of the Houston-Louisville game in the national semifinals. We sent an unpaid assistant to Wichita to see the game. He called me at halftime and said, 'This game is over.' Houston was thoroughly dominating Louisville, and Elvin was dominating the game."

In the second half, the Cougars gradually stretched their lead to 23 points with 4:28 remaining before Louisville cut the gap to 16 by game's end. Hayes, who hit 16 of 31 shots, was the high-point man with 35 points. He also led both teams with 24 rebounds and blocked four shots.

Unseld ended up with 23 points and 22 rebounds. Butch Beard chipped in 21 points for the Cardinals before fouling out. Other contributors for Houston were Lee with 18 points, Chaney with 17, and Ken Spain with 12, as well as Lewis with 9 points and ten assists.

The Cardinals were convinced the Cougars deserved their No. 1 ranking. "I've never seen anything like them," said Coach Dromo. "That is the strongest college team ever put together. Chaney was the difference out there tonight. He stopped our outside shooting and forced us out of our game plan. And Hayes is everything they said he was, too."

Dromo's players were also impressed. "They cut off every offensive attack we tried," said forward Jerry King.

"I've played against some great guards," guard Fred Holden said, "but I've always been able to pass it around to somebody. Chaney's hands are so quick and his arms are so long, it was impossible to pass or shoot over him."

Guy V. Lewis also complimented the play of Chaney: "I've never seen a player have such a half defensively as Chaney did in the first half tonight."

Years later, Cougar reserve guard Tom Gribben summed up the Louisville game from 1968: "Elvin Hayes put on a clinic that night in Wichita. He was one of the greatest natural athletes I've ever seen. I have never seen a team so beaten and demoralized as Louisville was during that game."

In the late game, TCU upset Big Eight champion Kansas State, 77–72, to set an all-Texas Midwest Regional Final for the second straight year. The Horned Frogs were the surprise champions of the Southwest Conference, having been led by first-year coach Johnny Swaim and junior forward James Cash. Cash became the first African American basketball player in the Southwest Conference, in no small part due to Hayes and Chaney opening the integration doors at a major Texas college a year earlier.

Cash became an all-conference player in 1967–68 and 1968–69, and he scored over a thousand points in his career. He also averaged 11.6 rebounds a game. More important, Cash was also an Academic All-American. Later, he became the first African American professor at the Harvard Business School.

Unlike the year before, when Houston held on to beat pesky SMU 83–75 in the Midwest Regional Final at Lawrence, Kansas, TCU never mounted a challenge to unseat the nation's No. 1 team. Houston used a full-court zone press to start the game to prevent TCU from stalling. The Cougars raced to a 15–0 lead and trounced the Horned Frogs 103–68. The win secured the Cougars's second straight trip to the Final Four and a rematch in the national semifinals against the UCLA Bruins.

The much bigger and taller Cougars cut off any kind of inside scoring from TCU, which was forced to shoot from outside over the UH 1-3-1 zone defense. Shooting mostly from the outside, TCU was limited to just 29.7 percent shooting on 27 of 91 field goal attempts. Houston dominated the boards, 76–55. The Cougars's press also forced TCU into 19 first-half turnovers. Hayes was his usual self, scoring 39 points and hauling in 25 rebounds.

TCU coach Johnny Swaim said, "Houston was just too much for us, but that doesn't make us too much different from any other team they've played this season. They're the strongest team I've ever encountered. To stop them, you'd have to have great speed, great outside shooting, and an awful lot of strength inside. Maybe UCLA has it, I don't know.

"After their game in the Astrodome, I would have told you that UCLA would win in LA. Now I'm not so sure of it, although I still think UCLA will win the game."

Swaim then went on to compliment Hayes and Chaney: "Elvin Hayes is the player people said he was. He took our entire offense away just by coming out on the floor . . . Chaney is the key to their defense, and he's super."

Guy V. Lewis explained why he elected to go with the full-court press to start the game: "I was afraid they might stall on us, so I told our boys to go out there and press them like mad. They did, and it won the game for us almost before it got started."

Chaney was surprised the Horned Frogs did not give the Cougars more of a game. "I expected them to play us a much closer game than they did," he said. "They weren't too good out there tonight. They couldn't handle our press. We rattled them quick, and they never could catch up. They weren't as good as many of the teams we played this season."

With the Midwest Regional championship in their hip pocket, the Cougars could now turn their attention to their rematch with UCLA in the national semifinals.

* * * * * * *

Since the Game of the Century, the Bruins had rolled through the rest of their schedule undefeated, and they went into the rematch with Houston with a 27–1 record. UCLA had won the West Regional by beating Santa Clara in the final, 87–66.

The verbal sparring for the Game of the Century rematch started early. On the Sunday before the game, just one day after Houston and UCLA had won their respective regional finals, Bruin coach John Wooden hinted that UCLA might stall against the Cougars.

"I'm surprised nobody has stalled against them. Maybe that's the best way to play them," Wooden said. "I really can't say if we're better off running or stalling against Houston."

Guy V. Lewis doubted UCLA would stall. "The game should be high-scoring and fast," he said. "I don't think Wooden has the slightest intention of stalling. He is trying to psych us. I think we could handle it all right if they do try it."

Lewis counted on UCLA using their vaunted pressing defense throughout the game: "They'll probably press from the time the ball is thrown in. The best defense against a press is to do very little dribbling.

Vern and Don know the situation and can handle it. UCLA will have to prove that they can beat us Friday. We did beat them the first time."

Ken Spain echoed Coach Lewis's comments. "I don't think they'll use a stall," Spain said. "I think their coach is just trying to psych us out. Well, it won't work. We're confident we can beat them again. We've gained a lot of confidence as a result of the win over UCLA earlier this year. We were confident before that game, but not nearly as much. That game also brought us all closer together, and we jelled as a team."

As a matter of fact, UCLA was devising a defense not based on a stall. Assistant Coach Jerry Norman designed the defense to stop Hayes and the Cougars.

UCLA reserve Bill Sweek described the defense in an interview years later: "Jerry Norman devised a diamond and one defense to stop Elvin Hayes. Kareem would be at the bottom of the diamond close to the basket; Mike Lynn and Lucius Allen would be on the wings. Mike Warren was at the top of the diamond. Lynn Shackelford's job was to shadow Elvin wherever he went. He made it to where he couldn't catch the ball."

Norman described how the Bruins would try to stop Hayes: "At the game in the Dome, we used a conventional defense in the first half, and Elvin got 29 points. We shadowed Hayes more in the second half with Jim Nielsen, and he only got 10 points.

"We knew we would probably play Houston again in the semifinals. There was no seeding in those days, and the Midwest would play the West. After Houston beat us, it seemed their confidence level went up. I would look at the box scores, since games weren't televised back then, and they were just decimating teams.

"We had to decide if we wanted to give Hayes his 35 points and let his teammates beat us or do we try and stop Hayes. Surprise is the biggest factor in basketball. We used the diamond and one because if you used a zone type 1-2-2 defense or a box and one, Elvin would be on one side of the court.

"We didn't want him setting up on the left side. We wanted Shackelford to stay between the ball and Hayes. We practiced this defense for a couple of weeks. We had one of our freshmen in practice act like he was Hayes. We finally decided to go with the diamond and one after Houston played Louisville in the Midwest regional semifinal.

"Louisville was the No. 2 seed, and we wanted to see how Wes Unseld did against Hayes. When our assistant that was there called us at halftime and said the game was basically over, that was when we decided to go with the diamond and one."

Going into the rematch, UCLA appeared confident. Bruin forward Mike Lynn said, "This is going to be the biggest game of our lives. It's a lot bigger than that game in Houston. This is for the national championship. Hayes has never won a national championship—and he won't get it, either."

John Wooden also appeared confident in the days leading up to the game. He said, "We have been improving rapidly over the last two months, and we will be very tenacious in our defense of the championship."

Wooden also defended Alcindor's poor showing against Houston in the Astrodome in January: "Lew played shyly. He was not aggressive, and it looked like he was playing in slow motion. Hayes will not play Lew alone. You don't play Lew one-on-one too effectively."

Since the Final Four was at the LA Sports Arena, which was not the Bruin home court, they had played five games on the floor during the season, including the Game of the Century in Houston. The crowd in Los Angeles would be made up of a large number of UCLA boosters.

Guy V. Lewis, however, didn't feel UCLA would have a home-court advantage, playing fairly near the Bruins's campus. "If it were a regular season game, I think it would definitely help them to play in Los Angeles," the coach said. "But this game means too much to us, and I don't think our kids will let the crowd bother them at all."

Unfortunately for the Cougars, the rematch with UCLA must have also meant a lot to the defending national champions. Before a jam-packed, pro-UCLA crowd of 15,472 at the Los Angeles Sports Arena, the No. 2–ranked Bruins demolished the No. 1–ranked Cougars, 101–69, ending Houston's 32-game winning streak.

With the game in favor of UCLA, 20–19, midway through the first half, the Bruins put on a torrid outside shooting display, led by Lucius

Allen, Mike Lynn, and Lynn Shackelford. By halftime, the Bruins's lead had grown to 53–31. UCLA was shooting 52.5 percent in the first half, while Houston was held to just 30.6 percent.

In the second half, UCLA continued its hot shooting and eventually stretched its lead to 40 points. The final score was 101–69, Houston's worst loss since the 110–80 debacle against Notre Dame in January 1965, when Hayes and Chaney were freshmen and not eligible for varsity competition.

For the game, the Bruins hit 51.8 percent of their shots, while Houston's cold shooting continued in the second half, ending up at 28.2 percent. It was the Cougars's worst night from the field in seven years. Coincidently, when UCLA lost the Game of the Century, the Bruins shot just 33 percent, their worst shooting performance in seven years.

Besides their hot shooting, the other significant aspect of the Bruin victory was the effectiveness of their diamond and one defense designed to stop Hayes. Hayes was held to career lows with ten points and five rebounds, as UCLA forward Lynn Shackelford did a masterful job of shadowing Hayes wherever he went on the court.

Former Bruin assistant coach Jerry Norman said in a 2013 interview, "Houston didn't expect the diamond and one, and it upset their whole team. They started grasping at straws. Shackelford did a remarkable job against Elvin. They never could get the ball in Hayes's hands close to the basket. Elvin got a couple of offensive rebound baskets because Shackelford couldn't block him out."

Ken Spain and Don Chaney tried to pick up the scoring void created by UCLA's diamond and one defense against Hayes. They each led the Cougars with 15 points, with Spain also recording 13 rebounds, while Chaney had five steals.

For UCLA, its balanced scoring attack was led by Lew Alcindor, Lucius Allen, and forward Mike Lynn's 19 points apiece. Lynn Shackelford recorded 17 points, and Mike Warren had 14.

After the game, Warren said, "This basically is a vindictive team, and that's the way we played it."

UCLA coach John Wooden added that the rout of the Cougars was "my most satisfying win." About UCLA's defensive strategy that shut down Elvin Hayes, he said, "We decided we would concede the outside shot to everybody but Hayes. He's such a great player. I had no idea we'd hold him like that."

The player assigned with the main job to guard Elvin, Lynn Shackelford, said years later, "This was the only time in my years at UCLA that we designed a special defense to stop a particular player and opponent. The diamond and one plan worked pretty well that night. In fact, years later, Coach Wooden said that the Houston game at the Final Four was the closest we came to reaching our potential in the Lew Alcindor era."

Guy V. Lewis was indeed impressed with the Bruins's performance, saying, "I thought that this UCLA team is the greatest collegiate basketball team I've ever seen . . . their first half was an unbelievable display of basketball. I don't think we could have beaten them with Bill Russell." He expressed his disappointment in his team: "We played like we were dead. It was a team effort; everybody looked bad."

Chaney added, "We went out pretty badly. We were way too tight."

Years later, in 2007, Chaney elaborated, "We felt we were ready going into the game. We felt we were as good as UCLA, even without George Reynolds. The way UCLA played, though, they would have beat us anyways. They had a great defensive scheme with the diamond and one and Lynn Shackelford following Elvin around."

"We weren't mentally ready," Theodis Lee observed after the game. "We let them push us out on offense. We were forcing things and making mistakes, and we had the whole town against us."

Ken Spain said, "Last week in Wichita, we had two great games. We never could get any momentum going against UCLA. We'd just stop. In a long year like this has been, you know you're going to hit your peak sometimes and go down from there."

All that now remained in the 1967–68 season for the Houston Cougars and the college careers of Elvin Hayes and Don Chaney was the third place game the next day against the Ohio State Buckeyes, who had lost to the North Carolina Tar Heels in the other national semifinal, 80–66.

An obviously flat Houston team fell, 89–85, to the unranked 20–8 Buckeyes.

"I said all along I felt the third-place game should be discontinued," Guy V. Lewis said. "I even said that last year after we beat North Carolina for third place. At this stage, if you're not playing for the championship, it's meaningless."

A couple telling statistics that demonstrated the Cougars's lethargy were the facts that they were outshot and outrebounded by the Buckeyes, the only time that happened in the 1967–68 season. Ohio State outshot Houston 44.2 percent to 40 percent and outrebounded the Cougars 58–54.

In the final game of their college careers, both Hayes and Chaney experienced a cold night from the field. Although Hayes scored 34 points, he hit only 14 of 34 from the field. Chaney hit just 4 of 15 in the game. Hayes, however, did add 16 rebounds, and Chaney contributed nine steals and 8 rebounds. Theodis Lee had a fine game with 27 points and 8 rebounds. Ken Spain had 10 points and 12 boards, while Vern Lewis had 6 points and a career-high 14 assists.

In the championship game, UCLA waltzed to its fourth title in five years with a 78–55 rout of the North Carolina Tar Heels. Lew Alcindor scored 34 points and managed 16 rebounds and nine blocked shots.

*   *   *   *   *   *   *

In spite of the disappointing end, the 31–2 Houston Cougars had a season for the ages. After toppling UCLA and ending the Bruins's 47-game winning streak in the Game of the Century, the Cougars were the No. 1 team in the land for more than two months and fashioned their own 32-game winning streak.

As a team, the Cougars led the nation in scoring at 95.7 points per game. They also led the nation in rebounding with 62.8 per game. Houston outscored its opponents by an average of 23.2 points per game. As for field goal percentage, the Cougars hit 48.1 percent of their shots for the season, while their opponents shot just 38.5 percent.

Besides being named the National Player of the Year, Elvin Hayes had a record-breaking season and career statistically. With his 1,214 points on the season, Hayes set a single-season NCAA record for points scored, passing the 1,209 Frank Selvy of Furman scored in 1953–54.

Hayes also set an NCAA record for field goals in a career with 1,215, and he set a NCAA Tournament record with 70 field goals in the Cougars's four games in the 1967–68 tournament. Hayes also ended up second all-time in NCAA scoring for a career, with 2,884 points.

For his three-year Cougar career, Hayes averaged 31 points and 17.2 rebounds per game, which are still school records. He also set school single-season scoring and rebound records with averages of 36.8 and 18.9 his senior season.

For his Cougar career, Don Chaney scored 1,133 points in three seasons, an average of 12.6 points per game. In addition, he averaged 5.3 rebounds per game. Unfortunately, no records were kept for steals when Chaney played for Houston. If so, he most certainly would have held the school record for that category and most likely would have been high up on the NCAA career list.

For their three years on the UH varsity, despite the 0–3 start to their sophomore year, Elvin Hayes and Don Chaney led the Houston Cougars to fashion an 81–12 record and make trips to the Final Four in 1967 and 1968.

More important, Hayes and Chaney, along with Warren McVea, integrated the University of Houston Athletic Department and helped open the doors for the integration of major college sports in the state of Texas and throughout the rest of the South.

All this materialized because Guy V. Lewis and Assistant Coach Harvey Pate convinced two 18-year-old African American men from Louisiana—where they were prohibited from playing major college basketball—to cross the state line into Texas, attend the University of Houston, and help change the face of college basketball in the South forever.

BIBLIOGRAPHY

INTERVIEWS

Achey, Calvin 3-15-13
Allen, Dave 4-11-08
Altenau, Mark 5-26-08
Arenas, Joe 10-5-07
Arrow, Betty 6-12-08
Arrow, Ronnie 6-10-08
Ashby, Vern 4-2-09
Azios, Ernie 6-27-08
Bahnsen, Gene 6-3-08
Baker, Tay 3-17-08
Ballard, Wayne 3-25-08
Bane, Bill 10-30-07
Beer, Tom 3-11-13
Bell, Carlos 12-9-07
Bell, Melvin 10-27-07
Bellard, Emory 11-14-07
Berger, Jim Pat 10-3-07
Berry, Royce 10-2-07
Birdsong, Otis 6-7-10
Blackman, Pete 1-20-09
Blackwell, Bob 7-26-09
Blanton, Gene 3-25-08

Blue, Vida 1-6-09
Blumenthal, Carol 6-24-08
Blumenthal, Doris 7-5-10
Boisture, Tom 9-26-08
Bonham, Ron 3-20-08
Booker, Odis 3-18-08
Bowman, Jim 3-30-08
Boyer, Glen 1-25-09
Brennan, Richard 6-3-08
Brezina, Greg 10-3-07
Bumbry, Ben 4-19-09
Burris, Bo 10-7-07
Byars, Rick 3-18-08
Caldwell, Joe 1-10-10
Canselo, Alan 12-8-07
Caraway, George 10-25-07
Carney, Leo 1-25-09
Casper, Art 9-20-07
Chaney, Don 10-23-07
Clark, Archie 3-1-09
Coffey, Junior 12-21-09
Cogdill, Gail 3-17-09

Cole, Larry 4-2-08

Cooper, Larry 8-22-07

Crawley, Richard 3-23-08

Cude, Roger 12-21-07

Daulong, Paul 11-8-07

Derryberry, Bob 7-15-08

Dickey, Jimmy, Sr. 10-3-07

Dierking, Fred 3-18-08

Disch, Jimmy 11-2-07

Donoher, Don 7-8-08

Drones, A. Z. 9-19-07

Drones, Jerry 10-17-07, 5-7-13

Dvoracek, Donald 2-24-09

Eblen, John 3-20-08

Edwards, Mitchell 7-14-08

Egan, John 3-20-08

Ellis, Richard 5-19-08

Elsasser, Larry 3-18-08

Elston, Gene 12-21-07

Engleke, Billy 3-22-08

Everly, John 3-10-13

Fairbanks, Chuck 12-4-07

Farr, Mel 12-21-07

Farr, Miller 12-19-07

Freberg, John 5-8-08

Gaines, Arthur 2-18-13

George, Terry 4-2-08

Gill, Bobby 1-19-09

Gnoss, George 3-1-09

Goss, Bob 3-20-08

Gower, Larry 1-17-09

Gribben, Tom 10-18-07

Grider, Gary 1-9-08

Guerrant, Cotton 11-14-07

Gugat, Rich 1-20-09

Hall, Eddie 7-16-08

Harkness, Jerry 3-24-08

Harper, Perry 3-21-09

Hayes, Elvin 11-9-07, 2-1-11

Hazzard, Walt 2-27-09

Hebert, Ken 9-25-07

Heidotting, Dale 3-18-08

Herskowitz, Mickey 8-5-08

Hilliard, Gene 1-24-09

Hodgson, Bob 1-24-09

Hoffman, Philip G. 6-4-08, 6-5-08

Hogue, Paul 4-11-08

Hollomon, Gus 12-20-07

Hollon, Bill 9-4-07

Hornsby, Spuds 6-2-08

Hudson, Lou 3-5-09

Hyland, Tom 4-19-09

Idzik, John, Jr. 3-19-09

Jackson, Lucious 7-31-08

James, Freddie 3-1-09

Jankans, John 6-25-09

Janssen, Carl 4-11-08

Jones, Dwight 6-9-10

Kalas, Harry 11-28-07

Kapner, Bernie 7-11-08

Kaspar, Neal 3-16-08

Keys, J. B. 5-15-13

Kilroy, Gene 7-16-14

Korpac, Al 6-28-09

Kruse, Rikki 9-28-07

Kundla, John 3-7-09

Lammers, John 3-21-09

Lattin, David 8-30-07

Lentz, Leary 1-9-08

Lewis, Guy V. 8-23-07, 3-16-10

Lewis, Vern 8-28-07, 1-31-13

Lifschutz, Reno 5-15-08

Liles, Laury 6-5-08

Lineberger, Phil 3-18-08

Littleton, Cleo 1-22-09

Litz, Elwood 12-16-07

Lobkovich, Jim 3-21-09

Lorch, Howard 10-17-07

Luckenbill, Ted 9-12-07, 6-5-08

Mallory, Willie 7-13-09

Manning, Guy 7-15-08

Margenthaler, Jack 11-21-07

Matson, Bruce 1-24-09

Matson, Ollie, Jr. 1-24-09

McDade, Joe Billy 6-24-08

McFerson, Jim 1-18-09

McKenna, Aaron 12-17-07

McLemore, McCoy 6-4-08

McVea, Warren 11-6-07, 12-12-07
McVey, Elliott 12-16-07
Mease, Quentin 8-14-07
Meredith, James 9-17-08
Milborn, Jim 1-25-09
Miller, Charlie 12-16-07
Miller, Ron 5-17-08
Montgomery, Howard 7-21-08
Moore, John 10-7-07
Mormino, Larry 5-18-08
Morse, Gene 7-14-08
Nance, Ted 10-20-07, 12-14-07, 6-7-08, 3-11-09, 3-12-13
Nelson, Al 6-24-09
Neuman, Denny 12-17-07
Newell, Bruce 12-17-07
Norman, Jerry 1-17-09, 3-15-13
O'Connor, Frank 3-20-09
Orsborn, Chuck 5-13-08
Ortegal, Bob 6-9-08
Otis, Paul 9-4-07
Owens, Mike 6-11-08
Ozug, Paul 9-18-07
Paciorek, Tom 9-25-07
Pate, Harvey 8-13-07, 8-29-07, 6-5-08, 6-15-09
Peacock, John 12-20-07
Perdix, Roger 3-1-09
Perdue, Jim 6-24-10
Phillips, Bum 9-18-07
Phillips, Gary 9-30-07, 6-5-08, 3-17-10
Phillips, Jess 12-17-07
Phillips, Wade 6-21-14
Phipps, Anson 12-18-07
Pierson, Lyle 3-10-09
Poff, Walt 4-19-09
Powers, Jody 1-11-08
Purvis, Gordon 3-22-08
Rangel, Mike 3-31-08
Reed, George 3-19-09
Richardson, Roosevelt 6-28-09
Robertson, Melvin 5-25-08
Rochelle, Richard 5-19-08
Roderick, George 6-4-08

Rosenblatt, Stan 6-12-08
Rule, Bob 12-12-07
Russell, Billy 6-25-09
Sash, Chuck 6-11-08
Schverak, Don 10-7-07, 3-18-08, 3-17-13
Shingleton, Larry 4-11-08
Sides, Barry 12-16-07
Sigler, Orvis 7-8-08
Simmons, Rufus 3-10-09
Slaughter, Fred 1-26-09
Sloniger, Wells 1-11-09
Smith, Bob 12-11-07
Smith, Bubba 12-13-07
Smith, Harold 5-10-13
Spears, James 1-7-07
Spears, Lee 1-6-07
Springer, Leonard 4-2-08
Starkey, Neal 3-29-08
Starks, Royce 3-1-09
Stembridge, Terry 4-10-08
Stotter, Rich 9-12-07
Strathe, James 1-24-09
Studley, Chuck 3-8-09
Swearengin, Sam 11-3-13
Sweek, Bill 3-14-13
Swindler, E. J. 6-4-08
Tarkanian, Jerry 12-4-07
Tarsikes, John 8-29-07
Tatman, Gil 6-27-09
Tenwick, Dave 6-13-08
Thacker, Tom 3-18-08
Thompson, Gary 1-26-09
Thompson, Jack 7-8-10
Thompson, Ocie 1-25-09
Toburen, Nelson 7-1-09
Tracy, John 10-22-07, 12-13-14
Tusa, Joe 7-26-08
Urbanek, Jim 1-7-08
Vanatta, Bob 7-14-08
Vischer, Christine 3-7-09
Walker, Chet 1-30-09
Walkosky, George 3-9-09
Washington, Gene 9-11-08

Watson, Lowell 3-20-08
Waxman, Dave 1-18-09
Wells, David 3-18-08, 3-20-08
Wells, Warren 12-20-07
West, Rollie 5-2-09
White, Richard 6-27-09
Wiesenhahn, Robert 5-18-08
Willey, Larry 5-18-08
Williams, Joel 2-12-13
Williams, Sam 7-11-08, 8-1-08
Wilson, Ben 6-25-09
Wilson, George 3-17-08

Wilson, John V. 6-9-08
Wilson, Tom 10-19-07
Wood, Chuck 4-17-08
Woodall, Dick 10-24-07, 2-20-13
Woodring, Phil 12-5-07
Worrell, Bill 6-3-08
Yates, Donald 6-25-09
Yates, Sonny 11-1-09
Yates, Walter 7-22-08
Yeoman, Bill 8-10-07, 3-11-13
Zagzebski, Ken 3-29-08
Zyroll, Tom 3-29-08

NEWSPAPERS

Abilene Reporter-News
Ada Evening News
Albany Times-Union
Amarillo Globe-Times
Arizona Gazette
Big Spring Herald
Boerne Star
Brownsville Herald
Capital Times
Charleston Daily Mail
Chicago Tribune
Corpus Christi Caller-Times
Corpus Christi Times
Daily Cougar
Dallas Morning News
Denton Record-Chronicle
El Paso Herald-Post
Eugene Register
Fresno Bee
Galveston Daily News
Grand Rapids Press
Great Bend Daily Tribune
Hayward Daily Review
Holland Evening Sentinel
Houston Chronicle
Houston Forward Times
Houston Informer
Houston Post

Houston Press
Jefferson City Daily Capital News
Lockhart Post-Register
Long Beach Independent
     Press-Telegram
Los Angeles Times
Loyola-Chicago Rambler Mania
Moberly Monitor-Index and Democrat
Modesto Bee
New York Times
Northwest Arkansas Times
Oakland Tribune
Pacific Stars and Stripes
Pasadena Star-News
Peoria Journal Star
Port Arthur News
Reno Evening Gazette
Salina Journal
San Antonio Express
San Antonio Express-News
San Antonio Informer
San Antonio Light
Seattle Times
Shreveport Times-News
Spokane Spokesman-Review
St. Petersburg Evening Independent
Syracuse Herald-American
Titusville Herald

Troy Times Record
USA Today
Victoria Advocate

Wall Street Journal
Washington Post
Wharton Spectator

PERIODICALS

Christian Science Monitor
Ebony
Parade

Sporting News
Sports Illustrated
Time

VIDEOS

"1968 Game of the Century." YouTube video, 7:43. Posted by "bambicha11," October 27, 2008. https://www.youtube.com/watch?v=9e31mA5clAg.

Berman, David, director. "The Strange Demise of Jim Crow." California Newsreel, 1998.

BOOKS

Bloom, John, and Michael Willard. *Sports Matters: Race, Relations, and Culture.* New York: New York University Press, 2002.

Cashion, Ty. *Pigskin Pulpit: A Social History of Texas High School Football Coaches.* Austin: Texas State Historical Association, 1998.

Einhorn, Eddie, with Ron Rapport. *How March Became Madness: How the NCAA Tournament Became the Greatest Sporting Event in America.* Chicago: Triumph Books, 2006.

Eisen, George, and David K. Wiggins. *Ethnicity and Sport in North American History and Culture.* Westport, Conn.: Greenwood Press, 1994.

Jones, K. C., with Jack Warner. *Rebound: The Autobiography of K. C. Jones and an Inside Look at the Champion Boston Celtics.* Boston: Quinlan Press, 1986.

Lapchick, Richard. *Broken Promises: Racism in American Sports.* New York: St. Martin's Press, 1984.

Lattin, David. *Slam Dunk to Glory: The Amazing True Story of the 1966 Season and the Championship Game That Changed America Forever.* Lakeland, Fla.: White Stone Books, 2006.

McMurray, Bill. *Texas High School Football.* South Bend, Ind.: Icarus Press, 1985.

Mease, Quentin R. *On Equal Footing: A Memoir.* Austin: Eakin Press, 2001.

Miller, Patrick, and David Wiggins. *Sport and the Color Line.* New York: Routledge, 2004.

Nicholson, Patrick J. *In Time: An Anecdotal History of the First Fifty Years of the University of Houston.* Houston: Pacesetter Press, 1977.

Olsen, Jack. *The Black Athlete: A Shameful Story*. New York: Time-Life Books, 1968.

Pennington, Richard. *Breaking the Ice: The Racial Integration of Southwest Conference Football*. Jefferson, N.C.: McFarland and Company, 1987.

Robertson, Oscar. *The Big O: My Life, My Times, My Game*. New York: St. Martin's Press, 2003.

Sailes, Gary, ed. *African Americans in Sport: Contemporary Themes*. New Brunswick, N.J.: Transaction Publishers, 1998.

Taylor, Otis, and Mark Stallard. *The Need to Win*. Champaign, Ill.: Sports Publishing LLC, 2003.

Walker, Chet, with Chris Messenger. *Long Time Coming: A Black Athlete's Coming of Age in America*. New York: Grove Publishing, 1995.

Wizig, Jerry. *Eat 'Em Up Cougars: Houston Football*. Huntsville, Ala.: Strode Publishers, 1977.

ARTICLES

Borucki, Wes. "You're Dixie's Southern Pride: American College Football and the Resurgence of Southern Identity." *Identities: Global Studies in Culture and Power* 10 (2003): 477–94.

Marcello, Ronald. "The Integration of Intercollegiate Athletics in Texas: North Texas State College as a Test Case, 1956." *Journal of Sports History* 14 (Winter 1987): 286–316.

Martin, Charles H. "Integrating New Year's Day: The Racial Politics of College Bowl Games in the American South." *Journal of Sports History* 24 (Fall 1997): 358–77.

———. "Jim Crow in the Gymnasium: The Integration of College Basketball in the American South." *International Journal of the History of Sport* 10 (1993): 68–86.

Smith, John Matthew. "Breaking the Plane: Integration and Black Protest in Michigan State University Football in the 1960s." *The Michigan Historical Review* 33 (2007): 1–21.

INDEX